The Beatles' Conspiracy:
John, Paul, George, Ringo and Bill

*Of that which you know, speak clearly;
of that which you don't, remain silent.*

Ludwig Wittgenstein
Tractatus Logico-Philosophicus (1922)

DAVID ELIO MALOCCO

Copyright © 2015, 2016, 2017 David Elio Malocco

All rights reserved.

ISBN: 1502544725
ISBN-13: 978-1502544728

DEDICATION

To Colette

ACKNOWLEDGMENTS

The author would like to thank all those who did not wished to be named in this section as well as Colette Kerr, Lisa Kerr, Emma Kerr, Pat Hannon, Gary Power, Geoff Baker, James I. Hannon, Noelle Hannon, Jed Epstein, Michael Manson, Pat Conroy, Joseph Armato, Joel Gilbert, Marjorie Riley, Peter Asher, John Evans, Michael Jacobs, Catherine Bach, Joel Silver, Raymond Murphy, Peter Veale, Dr. Richard Combs, Giuseppe Luchesse, Massimo Russo, Teresa Stokes, Albert Blake, Gerard Ryan, Michael Murray, Andrew Roche, Bobby Elwood, David Greene, George Mitchell, Brian Curless, Steven Murphy, Samantha Bernstein, Valerie Martin, John Dunne, Claudia Schwarzmeier, Harry Keane, Marie Woodlock, Jane Blake, Julie Werbell, Nancy Paladino, Niamh O'Donoghue, Alice Horta, Joseph Carr, Anthony O'Brien, Susie McGivern, George Brown, Ann Moore and Marcus Flood.

THE BEATLES CONSPIRACY: John, Paul, George, Ringo and Bill

THE ALBUM

SIDE ONE
THE OFFICIAL STORY

Track 1	An Introduction.	Page 002
Track 2	The Quarrymen	Page 013
Track 3	The Early Years	Page 041
Track 4	The Jesus Controversy	Page 069
Track 5	A New Departure	Page 083
Track 6	The Manson Connection	Page 105
Track 7	The End of the Road	Page 124

SIDE TWO
THE BOOTLEG VERSION – THE REAL STORY

Track 1	The Paul is Dead Theory	Page 133
Track 2	The Documentary Evidence	Page 155
Track 3	The Secret They Won't Reveal	Page 183
Track 4	The PID Clues	Page 242
Track 5	Divisions & Lack of Music	Page 270
Track 6	The Forensic Evidence	Page 285
Track 7	The Closing Arguments	Page 302

This is not an authorized biography of The Beatles.

Unless something happens there's nothing to stop Paul and I writing hits when we're old.

John Lennon

W ell, unfortunately John, something did happen.

This book is the result of two years of research involving the examination of fifteen books, over two hundred and fifty video and film clips, the inspection of three hundred photographs, interviews with thirty two close associates of *The Beatles*, several meetings (some clandestine) with various people in London, Liverpool, Rome, New York, Los Angeles, Scotland, Paris, Madrid and Dublin and the forensic examination of over three thousand internet posts and accompanying documentation.

This does not include listening to and reading the lyrics to every song on every album *The Beatles* ever made as well as many others.

Before I agreed to write the book I knew very little about the PID (Paul Is Dead) conspiracy theory but, to be honest, I was hugely sceptical. In fact, I thought it was ludicrous. The first dozen or so people I interviewed did nothing to change this opinion but then, I began to wonder, just wonder if it was, at all, even possible.

Was there *any* type of conspiracy?

What I found in the course of writing the book was that much of what is written about *The Beatles* is not exactly true. Some of the conspiracy theories, particularly the more extreme ones, are utter nonsense and include deliberate falsehoods, altered photographs, fabricated video footage and calculated deceptions.

But…

There is also a huge amount of disinformation from the official side. Even John Lennon and Paul McCartney have frequently contradicted both each other and themselves about who wrote what and what happened where. Furthermore, some of the information given to me through interviews lacked credibility and when I double checked them I found out they were untrue.

During the course of the book I have changed my mind on several occasions as to whether or not there was a conspiracy. But just as the first proof of the book was finished I began to receive information which drastically altered my vision of the theory. This evidence helped convince me of the real truth regarding one conspiracy theory and brought me very close to the truth of another.

Accordingly, dear reader, I ask you one favour. If you already believe the conspiracy theory, suspend your belief. If you do not believe it, open your mind to it. And, if you're not sure, I'm pretty certain you will be by the time you finish the last chapter.

Personally, I have never been a *Beatles'* fan. They were a little before my time. So, there is no hidden agenda in writing this book, no axe to grind, no publisher to satisfy, and no vested interest.

It is simply a search for the truth involving an honest appraisal of the proven facts. As with any work of this size there may be minor errors which if you bring to my attention I will correct as quickly as I can.

This book is not an authorized biography of any of *The Beatles* their personal representative, agents, companies, or anyone directly or indirectly involved with them. Finally, thank you for buying the book and I really hope you enjoy *The Beatles Conspiracy - John, Paul, George, Ringo and Bill*. So, who were *The Beatles*? They were a British rock band formed in Liverpool,

England in 1960, consisting of John Lennon, James Paul McCartney, George Harrison and Ritchie Starkey *aka* Ringo Starr.

They are widely regarded as the greatest and most influential band of the rock era. In the early 1960s, their enormous popularity first emerged as *Beatlemania*, but as their song writing grew in sophistication they came to be regarded as an embodiment of the ideals and values shared by the period's socio-cultural revolutions.

Formerly called *The Quarrymen*, *The Beatles* built their reputation by playing working class clubs in Liverpool in England and Hamburg in Germany before being moulded by manager Brian Epstein and producer George Martin both of whom greatly enhanced their musical reputation and potential. Their first hit came in 1962 with *Love Me Do* and they quickly became mega stars in both Britain and America earning the nickname *The Fab Four*.

From 1965 onwards, *The Beatles* produced what many critics consider their finest material, including the innovative and widely influential albums *Rubber Soul* (1965), *Revolver* (1966), *Sgt. Pepper's Lonely Hearts Club Band* (1967), *The White Album* (1968) and *Abbey Road* (1969).

They eventually disbanded in 1970, and John, Paul and George and to a somewhat lesser extent Ringo, enjoyed successful musical careers on their own and with others. John Lennon emigrated to America and lived in the Dakota Building in Manhattan's New

York City with his Japanese wife, Yoko Ono. Many fans blamed Ono for the break-up of the group but she was not responsible.

According to statistics from the RIAA, *The Beatles* are the best-selling music artists in the United States, with 177 million certified units. They have had more number-one albums on the British charts and sold more singles in the UK than any other musical act in the world.

In 2008, the group topped Billboard magazine's list of the all-time most successful "Hot 100" artists. As of 2014, they hold the record for most number-one hits on the Hot 100 chart with twenty.

They have received ten Grammy Awards, an Academy Award for Best Original Score and fifteen Ivor Novello Awards. They are the best-selling band in history, with estimated sales of over 600 million records worldwide. They were, at the height of their fame, the most influential rock group in the world.

Most people know that part of their story but not many know the conspiracy story which has shadowed them for nearly fifty years. Proponents of that theory claim that Lennon, Harrison, Starr and their manager Epstein were also involved in the biggest cover-up in rock and roll history when they conspired, with others, to conceal from the general public, the death of their most popular member, bass guitarist James Paul McCartney. Many PID (Paul is Dead) theorists are convinced that McCartney died, possibly in a car crash, or was murdered perhaps in a botched kidnap attempt, or simply disappeared sometime between the 11 September and 9 November 1966. And when I say "many" I mean millions.

The theory continues that the band with the assistance of others, replaced James Paul McCartney with a lookalike, possibly William Pepper aka William "Shears" Sheppard, who for nearly fifty years has masqueraded as original *Beatles'* member McCartney.

This is one of several theories about *The Beatles* discussed in this book. Some theorists claim and the evidence now uncovered confirms, that there were, at different times, up to three Paul McCartney lookalikes employed by the group's management.

Theorists also claim that a huge amount of money was spent to ensure the silence of others, including Sir Paul McCartney's former wife Heather Mills; a lady, who on national television in Britain and in America, said she feared for her life and that if anything ever happened to her she had "a box of evidence" secreted away that would rock the world.

At first glance, any reasonable person would have to admit that *The Beatles'* Conspiracy is probably the most preposterous of all the conspiracy theories that are out there. Preposterous, that is, until you check the forensic evidence.

In 2009 two eminent Italian scientists conducted a forensic examination and determined that it was highly unlikely that Sir Paul McCartney was the original *Beatle* James Paul McCartney. You see, unlike many of the protagonists in this incredible story, forensic evidence, properly acquired, doesn't lie.

This book examines the documentary evidence upon which this theory is based, including the "60IF" document; the "Last Testament of George Harrison" tapes; the forensic comparison examination carried out by the Italian scientists; and, over one hundred hidden messages deliberately left by *The Beatles* themselves in their album covers, lyrics and in backward masking.

As Fox Mulder would say: The truth is out there.

Many of the clues can be subjectively interpreted.

But the constant repetition of many more begs the question: why would they do this? Theorists say they wanted to let their fans know what happened to their colleague, James Paul McCartney, but were prevented from doing so directly; and, that the hoax was only meant to last for a short transition period.

Cynics claim it was a deliberate attempt by them and their management to sell more records at a time when their popularity was on the wane.

Either way it involved a huge betrayal of their fans.

From a forensic examination of known facts and honest, never before disclosed testimony from those closest to the truth, this book reveals with absolute certainty what is true, what is false and what cannot be explained. The author examines the group's involvement with the notorious London gangsters, Ronnie and Reggie Kray; British occultist, sexual pervert and Satanist, Aleister (*The Beast-666*) Crowley and American mass murderer Charles Manson.

That some members of the group were heavily influenced by the dark forces of Crowley and Manson may be explained by the lyrics in their music. In fact, some suggest that both Aleister Crowley and Charles Manson contributed to the lyrics of several of their tracks. But how much is true and how much is fabricated? In order to perpetrate this elaborate hoax each member of *The Beatles* would have had to agree to be part of the conspiracy. Others too would have known that James Paul McCartney was replaced in 1966. This begs the question: Why didn't people, like his best friend, manager, lawyer, psychiatrist or dentist never break their silence? After all, they had nothing to gain by being part of the fraud.

Maybe it was because James Paul McCartney's best friend, Tara Browne, was killed in an automobile "accident" on the 18 December 1966. His manager, Brian Epstein, died from an "accidental" drug overdose on the 27 August 1967. His lawyer, David Jacobs, "hung himself" on the 16 December 1968. His psychiatrist Dr. Richard Asher "was found hanging" in the basement of his house on the 25 April 1969 and his dentist Dr. John Riley died in a "mysterious road accident" in Ireland in 1986. Coincidence? Perhaps. But, then there are other unexplained deaths like those of Mal Evans, Brian

Jones, Kevin MacDonald, John Lennon and the attempted murder of George Harrison. So many suspicious deaths. Why?

As one insider told me: *Dead men can't talk.*

Prepare to be shocked as the greatest mystery never told in the history of rock and roll is unravelled: the real truth behind music legend Sir Paul McCartney, Bill Pepper-Shears-Sheppard and *The Beatles'* conspiracy.

What they actually said in interviews.

> **But I think it's people on the outside who perceive Paul as thinking he's the only one left. Actually, it's me. I am the last remaining Beatle**
>
> Ringo Starr (2011) *Daily Mail*
>
> **The last time I saw Paul? It was his funeral, I think.**
>
> Michael McGear on *Mike Douglas Show*
>
> **You know why I've left you. Protect me and I'll say nothing. Something so awful happened. Someone I'd loved for a long time, I found out he had betrayed me immensely and I don't mean infidelity or anything like that. Like beyond belief. …I've got to protect myself. I have to protect myself. People don't want to know what the truth is because they could never ever handle**

> **it, they'd be too devastated.**

Heather Mills McCartney on National TV

Later in the interview speaking about the concern for her continued safety she added:

> **I have a box of evidence that is going to a certain person should anything happen to me.**

When the interviewer Billy Bush asked her if the evidence was against Paul or the paparazzi, she replied:

> **I can't answer that 'cause I'm in the middle of divorce proceedings and it will be used against me. This evidence is against a certain party that behaved in a terrible way and I don't ever want the evidence to have to go out but if I'm going to be portrayed as this horrific person for my daughter to grow up… then this evidence is there for her to make up her mind when she's older.**

Billy Bush then asked her:

> **Knowing what you know now about Paul, would have married him in the first place?**

Heather Mills replied:

> **Never!**

And finally Jane Asher in 2004 said:

> **Life is bloody dark and awful. It doesn't mean I go round being permanently depressed. But I**

would if I really started to think about things. I don't think there's any meaning to anything. I have slightly more of an acceptance that you're hurtling towards the abyss. At least you won't know anything once you're in it.

Jane Asher speaking in 2004 reflecting on life.

So I suddenly realized that I didn't actually know how to set up a band. When you think about it, I'd never actually done it before. I'd joined the Beatles as an already set-up affair.

Sir Paul McCartney

In the beginning there were six.

Essentially, there were six core members of *The Quarrymen* the band formed by John Lennon which was the forerunner of *The Beatles*. They were: John Lennon; James Paul McCartney; George Harrison;

Ringo Starr; Pete Best; Stuart Sutcliffe and their managers, Allan Williams and Brian Epstein

JOHN LENNON

John Winston Lennon was born in Liverpool Maternity Hospital in England on the 9 October 1940 to Julia Stanley and Alfred Lennon. His father, Alfred was a merchant seaman of Irish descent. Initially, Alfred, although away most of the time at sea, was a good provider to his family and sent home regular weekly payments. But the couple eventually became estranged in early 1944 and Julia took up with another partner. At one stage, John's father returned and tried to take him to New Zealand but John refused to leave his mother. His aunt, Mimi Smith, made several complaints to Liverpool Social Services about the unsuitability of her sister, Julia, to care for John and it was arranged that he live with Mimi and her husband George Smith, who had no children of their own, at Mendips, 251 Menlove Avenue, Woolton. His mother kept in regular contact with him and they visited each other often. She introduced him to the music of Elvis Presley and Fats Domino.

John spent a lot of time with his cousin, Stanley Parkes, who was seven years older. They went to the cinema and local theatres a lot to watch British stars like Arthur Askey, Max Bygraves, Dickie Valentine, Joe Loss, and John's favourite George Formby. John was a bit of a rebel at school and after the death of his uncle from a diseased liver when John was 14 it became more difficult to keep him in check. Although John was raised in the Anglican Protestant faith he had little time for organized religion.

He attended Dovedale Primary School and later Quarry Bank High School in Liverpool. Fellow students described him as "happy", "easy going" and "good humoured". Teachers described him as "hopeless", "a clown" and "a waster". In truth, all of these descriptions were accurate.

In 1956, his mother Julia bought him his first guitar, a Gallotone Champion acoustic on condition that he didn't tell his aunt Mimi who wasn't convinced that John's love of music would help him in any meaningful career.

Tragedy struck on the 15 July 1958 when John's mother was knocked down by a car and killed. John was just seventeen. He later attended Liverpool College of Art only to be expelled in his final year.

Before entering the College of Art John Lennon formed a skiffle band in September 1956. He called the band *The Quarrymen* after the Quarry Bank High School. John first met James Paul McCartney at *The Quarrymen's* second performance, held in Woolton on 6 July 1957 at the St. Peter's Church garden fête. He then asked McCartney to join the band. McCartney agreed.

McCartney's father did not fully approve of his friendship with Lennon and believed that he would get the young Paul (as his family called him) into trouble. But he mellowed somewhat and allowed them rehearse in the front room of the McCartney residence at 20 Forthlin Road.

During this time, John Lennon who was just 18, wrote his first song, *Hello Little Girl*, which five years later became a Top Ten hit for a band called *The Fourmost*. Lennon and McCartney are responsible for nearly all the music recorded by *The Beatles*.

John married childhood sweetheart Cynthia Powell in 1962 just before the group became world famous. The marriage lasted six years. During their marriage Cynthia gave birth to one son, Julian. In 1968 they divorced and a year later Lennon married Japanese artist Yoko Ono with whom he had a son called Sean.

John Lennon was shot dead outside his Manhattan apartment block, *The Dakota*, on the 8 December 1980. Mark David Chapman was convicted of his killing. After he had killed him, Chapman leaned nonchalantly against the wall of the *Dakota*, proclaiming "I acted alone. I acted alone" and then began flicking through a copy of the book *Catcher In The Rye*, J.D. Salinger's famous novel of adolescent alienation, whose central character was apparently the inspiration for what he had just done. Chapman remains in prison until this day. His next parole date is August 2018.

In his book *John Lennon: Life, Times And Assassination* (2010) Phil Strongman argues that Chapman was a CIA operative hypnotically controlled by them to kill Lennon. *Catcher In The Rye* was part of Chapman's hypnotic programming, a trigger that could be "fired" at him by a few simple keywords [via] a cassette tape message, telex or telegram or even a mere telephone call. It's certainly true that conspiracy theorists have long suspected both the Americans and their Communist foes of using such techniques to activate 'sleeper' assassins, as fictionalised in the film *The Manchurian Candidate*. And did Chapman really shoot John Lennon or was he shot by the Dakota's doorman Jose Sanjenis Perdomo who just happened to be a former CIA agent, and if so, why?

Paul McCartney

James Paul McCartney was born on the 18 June 1942, in Walton Hospital, Liverpool, England, to Mary Patricia Mohin and Jim McCartney. His mother was a midwife at the hospital and his father was a volunteer firefighter. He had one younger brother, Michael, who was born on the 7 January 1944.

Like many Liverpool families at the time, the McCartney and Mohin families were of Irish descent. Jim worked for most of his life in the cotton trade, while Mary was a trained nurse and midwife. The two boys were baptized as Roman Catholics following their mother's faith. But they did not attend Catholic schools and were not encouraged in the faith.

Paul attended Stockton Wood Road Primary School and later Joseph Williams Junior School. After he finished school he gained admission to the Liverpool

Institute. It was at the Institute that Paul first met George Harrison on the bus to the Institute from his suburban home in Speke. George was a year younger than Paul.

McCartney's mother Mary was the family's primary wage earner. It was her money that enabled the family to move to 20 Forthlin Road in Allerton, where they lived until 1964. She was a hard worker who was careful with her money.

On the 31 October 1956 Mary McCartney died of an embolism after an operation to stop the spread of breast cancer. Paul was just fourteen years of age and the death affected him badly. After Mary's death, Jim married Angela Williams in November 1964 and adopted her daughter from a previous marriage, Ruth McCartney.

Paul's father Jim was a musician of note who led *Jim Mac's Jazz Band* in the 1920s. Jim excelled both on the trumpet and piano. He encouraged his sons to play the piano and provided them with music lessons. Jim bought Paul a trumpet for his fourteenth birthday. But Paul was more interested in learning the guitar and in singing. He later traded in the trumpet for a Framus Zenith (model 17) acoustic guitar.

Initially, Paul had difficulty playing the guitar because he was left handed so he decided to reverse the order of the strings. It was around this time that Paul wrote his first song *I Lost My Little Girl*, and the basis for a song that would later become *When I'm Sixty-Four*. He says that he was, at the time, heavily influenced by

Little Richard. When Paul accepted John's invitation to join the band he asked John to recruit his friend George Harrison but at 14 John felt he was too young.

Harrison later joined in 1958 as lead guitarist, followed by Lennon's art school friend Stuart Sutcliffe on bass, in 1960. By May 1960 the band had tried several names, including *Beatals, Johnny and the Moondogs* and the *Silver Beetles*. They adopted the name *The Beatles* in August 1960 and recruited drummer Pete Best shortly before a five-engagement residency in Hamburg. At first Jim McCartney refused to allow his son go to Hamburg but when he was advised by the band's then manager Allan Williams that Paul would earn £15 per week, double what he was earning, he let him go. Jim died of bronchial pneumonia on the 18 March 1976. His other son Michael, who sometimes calls himself Michael McGear, is still alive and is a musician and artist.

McCartney became the centre of the conspiracy theory when rumours of his supposed death surfaced around 1966. It was believed that he had died or was seriously injured in a car crash and that the group were anxious not to disclose the details of the accident. At the time McCartney was engaged to British actress Jane Asher and for several years McCartney actually lived in her parent's house in Chelsea in London. But while dating her he was also seeing other women; a fact which was an open secret in London.

Later the engagement was abruptly cancelled and

McCartney married Linda Eastman, an American photographer in 1969. PID conspirators claim that Eastman was aware that the person she married was not the original *Beatle* James Paul McCartney.

The couple had three children, Stella, James and Mary. McCartney later adopted Heather whose biological parents are Eastman and her first husband Joseph See. Linda Eastman died from cancer in April 1998. McCartney then married British human right's activist Heather Mills in 2002. They had one daughter called Beatrice. The marriage lasted six years before a bitter divorce in 2008. He later married Nancy Shevell.

GEORGE HARRISON

George Harrison was born in Liverpool on the 25 February 1943 to Harold Hargreaves Harrison and Louise French. The youngest of four children, George had one sister, Louise, and two brothers, Harry and Peter.

His mother Louise was a shop assistant from a Catholic family with Irish roots, and his father was a bus conductor who had worked as a ship's steward on the White Star Line.

His mother was a major influence in his music career and encouraged him greatly. While pregnant with George, she often listened to the weekly broadcast Radio India. Harrison's biographer Joshua Greene wrote in *Here Comes the Sun: The Spiritual an Musical Journey of George Harrison* (2007):

> **Every Sunday she tuned in to mystical sounds evoked by sitars and tablas, hoping that the exotic music would bring peace and calm to the baby in the womb.**

Harrison's family were essentially working class. He was born and lived the first six years of his life at 12 Arnold Grove, Wavertree, Liverpool, in a terraced house in a cul-de-sac. The home had an outdoor toilet and its only heat came from a single coal fire.

In 1949 the family were offered a council house and moved to 25 Upton Green, Speke. In 1948, at the age of five, Harrison enrolled at Dovedale Primary School and later attended the Liverpool Institute from 1954 to 1959.

Towards the end of 1956 George's father, although apprehensive about his son's interest in pursuing a music career, bought him a Dutch Egmond flat top acoustic guitar. A friend of his father's gave him guitar lessons. Harrison formed a skiffle group called the *Rebels* with his brother Peter and a friend, Arthur Kelly. He met Paul McCartney on the bus to school and they became great friends, bonding over their shared love of music.

Harrison's first audition for *The Quarrymen* took place in March 1958 at Rory Storm's *Morgue Skiffle Club*. He played *Guitar Boogie Shuffle*. Although Lennon was impressed he felt he was too young.

McCartney persisted in putting him forward and his second audition took place on the upper deck of a Liverpool bus when he played the lead for the instrumental *Raunchy*. By the time he had turned 15 Lennon accepted him into the band. George decided to leave school and worked for several months as an apprentice electrician at Blacklers, a local department store. In 1960 the band had their first tour of Scotland. Harrison used the pseudonym "Carl Harrison," paying tribute to Carl Perkins. Later that year their unofficial manager, Allan Williams, arranged a residency for the band in Hamburg, Germany. While there he took guitar lessons from Tony Sheridan while they briefly served as his backing group. The band's first residency in Hamburg ended prematurely when Harrison was deported for being too young to work in nightclubs.

In 1966 when *The Beatles* were at the height of their fame he married British model Pattie Boyd whom he met on the set of the film *A Hard Day's Night*. They were not blessed with any children. In 1973, Boyd's marriage to Harrison began to fail and she had an affair with *Faces* guitarist Ronnie Wood. The couple separated in 1974 and their divorce was finalized in 1977.

Boyd said her decision to divorce was based largely on his repeated infidelities, culminating in an affair with Ringo Starr's wife Maureen. Boyd later married Eric Clapton. The following year Harrison married Olivia Trinidad Arias, with whom he had one son, Dhani. After *The Beatles* split Harrison began a successful solo career as a composer, performer and film producer. On the 30 December 1999 he survived an attempt on his life when thirty four year-old Michael Abram broke into his home and stabbed him forty times with a kitchen knife. Later, Harrison said of him:

> **He wasn't a burglar, and he certainly wasn't auditioning for the Traveling Wilburys.**

Abram, of Huyton, Merseyside, was sent to the Scott Clinic in St. Helens after being cleared of attempted murder at Oxford Crown Court on the grounds of temporary insanity. Abram spent only two years in "prison." On his release he expressed remorse for the attack, but blamed doctors for failing to diagnose his schizophrenia. According to the *Daily Mail* of the 5 July 2001 he said on his release:

> **I would give anything not to have done what I did in attacking George Harrison. But looking back on it now, I have come to understand that I was very ill at that time, really not in control of my actions. I can only hope the Harrison family might somehow find it in their hearts to accept my apologies. I hope now they can understand what happened to me and appreciate that it was not my fault. Physically I did it, but I was not in control of my own mind at the time.**

Mark Chapman, the man convicted of murdering John Lennon also claimed to have no control over his actions. Harrison never fully recovered and died later on the 29 November 2001, aged 58, from metastatic non-small cell lung cancer.

Ringo Starr

Ringo Starr whose real name is Richard Starkey, Jr. was born into poverty on the 7 July 1940, at 9 Madryn Street, in Dingle, Liverpool. He was the only child of Elsie Gleave and Richard Starkey, Sr. and they called him Ritchie. Elsie and Richard enjoyed singing and dancing, so much so that Richard quickly lost interest in his family and chose instead to spend long hours drinking and dancing in pubs, sometimes for several consecutive days.

In 1944 his parents moved to 10 Admiral Grove in Dingle, separated and then divorced within a year. Elsie struggled to survive on her ex-husband's support payments of thirty shillings a week, so she took on several menial jobs cleaning houses before securing a position as a local barmaid, an occupation that she enjoyed for twelve years.

Ringo was a sickly child, contracting appendicitis and later peritonitis, causing him to fall into a coma that lasted for three days when he was only six. He spent a year recovering in Liverpool's Myrtle Street Children's hospital and was discharged in May 1948. His mother smothered him and was overprotective, causing him to miss school for several years.

He received private tuition from his surrogate sister and neighbour, Marie Maguire Crawford, and was just back on course academically when he contracted tuberculosis and was admitted to a sanatorium, where he remained for two years. While there he joined the hospital band as a drummer using a makeshift drum kit. It was the spark to drive him forward as a percussionist.

Soon afterwards, he began studying music and went back to school, St Silas, a Church of England primary school. After primary school he attended Dingle Vale Secondary modern school, where he showed an aptitude for art and drama, as well as practical subjects including mechanics.

On the 17 April 1953, Starkey's mother married Harry Graves, an ex-Londoner who had moved to Liverpool following the failure of his first marriage. Harry was a huge fan of big band music and introduced Ritchie to recordings by Dinah Shore, Sarah Vaughan and Billy Daniels.

The pair of them struck up a genuine friendship. He became the father Ritchie never had. Starkey later said he learned gentleness from Harry. After he returned home from the sanatorium in later 1955 Starkey worked briefly with British Rail and later as a waiter on a ferry.

In the middle of 1956 his stepfather secured him a job as an apprentice machinist at a Liverpool equipment manufacturer. While working there he met Roy Trafford. The pair were joined by Starkey's neighbour and co-worker, the guitarist Eddie Miles, forming the *Eddie Miles Band*, later renamed *Eddie Clayton and the Clayton Squares* after a Liverpool landmark. His step father then bought him a makeshift drum kit and in November 1959, Starkey joined *Al Caldwell's Texans*, a skiffle group who were looking for someone with a proper drum kit so that the group could progress from one of Liverpool's best-known skiffle acts to a fully-fledged rock and roll band.

They later changed their name to *Rory Storm and the Hurricanes* before recruiting Starkey. By the early 1960 the *Hurricanes* had become one of Liverpool's leading bands. In May, they were offered a three-month residency at a *Butlin's* holiday camp in Wales which led to other opportunities. They later accepted a residency in Hamburg, joining *The Beatles* at Bruno Koschmider's *Kaiserkeller* on 1 October 1960, where Starkey first met the band.

In 1965 he married long term friend and hairdresser Maureen "Mo" Cox after he found out that the 18 year old Mo was pregnant with his child. Manager Brian Epstein tried to keep the marriage quiet but when word got out they were besieged by over 100 photographers in Brighton & Hove where they were honeymooning. They were married for ten years and had three children, Zak, Jason and Lee.

Their marriage really broke up in 1970 following her affair with George Harrison, an incident that so angered John Lennon that he once referred to it as "virtual incest." In 1976, Maureen started to live with Isaac Tigrett, one of the founders of the *Hard Rock Cafe* and they eventually married in 1989.

In 1981 Starr married Barbara Bach, an American actress and model best known for her role as the Bond girl Anya Amasova in the film *The Spy Who Loved Me*. They remain married and have each been treated for alcoholism.

Ringo has, on more than one occasion, claimed that he is the only surviving *Beatle*.

Stuart Sutcliffe

Stuart Sutcliffe was born on the 23 June 1940 at the Simpson Memorial Maternity Pavilion Hospital in Edinburgh, Scotland to Millie and Charles Sutcliffe. His father was a senior civil servant and later ship's engineer, and so was often absent during Stuart's early childhood. Stuart had two younger sisters, Pauline and Joyce.

When he was four his family moved to Liverpool and he attended Park View Primary School in Huyton and later Prescot Grammar School. Afterwards he went to the Liverpool College of Art where he was regarded as a highly gifted student.

While studying at Liverpool College of Art, Stuart worked part time as a bin man for the Corporation. Bill Harry introduced Sutcliffe to Lennon and they became close friends. Sutcliffe and Harry shared a dingy flat at 9 Percy Street, Liverpool, before being evicted and moving to another dingy flat in Hillary Mansions at 3 Gambier Terrace. Lennon moved in with Sutcliffe in early 1960. They were so broke that on one occasion they burned the flat's furniture to keep warm. One night at the *Casbah Coffee Club* Lennon and McCartney realizing that Sutcliffe was not only a talented artist but also an accomplished guitarist, persuaded Sutcliffe to buy a Höfner President 500/5 model bass guitar on hire-purchase from Frank Hessey's Music Shop. And so, in May 1960 Sutcliffe joined Lennon, McCartney, and George Harrison in their band which was, at that time known as *The Silver Beatles*. Sutcliffe began acting as a booking agent for the group, and they often used his Gambier Terrace flat as a rehearsal room.

The group later changed their name following a discussion one afternoon in the Renshaw Hall bar when Sutcliffe, Lennon and his girlfriend, Cynthia Powell, thought up names similar to Buddy Holly's band, the *Crickets*. They eventually came up with *Beatals*. But Lennon later changed the name to *The Beatles* because he thought the original name sounded too French.

When *The Beatles* auditioned for Larry Parnes at the Wyvern Club, Seel Street, Liverpool, their then road manager, Allan Williams, claimed that Parnes would have taken the group as the backing band for Billy Fury for £10 per week but for Sutcliffe, who didn't impress him, and the fact that they did not have a permanent drummer.

Despite this setback Sutcliffe's popularity grew after he began wearing Ray-Ban sunglasses and tight trousers and within a short period he was becoming the fan's favourite. This caused friction in the band as Lennon and McCartney became increasingly more jealous over his popularity. In any event, it all ended in farce when on the 5 December 1960 Harrison was sent back to England because he was too young to play in nightclubs and McCartney and Best were deported for attempted arson at the *Bambi Kino*. This left Lennon and Sutcliffe alone in Hamburg. Lennon took a train home, but as Sutcliffe had a cold, he stayed in Hamburg until the 20 January 1961 when he returned home. In March 1961 he went back to Hamburg with the other *Beatles* for their second residency.

However, in July 1961, Sutcliffe decided to leave the group after being awarded a postgraduate scholarship at the Hamburg College of Art under the tutelage of Paolozzi. On the 10 April 1962, he suddenly became ill and was taken to hospital, but died in the ambulance on the way. The cause of death was later revealed to have been an aneurysm in his brain's right hemisphere.

PETE BEST

Randolph Peter Best was born in Madras (now Chennai) in British India on the 24 November 1941 to Alice Mona Shaw and Donald Peter Scanland. His father was a marine engineer who subsequently died during World War II. His mother Mona was training to become a doctor when she met Johnny Best.

Johnny's family were well known business people in Liverpool who once owned the Liverpool Stadium. Johnny and Mona married on the 7 March 1944 at St. Thomas's Cathedral, Bombay, and effectively became Pete's dad. The family returned to Liverpool on Christmas day 1945 sailing on the *Georgic*, the last troop ship to leave India. Initially, the family lived at John Best's family home Ellerslie Manor, in West Derby, and then moved to a small flat on Cases Street, Liverpool. In 1948 they moved to 17 Queenscourt Road where they remained for nine years.

In 1957 they purchased a large Victorian house at 8 Hayman's Green. Previously owned by the West Derby Conservative Club, the 15 bedroomed house was set in an acre of land. Mona later opened *The Casbah Coffee Club* in the large cellar of the house.

It was later to become one of Liverpool's most famous clubs. Best attended Blackmoor Park primary school in West Derby and the Collegiate Grammar School in Shaw Street. After his mother bought him a drum kit from Blackler's music store Best joined up with Chas Newby, Bill Barlow and Ken Brown and formed his own band, *The Black Jacks*. Brown had, at one time been a member of *The Quarrymen*.

The Black Jacks later became the resident group at *The Casbah*, after *The Quarrymen* cancelled their residency because of an argument about money.

After leaving the music scene Best worked as a civil servant for the employment exchange in England for

20 years before retiring in 1989. Since then, he's been playing music, written a book and released a DVD about his experience with *The Beatles*.

Lennon, McCartney, and Harrison all later stated that they regretted the manner in which Best was sacked. Lennon admitted that "we were cowards when we sacked him. We made Brian do it." McCartney said: "I do feel sorry for him, because of what he could have been on to." While Harrison admitted: "We weren't very good at telling Pete he had to go. Historically it may look like we did something nasty to Pete and it may have been that we could have handled it better." Ringo Starr was not involved in the sacking and knew nothing about the details.

Beatles' biographer Mark Lewisohn wrote:

> **Despite his alleged shortcomings, it was still shabby treatment ... the most underhand, unfortunate and unforgivable chapter in The Beatles' rise to monumental power.**

Pete has been married for over fifty years to Kathy Best. They have two daughters and four grandchildren. On the 25 July 2011 the city of Liverpool honoured Pete Best with the announcement that two new streets in the city would be named *Pete Best Drive* and *Casbah Close*.

Allan Williams

The Beatles built their reputation playing clubs in

Liverpool and Hamburg over a three-year period from 1960. Their first manager and initial booking agent was Allan Williams. Allan Richard Williams was born on the 17 March 1930 in Bootle, Liverpool. A former businessman and promoter, it was Williams who personally drove the van to take the young band to Hamburg, Germany in 1960.

Allan left home in his mid-teens to sing with Joe Loss in the Isle of Man. Later he sang with the *D'Oyly Carte Opera Company*. In 1958 he rented a shop at 21 Slater Street, Liverpool, which he converted into a coffee bar. He called the venue the *Jacaranda*, after an exotic species of ornamental flowering tree, *jacaranda mimosifolia*.

It soon became known as *The Jac* and was popular with a lot of emerging band members at the time including John Lennon and Stuart Sutcliffe who attended the nearby Liverpool Art College. When they asked him for the opportunity to play at *The Jac* he agreed subject to the proviso that they first help him redecorate the premises.

Between May and August 1960, Williams secured a number of bookings for the group one of which was backing for a local stripper. But it was really in Hamburg where his best contacts were. In the 1958 documentary *The Compleat Beatles*, Williams tells the story of having to reassure Howie Casey, leader of *The Seniors* who were already established in Hamburg about introducing Hamburg to *The Beatles*. Casey had said:

Listen, we've got a good thing going here in Hamburg. But if you send that bum group, The Beatles, you're going to louse it up for all of us.

Nevertheless, in August 1960, with Pete Best as the group's new drummer, Allan Williams and *The Beatles* left Liverpool in a small, crowded van and drove to Hamburg for the first time.

The band, now a five-piece, were contracted to club owner Bruno Koschmider for what was to be a ten week residency. Koschmider had converted a couple of strip clubs in the district into music venues, and he initially placed *The Beatles* at the *Indra Club*. Then after it was closed down due to noise pollution he moved them to the *Kaiserkeller* in October.

But when he discovered that they had been performing at the rival *Top Ten Club* in breach of their contract, he gave the band one month's termination notice. He also informed the authorities that Harrison was too young to be playing in night clubs. Harrison had obtained permission to stay in Hamburg by lying to the German authorities about his age.

One week later, he had McCartney and Best arrested for attempted arson and they had to leave the country for a while. But they returned and completed five residencies in Hamburg. He continued to get them bookings, until he fell out with the group in 1961 over the payment of his ten per cent commission. In 1962 Brian Epstein became the band's manager despite having been warned by Williams:

Do not to touch them with a fucking bargepole, they will let you down.

In 1975, he published a memoir, *The Man Who Gave The Beatles Away*.

BRIAN EPSTEIN

English music entrepreneur Brian Samuel Epstein was born in Rodney Street, Liverpool, on the 19 September 1934 to furniture store owner Harry Epstein and Malka "Queenie" Hyman. The family lived at 197 Queens Drive, Childwall, in Liverpool, and would remain there for the next 30 years.

After being expelled from several schools Brian went to work in the family business before being conscripted to do his national service as a data entry clerk into the Royal Army Service Corps. After this, his parents, now aware of the fact that he was homosexual, allowed him to go to London to become an actor.

Epstein attended the *Royal Academy of Dramatic Art* (RADA), in London where his classmates included actors Susannah York, Albert Finney and Peter O'Toole. But, missing the world of business he dropped out after the third term and returned to Liverpool where his father put him in charge of the music department of his new store, *NEMS*, on Great Charlotte Street.

Epstein worked tirelessly to make it a success and so

impressed his father that after he opened another store at 12–14 Whitechapel, Epstein was put in charge of the entire operation. Epstein began to take an interest in *The Beatles* when he saw them in various issues of *Mersey Beat* and on numerous posters around Liverpool. He knew Bill Harry, editor of *Mersey Beat* who had persuaded Brian to let him sell the magazine in his stores. After the group had recorded the *My Bonnie* single with Tony Sheridan in Germany, they were again featured in the magazine. Epstein made enquiries.

In August 1961, Epstein started a regular music column in the *Mersey Beat*, called "Stop the World— And Listen To Everything In It: Brian Epstein of NEMS." Epstein first saw *The Beatles* perform live in the *Cavern Club* on the 9 November 1961. He was later to write:

> **I was immediately struck by their music, their beat and their sense of humour on stage and, even afterwards, when I met them, I was struck again by their personal charm. And it was there that, really, it all started.**

The Beatles played at the *Cavern* over the next three weeks, and Epstein was always there to watch them. He then contacted their previous manager Allan Williams to see if there were any contractual ties. Satisfied that there were none he arranged to meet them at his offices on the 3 December 1961.

Lennon, Harrison and Best turned up with Bob Wooler, the resident DJ at the *Cavern*, who Lennon introduced as his dad. When asked about the absence of Paul McCartney, George said he was having a bath and would be late. On noticing that this upset Epstein, Harrison is reputed to have quipped:

Don't worry. He may be late, but he'll be very clean.

Epstein indicated that he would like to manage them as a band and two further meetings followed on the 6 and 10 December 1961. The reaction of their respective families was mixed. McCartney's father was sceptical about him getting involved with a Jewish manager.

Pete Best's mother, Mona, was impressed by Epstein and thought he could be good for them. Lennon's aunt and guardian, Mimi Smith, was positively against the idea while Harrison's family were cautious but in favour.

On the 24 January 1962 John, Paul, Pete and George signed a five-year contract with Epstein which gave him between 10 and 15% of their income. A new contract was signed in October 1962 which gave him 15 to 25% of their income depending on how much he helped them make. The members of the band would then share any residual income after deduction of expenses. In many respects they were the first boy band.

On the 1 October 1962, four days before the release of *Love Me Do*, Epstein signed Lennon and McCartney to a three-year NEMS publishing contract.

It was a bold and brave move for a businessman who lacked any artist management experience but Epstein proved to be adept at improving their image and general performance. He made them wear suits, despite Lennon's initial protestations and banned them from smoking, swearing, eating or drinking while on stage. Within a relatively short period of time he had moulded them into a very professional act.

Meanwhile Epstein endeavoured to free them from their contractual obligations with Bert Kaempfert Productions. He eventually negotiated a one-month-early release from their contract in exchange for one last recording session in Hamburg. It was on their return to Hamburg to undertake the session when they heard the tragic news of the untimely death of their friend and colleague Stuart Sutcliffe.

Later, Epstein began negotiations with record labels Columbia, Pye, Philips, and Oriole for a recording contract but he enjoyed little success. After an early February audition, Decca Records rejected the band with the comment "Guitar groups are on the way out, Mr. Epstein". Unperturbed, Epstein secured the services of producer George Martin and three months later he signed *The Beatles* to EMI's Parlophone label.

It was a major coup for Epstein and his merry band of mop heads, considering that EMI producers Norrie Paramor, Walter Ridley and Norman Newell had already declined to sign them. It wasn't a great recording contract but at least it was a recording contract and *The Beatles* were on their way to world domination.

Then they sacked Pete Best. The deal gave them, John Lennon, Paul McCartney, George Harrison and Pete Best one penny (1d) for each record sold, which split among the four members, meant they would earn a farthing per copy. The royalty rate was further reduced by fifty per cent for singles sold outside the UK. Martin scheduled the first recording session to be on the 6 June 1962, at Abbey Road Studios but it didn't go smoothly.

Martin was less than impressed with the band's drummer, Pete Best, and he and his experienced team of sound engineers suggested that they use an experienced studio session drummer to make the recording more professionally sounding. This was not an unusual practice as many bands changed musicians for recordings. What happened next has always been disputed with different versions depending on who is telling them. The general consensus is that when they heard that Martin didn't want Best as the recording drummer, Lennon, McCartney and Harrison, fearful that EMI might pull out, instructed Epstein to sack Pete Best. Epstein wasn't happy with the task. He knew Best was not the greatest drummer ever, but he was very popular with the fans. In his autobiography, *A Cellarful of Noise* (1964) which was actually written by Derek Taylor *The Beatles'* press office, Epstein wrote that he "wasn't sure" about Martin's assessment of Best's drumming:

> **I was not anxious to change the membership of the Beatles at a time when they were developing**

> **as personalities. I asked the Beatles to leave the group as it was.**

But, ultimately, Epstein decided that if the group was to remain happy, Pete Best must go. Pete Best played his last two gigs with *The Beatles* on the 15 August 1962 at the *Cavern Club,* Liverpool. He was due to play his last show on the following day at *The Riverpark Ballroom*, Chester; however, Johnny Hutchinson drummed on this occasion after Epstein summoned Best to his office and summarily dismissed him, ten weeks and one day after the first recording session.

Pete Best had been with the group for two years and four days. He has always maintained that he was never given a satisfactory explanation for his dismissal. Epstein initially offered the vacant position to Johnny Hutchinson, who played in a group called *The Big Three* but he turned down the offer saying:

> **Pete Best is a very good friend of mine. I couldn't do the dirty on him.**

However, Hutchinson did play for *The Beatles* at short notice when Best did not turn up on the evening of his dismissal, and for two subsequent bookings, until Ringo Starr could join. Starr was well known to the group, as he was then playing with the hugely popular band *Rory Storm and the Hurricanes*. Starr had also occasionally replaced Best when the drummer was ill, and had performed at a recording session with Lennon, McCartney and Harrison in Hamburg. George Martin was shocked to discover that Epstein had dismissed Best and is alleged to have told Mona

Best when she phoned him about the matter:

> **I never suggested that Pete Best must go. All I said was that for the purposes of the Beatles' first record I would rather use a session man. I never thought that Brian Epstein would let him go. He seemed to be the most saleable commodity as far as looks went. It was a surprise when I learned that they had dropped Pete. The drums were important to me for a record, but they didn't matter much otherwise. Fans don't pay particular attention to the quality of the drumming.**

Pete Best's friend, Neil Aspinall was working as road manager for the group at the time and was waiting for him downstairs in Epstein's NEMS record shop after the dismissal meeting. Furious at what had happened he threatened to leave the band but Pete persuaded him to remain on. At the next concert he asked John Lennon why Pete had been sacked to which Lennon replied:

> **It's got nothing to do with you, you're only the driver.**

Bill Harry, the editor of *Mersey Beat* reported Best's dismissal on the front-page of the magazine. Many *Beatles'* fans were genuinely upset. So much so that the group encountered some jeering and heckling in the street and on stage for weeks afterwards with some fans chanting "Pete forever, Ringo never!"But within a couple of months all had been forgiven if not forgotten and Ringo Starr became the fourth but not final member of the *Fab Four*.

*Do not to touch them with a fucking bargepole,
they will let you down.*

Allan Williams to Brian Epstein

PLEASE PLEASE ME (1963)

The first single released by *The Beatles* was *Love Me Do* with *P.S. I Love You* on the B side. It was released in the United Kingdom on the 5 October 1962 and it reached Number 17. When it was released two years later in the United States, it reached number one.

One of the reasons why it probably didn't do better in the UK was that the group were completing their fifth residency in Hamburg and had little time to promote it in the UK. In 1962 the group were really only known in Liverpool and Hamburg. The song was written by Lennon and McCartney.

Please Please Me was their second song to be released as a single in the UK on the 11 January 1963. Originally written entirely by Lennon its ultimate form was significantly influenced by their producer George Martin.

It reached number one on the New Musical Express chart, which was the top chart at the time, on the 22 February and later hit number one on the Melody Maker chart. Even though Brian Epstein bought 2,000 copies of the single, it stalled on the third chart the Record Retailer Chart at number two. The Record Retailer chart ultimately evolved into the UK Singles Chart. The flip side of the single had the track *Ask Me Why*.

Buoyed by the success of their first two singles George Martin decided to have the group make an LP. At the time, LPs released in the UK usually had seven songs on each side. They already had four songs, *Love Me Do*, *P.S. I Love You*, *Please Please Me*, and *Ask Me Why*.

They needed ten more songs. Martin decided they could record them all in a single day. No one has ever satisfactorily explained why he deemed it necessary to record an entire album in a single day and one can only surmise that he was under certain financial constraints. Mark Lewisohn in *The Beatles Recording Sessions* (1988) quotes George Martin as saying:

> **There wasn't a lot of money at Parlophone. I was working to an annual budget of £55,000.**

This budget was for all the artists on Martin's books. The whole day's session cost just over £400 which in today's terms would be the equivalent of around £10,000. All the musicians were paid in accordance with their rates as members of the Musicians' Union. Each member of the group was paid a flat fee of £7.50 per session fee for each three-hour session.

Initially Martin thought about recording the album live at *The Cavern* and visited the venue in December to check out the acoustics. But because of a combination of technical problems and time restraints he opted to make the recording in the EMI Studios in Abbey Road. George Martin in the book *With a Little Help from My Friends: The Making of Sgt. Pepper* (1994) by George Martin and William Pearson commented about the recording session:

> **It was a straightforward performance of their stage repertoire; a broadcast, more or less.**

The session began at 10:00 a.m. on Monday morning the 11 February 1963 and finished at 10:45 p.m. Essentially, it was a thirteen hour live act with a couple of breaks thrown in between. In three sessions of three hours each (Martin had over optimistically booked just two) the group produced an authentic representation of the band's *Cavern Club*-era sound. *Beatles'* expert Mark Lewisohn was hardly exaggerating when he wrote:

> **There can scarcely have been 585 more productive minutes in the history of recorded music.**

Initially Martin had decided to call the album *Off the Beatle Track* before realizing the popularity of the single *Please Please Me*. He then thought it better to capitalize on that success.

An eleventh song *Hold Me Tight* was recorded during these sessions but as it was considered to be surplus to requirements it was not included on the album. The album was released as a mono LP album on the Parlophone label in the UK on the 22 March 1963 and reached the top of the UK album charts in May 1963 where it remained for thirty weeks before being replaced by their second album *With the Beatles*.

In 2012, it was voted 39th on *Rolling Stone* magazine's list of the "2500 Greatest Albums of All Time".

It wasn't just the album that was an immediate success. The following month the group released their third single *From Me To You* also reaching number one which initiated an almost unbroken string of seventeen British number-one singles for them, including all but one of the eighteen they released over the next six years.

Their fourth single *She Loves You* released in August

achieved the fastest sales of any record in the UK up to that time. It sold an incredible three-quarters of a million copies in under four weeks and became their first single to sell a million copies. The group toured the UK three times in the first half of the year. They became a sensational overnight success. Everywhere they went they were greeted with frenzied adulation, riotous enthusiasm and screaming fans. The media called the frenzy *Beatlemania* and it was contagious.

In 2014 boy band *One Direction* were considered to be the most popular band in the world. If you take the adulation of their fans and multiply it by ten then you will have an indication of what *Beatlemania* was like at the time.

In late October, *The Beatles* began a five-day tour of Sweden which was their first time abroad since the final Hamburg engagement of December 1962. They returned to the UK on the 31 October to be greeted by several hundred screaming fans and about one hundred members of the press at Heathrow Airport. The following day the group began its fourth tour of Britain within nine months. Meanwhile, *Beatlemania* intensified and police were obliged to resort to using high-pressure water hoses to control concert crowds to avoid riots taking place.

WITH THE BEATLES (1963)

EMI actually delayed the release of the *With the Beatles* until they were sure the sales of *Please Please Me* had peaked. *With the Beatles* was released in November 1963 with 270,000 advance orders. It sold half a million copies in one week, holding the number one position for twenty one weeks and remaining on the charts for forty weeks.

Reversing their usual practice EMI released the album before releasing their single *I Want to Hold Your Hand*. It was an inspired decision. Critics loved the album, loved the single and loved the group. William Mann of *The Times* suggested that Lennon and McCartney were "the outstanding English composers of 1963." They were now the darlings of the music establishment and the album *With The Beatles* became the second album in UK chart history to sell a million copies. They then became known as the *Fab Four*.

They had conquered the UK but the question on everyone's lips was whether or not they could crack America.

The initial invasion of America by *Beatlemania* was hindered by a succession of legal and business arguments and disputes. Capitol Records were EMI's American subsidiary. They prevented the group's releases in the United States for more than a year by initially declining to issue their music, including their first three singles. The group's management entered negotiations with the independent US label Vee-Jay which resulted in the release of some of the songs in 1963.

They also prepared an album called *Introducing The Beatles* which consisted of most of the songs of

Parlophone's *Please Please Me*. However the album wasn't released because of infighting and a subsequent management shake-up. When it was discovered that the label did not report royalties on their sales the licence Vee-Jay signed with EMI was rescinded. EMI entered into a new license agreement with the Swan label for the single *She Loves You*, but once again legal issues with royalties and publishing rights hindered any successful marketing of the group in the US.

Accordingly, Brian Epstein made an executive decision to launch a $40,000 American marketing campaign for the group. He also persuaded disc jockey Carrol James to begin playing their records.

In December 1963 they were introduced in the Tidewater area of Virginia by Gene Loving of radio station WGH-AM, accompanied by a full marketing campaign, including *Beatles'* shirt giveaways. By January 1964 their records were being played on radio stations in New York followed by the rest of the country. They had arrived in America but had yet to visit.

Released on the 26 December 1963 their single *I Want to Hold Your Hand* became a number one hit in America selling over one million copies. Shortly afterwards, Vee-Jay released *Introducing The Beatles* to coincide with Capitol's debut album *Meet the Beatles!* Meanwhile Swan reactivated production of *She Loves You*. America waited with bated breath for the arrival of the *Fab Four*.

An estimated 4,000 crying and screaming fans waved goodbye to their idols at Heathrow Airport on the 7 February 1964. Ten hours later a similar uproarious crowd greeted them at New York's John F. Kennedy airport. *Beatlemania* invaded America.

Two days later they gave their first live television performance on the *Ed Sullivan Show*. The show was watched by approximately 73 million viewers in over 23 million households. They equated to an incredible 34 per cent of the American population.

The Beatles were the headline act and it wasn't as if there was nothing else to report on in America. Madeline McCullough in a paper on mass hysteria *Mass Hysteria Case Study: Don't Worry it's Just Beatlemania* (Elliott School of Communication, Wichita State University) wrote:

> **The Beatles were a huge news story, but certainly not the only big story in 1964, 1965 and 1966. The Rev. Dr. Martin Luther King, Jr. delivered his "I Have a Dream" speech in August 1963, six months before the Beatles first U.S. appearance on Feb. 7, 1964. The November before their debut on Sullivan's show President John F. Kennedy was assassinated. And just a month prior the United States Surgeon General Luther Leonidas Terry reported in January that smoking may be hazardous to your health. The U.S. Post Office was adopting the ZIP code system, Valium and Lava Lamps made their debut and Andy Warhol, Jasper Johns and Roy Lichtenstein exhibited their work in the first large-scale exhibition of Pop Art at the Guggenheim**

Museum in New York City. It the midst of all this four Brits were capturing the nation's attention, the world's attention, in a big way.

Biographer Jonathan Gould in his *book Can't Buy Me Love: The Beatles, Britain, and America* (2008) wrote that it was:

the largest audience that had ever been recorded for an American television program.

But according to Bob Spitz in *The Beatles: The Biography* (2006) not everyone was a fan of *The Beatles* and they encountered their fair share of criticism.

The group played to rapturous acclaim at the Washington *Coliseum* and later at New York's *Carnegie Hall* before flying south to conquer Florida. They then appeared again on the weekly *Ed Sullivan Show* before another 70 million viewers, before returning to the UK on the 22 February, 1964. Not everyone loved the *Beatles* but enough did to make the group hugely successful in America.

A HARD DAY'S NIGHT – THE MOVIE (1964)

Realizing the lucrative potential of their soundtracks United Artists Records trumped Capitol Records and persuaded their film department to offer the group a three picture deal. It was an offer they couldn't refuse. Richard Lester directed the *Fab Four* in *A Hard Day's Night*. The mockumentary took just six weeks to make and premiered in July in London and New York the following month receiving rave reviews on both sides of the Atlantic. In an unprecedented week in April 1964 *The Beatles* held twelve positions on the Billboard Hot 100 singles chart, including the top five. Their trademark German inspired collarless suits and unusually long mop head style haircuts became a symbol of revolution to the new era of a questioning youth culture.

They had conquered the UK and the USA it was now time to tackle the rest of the world. They began touring in June 1964 and staged thirty seven shows over twenty seven days in countries as diverse as Denmark, Holland, Hong Kong, Australia and New Zealand. They then flew on to America where they attracted audiences of between 10 to 20,000 in cities from New York to San Francisco.

That August they met Bob Dylan in their New York hotel suite. They exchanged music styles and he introduced them to drugs in general and cannabis in particular. Despite their squeaky clean image the group had already been experimenting with drugs since their Hamburg days.

A HARD DAY'S NIGHT – THE ALBUM (1964)

The group adopted the name of their first film, *A Hard Day's Night*, for their third studio album. It was recorded at EMI Studios in London and Pathé Marconi Studios, in Paris on the 29 January, 25-27 February, 1 March and 1-4 June and finally released on the 10 July 1964.

One side contained songs from the soundtrack to their film while the other side contains songs written for, but not included in the film. The American version of the album was released two weeks earlier by United Artists Records, with a different track listing.

The title of the album was selected by the film director Richard Lester after a comment made by Ringo Starr. In an 1980 *Playboy* interview Lennon is quoted as saying:

> **I was going home in the car and Dick Lester suggested the title, 'Hard Day's Night' from something Ringo had said. I had used it in 'In His Own Write', but it was an off-the-cuff remark by Ringo. You know, one of those malapropisms. A Ringo-ism, where he said it not to be funny ... just said it. So Dick Lester said, 'We are going to use that title.'**

The album contained thirteen original songs all of which were written by Lennon and McCartney including *A Hard Days' Night* and *Can't Buy Me Love* previously released on the 26 March 1964. Both singles became transatlantic number ones. Lennon wrote ten out of the thirteen tracks on the album, all except *And I Love Her, Can't Buy Me Love,* and *Things We Said Today*. This is also one of three Beatles albums, along with *Let It Be* and *Magical Mystery Tour* on which Ringo Starr does not sing lead vocal on any songs.

In 2000, the magazine *Q* placed the album at number five in its list of the 100 Greatest British Albums Ever. In 2012, *Rolling Stone* magazine voted it 307th on *Rolling Stone* magazine's list of the "500 Greatest Albums of All Time".

Critics loved it. Tom Ewing from *Pitchfork Media*, commented that the lack of rock and roll covers allows listeners to

> **take the group's new sound purely on its own modernist terms, with audacious chord choices, powerful harmonies, gleaming guitar, and Northern harmonica.**

Many critics wrote about how the group's music had matured and become sophisticated. Others specifically singled out George Harrison's contribution. Richie Unterberger in *The Beatles Biography* (2009) wrote:

> **George Harrison's resonant 12-string electric guitar leads were hugely influential; the movie helped persuade The Byrds, then folksingers, to plunge all out into rock and roll, and the Beatles would be hugely influential on the folk-rock explosion of 1965. The Beatles' success, too, had begun to open the US market for fellow Brits like the Rolling Stones, the Animals, and the Kinks, and inspired young American groups like the Beau Brummels, Lovin' Spoonful, and others to mount a challenge of their own with self-penned material that owed a great debt to Lennon-McCartney.**

In *A Hard Day's Night* all songs were credited to John Lennon and Paul McCartney. In the UK three singles were released from the album. *A Hard Day's Night* with *I Should Have Known Better* on the flip side was released on the 13 July 1964. *And I Love Her* and *If I Fell* on the flip side was released on the 20 July 1964. *I'll Cry Instead* with *I'm Happy Just to Dance with You* was released on the 20 August 1964.

In the USA United Artists Records released the American version of the album on the 26 June 1964 in both mono and stereo. *The Beatles'* fourth album in the United States went straight to number one on the Billboard album chart, and stayed there for fourteen weeks.

BEATLES FOR SALE (1964)

Just a month after the release of the film *A Hard Day's Night* the group were back in the studio recording their fourth studio album, *Beatles for Sale*. The first session took place between the 11 and 14 August 1964. The final session was on the 26 October 1964. Not surprisingly they had exhausted their repertoire of songs and their hectic schedule did not allow them the opportunity to replenish their store.

Originally they wanted the album to continue in the format established by *A Hard Day's Night* containing only original songs but as Lennon readily admitted: "Material's becoming a hell of a problem."

Consequently, six covers were necessary to complete the album which was recorded between August and October 1964. But the eight originals which made up the rest of the album eloquently demonstrated the bludgeoning maturity of the Lennon and McCartney song writing partnership. It couldn't get any better, or could it?

Beatles for Sale was released on the 4 December 1964 and for the first time showed the influence Bob Dylan had on the group's principal songwriter, John Lennon. Lennon had met him in New York on the 28 August 1964 while on tour.

The album did not produce a single for the UK but non-album tracks *I Feel Fine* and *She's a Woman* were released as singles in the UK. They were followed up in the United States by *Eight Days a Week*, which became their seventh number one in March 1965.

The album reached number one in the UK and retained that position for 11 of the 46 weeks that it spent in the Top 20. It was their fourth album in 21 months. Much of the production on the album was carried out on days off from performances in the UK, and most of the song writing was completed in the studio itself. The constant rounds of films, recordings, performing, appearances and song writing were beginning to take their toll on the group.

As George Martin later said:

> **They were rather war-weary during Beatles for Sale. One must remember that they'd been**

> battered like mad throughout '64, and much of '63. Success is a wonderful thing, but it is very, very tiring.

Even the prolific Lennon and McCartney song writing team could not keep up with the demand for their songs. The album included six covers, the same number as their first two albums. McCartney later said that the album was basically their stage show, with some new songs. The group's road manager, Neil Aspinall, later reflected:

> No band today would come off a long US tour at the end of September, go into the studio and start a new album, still writing songs, and then go on a UK tour, finish the album in five weeks, still touring, and have the album out in time for Christmas. But that's what the Beatles did at the end of 1964. A lot of it was down to naivety, thinking that this was the way things were done. If the record company needs another album, you go and make one.

The reaction of critics was, in the main, positive but several commented on the group's exhaustion with Erlewine writing

> The weariness of Beatles for Sale comes as something of a shock.

In early 1965, Lennon and Harrison were introduced to LSD by, of all people, their dentist and became regular users. The identity of the dentist who first introduced *The Beatles* to LSD was finally revealed in the book *The Fab Four: The Gospel According to the*

Beatles (2007) by Steve Turner as John Riley, a distinguished professional with a practice in London's Harley Street. Riley's identity has been shrouded since that fateful occurrence in 1965, but in 2007, twenty years after his death, Turner lifted the lid on the controversial dentist, who spiked the stars' coffees with the drug when they went to dinner with him. Lennon was later to comment on his first trip as follows:

> **It was just terrifying, but it was fantastic. I was pretty stunned for a month or two.**

McCartney began using LSD on a regular basis in late 1966 and became the first *Beatle* to discuss LSD publicly when he admitted in a magazine article that it opened his eyes and made him a better, more honest, more tolerant member of society. The group's squeaky clean image was fast wearing off.

McCartney discussed LSD while chatting with a reporter who had enquired about it. His LSD quote appeared in *Queen*, a UK-based magazine at the time.

The quote was also then reprinted by *Life* magazine in their 16 June 1967 feature, "The New Far-Out Beatles: They're grown men now and creating extraordinary musical sounds' by Thomas Thompson. In both articles, Paul McCartney was quoted as saying:

> **After I took it (LSD), it opened my eyes. We only use one-tenth of our brain. Just think what we could accomplish if we could only tap that hidden part. It would mean a whole new world.**

Before this damaging revelation surfaced and in a blatant effort to court popular opinion, at least among younger voters, the *Fab Four* were each nominated for MBE (Member of the British Empire) awards by the then British Prime Minister Harold Wilson. The honours were conferred in June 1965 amid much controversy.

John Lennon returned his MBE to the Queen on the 25 November 1969, as an act of protest against the Vietnam war. The insignia was accompanied by handwritten letters to the Queen, prime minister Harold Wilson, and the secretary of the Central Chancery, explaining his actions. The letters were written on notepaper headed Bag Productions and the one to the Queen read:

> **Your Majesty, I am returning my MBE as a protest against Britain's involvement in the Nigeria-Biafra thing, against our support of America in Vietnam and against 'Cold Turkey' slipping down the charts. With love. John Lennon of Bag.**

Cold Turkey is a song written by John Lennon, released as a single in 1969 by the *Plastic Ono Band*. It peaked at number 30 on the charts.

HELP! – THE MOVIE (1965)

Help was the second feature film made by *The Beatles* and directed by Richard Lester. Because of the commercial success of *A Hard Day's Night*, Lester was given a much bigger budget, $1,500,000 for this movie. The producers needn't have worried about their investment. The movie returned $12,066,667. As well as the *Fab Four* the film starred Leo McKern, Eleanor Bron, Victor Spinetti, John Bluthal, Roy Kinnear and Patrick Cargill.

It is a comedy adventure Bond spoof which sees the group combat an evil cult. The soundtrack was released as an album, also called *Help!* The film was originally entitled *Eight Arms To Hold You* but the name was changed at the last moment. The movie itself was shot in colour in several exotic foreign locations. It was also given a fuller musical score than the previous movie and included pieces of well-known classical music including Wagner's *Lohengrin Act III Overture*, Tchaikovsky's *1812 Overture*, Beethoven's *Ninth Symphony* and, during the end credits and with their own comic vocal interpretation, Rossini's *Barber of Seville* overture.

Help! was shot in London, Salisbury Plain, the Austrian Alps, New Providence Island, Paradise Island in the Bahamas and Twickenham Film Studios. Principal photography began in the Bahamas on the 23 February 1965 and finished on the 14 April at Ailsa Avenue in Twickenham. The film was released at the end of July 1965 and was a mishmash of slapstick pseudo comedy which pleased no one. In 1970, John Lennon said they felt like extras in their own movie:

The movie was out of our control. With A Hard

Day's Night, we had a lot of input, and it was semi-realistic. But with Help!, Dick Lester didn't tell us what it was all about.

McCartney said about the movie:

Help! was great but it wasn't our film – we were sort of guest stars. It was fun, but basically, as an idea for a film, it was a bit wrong.

But Ringo Starr was the most honest when he said about the film:

A hell of a lot of pot was being smoked while we were making the film. It was great. That helped make it a lot of fun. In one of the scenes, Victor Spinetti and Roy Kinnear are playing curling: sliding along those big stones. One of the stones has a bomb in it and we find out that it's going to blow up, and have to run away. Well, Paul and I ran about seven miles, we ran and ran, just so we could stop and have a joint before we came back. We could have run all the way to Switzerland. If you look at pictures of us you can see a lot of red-eyed shots; they were red from the dope we were smoking. And these were those clean-cut boys! Dick Lester knew that very little would get done after lunch.

In the afternoon we very seldom got past the first line of the script. We had such hysterics that no one could do anything. Dick Lester would say, 'No, boys, could we do it again?' It was just that we had a lot of fun – a lot of fun in those days.

On that score he was right. The *Fab Four* were not

just enjoying their success but they were having fun and hanging out with each other.

Help! – THE ALBUM (1965)

Lennon dominated the soundtrack for the movie and wrote and sang lead on most of its songs, including the two singles: *Help!* and *Ticket to Ride*. The accompanying album which was the group's fifth studio LP, contained all original material save for two covers, *Act Naturally* and *Dizzy Miss Lizzy*. With the exception of *Let It Be's* brief rendition of the traditional Liverpool folk song *Maggie Mae* these were the last covers the band would include on an album. The album is famous for the inclusion of the McCartney classic *Yesterday*. The song would inspire the most recorded cover versions of any song ever written.

McCartney said he composed the melody in a dream while staying at the family home of Jane Asher in Wimpole Street, London. He said in *Anthology*:

> **I was living in a little flat at the top of a house and I had a piano by my bed. I woke up one morning with a tune in my head and I thought, 'Hey, I don't know this tune - or do I?' It was like a jazz melody. My dad used to know a lot of old jazz tunes; I thought maybe I'd just remembered it from the past. I went to the piano and found the chords to it, made sure I remembered it and then hawked it round to all my friends, asking what it was: 'Do you know this? It's a good little**

tune, but I couldn't have written it because I dreamt it.'

However, there is a growing band of anti-McCartneyites who claim Sir Paul McCartney never wrote any of the classics attributed to him.

The songs played during the film are: *Help!*, *You're Going to Lose That Girl*, *You've Got to Hide Your Love Away*, *Ticket to Ride*, *I Need You*, *The Night Before*, *Another Girl*, *She's a Woman*, *A Hard Day's Night*, *I'm Happy Just to Dance with You* and *You Can't Do That*.

The seven main songs formed the first side of the album while the second side consisted of other new *Beatles'* songs recorded at the same time or shortly afterwards. The month following the release of their second feature the group were back in America for another tour. The tour opened on the 15 August 1965 with a concert before a world-record crowd of 55,600 at New York's Shea Stadium. Lewisohn described it as "perhaps the most famous of all Beatles' concerts."

A further nine successful concerts followed throughout the States. Before their last concert they were invited to Beverly Hills, to meet the legend, Elvis Presley. That September an American Saturday-morning cartoon series, *The Beatles*, was launched. It represented an historical milestone being the first weekly television series to feature animated versions of real life people. The end of the tour represented another milestone in *The Beatles'* story.

Something happened. Something changed and they

would never be the same again.

Rubber Soul (1965)

After a ten day break the group re-entered the recording studio in October 1965 to work on their next album *Rubber Soul*. It was released eight weeks later.

Critics interpreted it as a major step forward in the maturity and complexity of the group's music. Lennon in a reference to the group's excessive use of marijuana called the album "the pot album."

It certainly was a new departure. Harrison's introduction of a sitar on *Norwegian Wood* was seen as a further progression by the group outside the traditional boundaries of pop and rock music.

Many of *Rubber Soul's* more notable songs were credited as being the product of Lennon and McCartney's collaborative song writing but, for the first time, it also featured distinct compositions from each. Lennon and McCartney now began to bicker about who wrote what.

Each claimed to be the main writer of *In My Life*. Insiders claim that it was during the production of *Rubber Soul* that differences of opinion, not always artistic, began to split the group.

For example, recording engineer, Norman Smith,

later claimed that the studio sessions revealed signs of growing conflict within the group. McCartney argued with Lennon and with Harrison while Starr just ignored his caustic remarks. Smith said:

> **The clash between John and Paul was becoming obvious, and as far as Paul was concerned, George could do no right.**

This sixth studio album, regarded as a kind of folk rock album, was recorded at EMI studios in London on the 17 June and between the 12 October to 11 November 1965. It was released on the 3 December 1965 in time for the Christmas market. Critics commented that it represented a major artistic achievement.

In 2012, *Rubber Soul* was ranked number five on *Rolling Stone* magazine's list of the "500 Greatest Albums of All Time". Nearly all of the album's songs were composed immediately after *The Beatles'* return to London following their North American tour and the influence of *Bob Dylan*, *The Byrds* and *The Beach Boys* was clearly evident. *Rubber Soul* replaced *The Sound of Music* soundtrack at the top of the charts, and held the top spot eight weeks. Pitchfork Media described the album as the most:

> **important artistic leap in The Beatles' career— the signpost that signalled a shift away from Beatlemania and the heavy demands of teen pop, toward more introspective, adult subject matter.**

Because they were exhausted from five years of virtually non-stop touring, recording, and film work, the group decided to take a three-month break during the first part of 1966 before recording their next album. Meanwhile on the 26 December 1965 McCartney crashed his moped, resulting in a chipped tooth as seen in the videos for *Paperback Writer* and *Rain* and a scar on his top lip, which he hid by growing a moustache.

On the 21 January 1966 George Harrison married Pattie Boyd, at the Esher Register Office, Surrey. Brian Epstein and Paul McCartney were best men. That evening Brian threw a party at his London home in Chapel Street, in honour of George and Pattie. The guests who attended included Paul with Jane Asher, John and Cynthia Lennon, Geoffrey Ellis, Wendy Hanson, and George and Judy Martin.

On Monday the 31 January Paul and Jane with George and Pattie attended Wyndham's Theatre, London for the premiere of the play *How's The World Treating You?* On Thursday the 3 February McCartney attended the performance of Stevie Wonder at the *Scotch Of St James* night-club, in London and hung out with him afterwards.

Brian Epstein had planned for the group to begin work in April 1966 on what would be their third film soundtrack. However, the band members could not agree on a suitable script so they scrapped the plans for the film and decided instead to record a new LP. As they had three months boxed off to make the film they found themselves, for the first time, with a decent period of time to make a creative album which they would later call *Revolver*. On the 1 May 1966 they performed for a crowd of 10,000 people during NME's annual Poll-Winners All-Star Concert at Empire Pool, in Wembley. It was to be their last British concert in front of a paying audience. The concert was far from a success and many critics began to wonder if their lacklustre performance had anything to do with the increasing amount of rumours which were then circulating that the group were about to split up.

Insiders speak of internal feuds, in-fighting and a jostling for position with McCartney insisting on always getting his own way. John Lennon had been the groups' dominant creative force between 1962 to 1965. But from 1965 McCartney began to exert his influence in the group beyond sharing the song writing, musical accompaniment and assisting with arrangement.

By 1966 McCartney had secured an approximately equal position with Lennon. The constant infighting was taking its toll on Lennon who appeared to be increasingly disinterested in *The Beatles*. The balance of power was slowly shifting to the McCartney camp. Meanwhile, George Harrison had discovered a newfound interest in Indian music and culture and began to exert his own influence on the band.

REVOLVER (1966)

Their next album *Revolver*, which was released in August 1966, marked another high for the group.

Scott Plagenhoef in *Pitchfork* identifies it as "the sound of a band growing into supreme confidence" and went on to talk about the group "redefining what was expected from popular music."

The album highlighted three features: sophisticated song writing; a substantially expanded repertoire of different musical styles from classical to rock; and, innovative studio experimentation. Even the cover, designed by their old friend from Hamburg, Klaus Voormann, was hailed as a classic.

Incidentally, the album was preceded by the single *Paperback Writer* with an accompanying music video regarded by critics as among the first true music videos.

For the first time three of Harrison's compositions earned a place in a *Beatles'* album. In 2003, *Rolling Stone* ranked *Revolver* as the third greatest album of all time. Strangely enough, the group failed to perform any of its songs in the American tour that followed its release.

The album marked the end of *The Beatles* as a live act performing to thousands of adoring fans whose screams completely blocked out the group's music. They were now a different group, in more ways than one. *Revolver* spent thirty four weeks on the British Albums Chart, earning the number one spot on 13 August 1966. It also reached number one on the Billboard Top LPs, where it stayed for six weeks.

One of the tracks *Taxman* was highly critical of the

high marginal tax rates paid by top earners like *The Beatles*, which were sometimes as much as 95 percent of their income. The song was written by George Harrison while Lennon helped him with some lyrics including the line

> **My advice for those who die:**
> **declare the pennies on your eyes.**

The lyrics mentions "Mr. Wilson" and "Mr. Heath", referring to Harold Wilson and Edward Heath, who were, respectively, the British Labour Prime Minister and Conservative Leader of the Opposition at the time.

Each band member contributed to the lyrics of *Eleanor Rigby* although McCartney is credited as the songwriter. Various differing meanings have been given to both songs.

One critic described *Here, There and Everywhere* as the most perfect song that McCartney has ever written. He is supposed to have written the song in early June 1966, toward the end of the *Revolver* sessions.

The group were under pressure to complete the album before their scheduled flight to Germany on the 23 June for a European tour. The recording sessions involved many arguments between the band members with McCartney walking out on several occasions, like for example during the recording of *She Said She Said*.

All songs on the *Revolver* album were written and

composed by Lennon and McCartney, with the exception of *Taxman, Love You To* and *I Want to Tell You*, which were composed by George Harrison.

Unfortunately, the release of the album was completely overshadowed by controversy following the negative reaction in America to John Lennon's remarks about *The Beatles* being more popular than Jesus.

*In a way, I think of Paul McCartney as 'Him'...
I do wake up some mornings and think, Jesus Christ,
am I really that guy that is in the same body as I'm
inhabiting?*

Sir Paul McCartney

How does a Beatle live?

In March 1966, the London *Evening Standard* ran a weekly series of articles entitled "How Does a Beatle Live?" which featured John Lennon, Ringo Starr,

George Harrison, and Paul McCartney respectively. The articles were completed by journalist Maureen Cleave, who knew the group well and Lennon intimately and had interviewed them regularly since the start of *Beatlemania* in the UK.

Three years previously she had written they were "the darlings of Merseyside", and had accompanied them on the plane on the group's first US tour in February 1964. For her lifestyle series in March 1966, she decided to interview the group separately. Cleave interviewed Lennon on the 4 March 1966 at his home, Kenwood, in Weybridge. Her article mentioned that Lennon was "reading extensively about religion". During the course of the interview Lennon made the following comment:

> **Christianity will go. It will vanish and shrink. I needn't argue about that; I'm right and I'll be proved right. We're more popular than Jesus now; I don't know which will go first—rock 'n' roll or Christianity. Jesus was all right but his disciples were thick and ordinary. It's them twisting it that ruins it for me.**

The interview was published in the *Evening Standard* in March 1966 and while it didn't go unnoticed neither did it provoke a public reaction. *The Beatles'* press officer Tony Barrow contacted *Datebook*, a US teen magazine, and sold them the rights to all four interviews. *Datebook* had already run pieces on British fashion designer Mary Quant and on the effects of LSD, so it seemed like a suitable publication to carry the interviews.

On the 16 June 1966 *The Beatles* received vaccinations against cholera and later attended at BBC Television Centre, London for a rehearsal for *Top Of The Pops*. The following day McCartney bought a farm in Kintyre in Scotland. The next day the group made an appearance on *Thank Your Lucky Stars*.

On Wednesday the 22 June they attended a private launch party for the club *Sibylla's* in London. On the 24 June they arrived in Munich for the start of their German tour. On the following day they received a threat from a Japanese national group relating to their forthcoming tour. They arrived in Tokyo on the 28 June.

On the 30 June they gave a press conference. One of the questions they were asked was:

> **When you have private and public troubles, official troubles, do you settle that by talking to one another or do you yell?**

To which John responded:

> **We don't have many troubles with each other, you know. Any ones that we do we talk it over.**

Five months after the *Evening Standard* interviews *Datebook* republished the interviews. It was July 1966. But the magazine's art editor Art Unger, realizing the controversial nature of the Lennon interview, boldly and deliberately positioned Lennon's quote about Christianity on its front cover. It became the spark that ignited into a fierce backlash against the group, at least in America. Tommy Charles saw an opportunity and took it. Tommy Charles or Tommy "Wanker" Charles as John Lennon liked to call him was a well-known DJ working for the WAQY radio station in Birmingham, Alabama. He heard about the quotation from his co-worker Doug Layton, and was, apparently, immediately incensed, saying something to the effect

> **That does it for me. I am not going to play the Beatles any more.**

Charles and Layton then went on air and invited listeners' comments on Lennon's views on Christianity. Not surprisingly, the response was overwhelmingly negative. Charles felt that the comments were sacrilegious and

> **that something ought to be done to show them that they can't get away with this sort of thing.**

The WAQY show was picked up by the Bureau Manager for United Press International News, Al Benn. He immediately filed a news report in New York. On the 4 August the South African government established a prohibition of radio broadcasting *Beatles'* records, because of Lennon's declarations about religion. The decision was maintained for several years.

On the 5 August the Spanish radio RKT established a censorship against the *Beatles* and the Jesus story made the front page of the *New York Times*. Soon, twenty more stations across America followed WAQY's lead with similar announcements. Some DJs went further organizing demonstrations with bonfires, and urging teenagers to burn their *Beatles'* records and other memorabilia.

On the 6 August McCartney gave an interview to David Frost's Phonograph, broadcast by BBC-radio. This was the negative and intimidating atmosphere into which the group entered as they left Britain on the 11 August 1966 for their American tour. Insiders say that McCartney initially did not want to take part in the tour but relented at the last minute. But McCartney was not the only member of the group to be nervous and upset at the prospect of public appearances. They had had a scary enough time that July while touring in Japan and the Philippines.

The Asian leg of the tour began with controversy when right-wing Japanese nationalists protested at the staging of their concerts in Tokyo at the *Nippon Budokan* in June and July because the stadium was built for the staging of the martial arts rather than musical performances.

Despite this the concerts went ahead with heavy security to protect the group from both fans and protesters. During the period they were basically under house arrest in their suite in the Tokyo Hilton. According to a roadie who will not give his permission to be identified, but whose evidence is corroborated by a former rent boy, he overheard McCartney insisting that a double be used for live performances by him in the future.

If this is true it is not the first time the group would have used a double for McCartney. And if he did use a double, he exercised sound judgment for things were to get much worse in Manila.

The problem arose when they unintentionally snubbed the nation's first lady, Imelda Marcos. Marcos had expected the group to attend a breakfast reception at the Presidential Palace. However, when presented with the invitation, their manager, Brian Epstein, not wanting to politicize the group, politely declined. But Epstein was soon to discover that the Marco's regime was unaccustomed to accepting "no" for an answer. Incensed when they didn't turn up for her 200 guests the snub was broadcast by the Philippine media. Almost immediately, their police protection disappeared.

A televised apology made by Epstein on Channel 5 was blacked out by the regime. The group and their entourage had to make their own way to the Manila International Airport. The halls of the hotel were dark and lined with staff who shouted at them in Spanish and English. Roads to the airport were blocked by the military and the situation was very tense. They were jostled and attacked at the airport by demonstrators and police and they feared for their lives. Their road manager, Mal Evans, was attacked and beaten. Upon leaving the country, band members publicly expressed resentment at their treatment, with John Lennon saying

> **If we go back, it will be with an H-bomb. I won't even fly over the place.**

America would be much better but not without incident. After the Jesus controversy an effort was made to diffuse the situation with Lennon being told by Epstein and Barrow that he had to apologize.

Their first concert was scheduled for Chicago on the 12 August 1966. A press conference was called at which Lennon tried to explain that he didn't mean anything derogatory but stressed that he was simply remarking on how other people viewed and popularized the band. He described his own belief in God by quoting the Bishop of Woolwich, saying:

> **not as an old man in the sky. I believe that what people call God is something in all of us.**

But he only apologized when pressed to do so by a journalist and said:

> **If you want me to apologize, if that will make you happy, then OK, I'm sorry.**

The apology, grudgingly given, did not diffuse the situation and the tour was marred by protests and disturbances including threats from the Ku Klux Klan that they would make them pay.

On the 13 August there was a public *Beatles'* records burning organized by the North American radio station Coob. Priest Thurman H. Babbs of Cleveland, Ohio, said that he would ask for the excommunication of any parishioner who went to listen to *The Beatles* or approved Lennon's views about

Christianity. Despite the protests the concerts in Detroit, Cleveland, Washington, Philadelphia, Toronto and Boston went ahead. On Wednesday the 17 August while in Toronto Lennon gave his support to Americans who were going to Canada rather than being sent to Vietnam. On the 19 August 1966 they were due to play in the Memphis Mid-South Coliseum. The Memphis city council voted to cancel the concert rather than have "municipal facilities be used as a forum to ridicule anyone's religion."

They issued a statement saying that *The Beatles* were not welcome in Memphis but they went anyway and the concert went ahead but not without incident. During the concert someone let off a firecracker and members of the band thought that a sniper had shot John Lennon and that they were all the target of gunfire. After this concert they performed at Cincinnati Crosley Field, St. Louis Busch Memorial Stadium, New York City Shea Stadium, Seattle Center Coliseum, Los Angeles Dodger Stadium and finally on the 29 August 1966 at San Francisco Candlestick Park. They gave a press conference in New York on the 22 August. The first question asked was:

> **Would any of you care to comment on any aspect of the war in Vietnam?**

Lennon answered:

> **We don't like it.**

When invited to elaborate he replied:

> **No. I've elaborated enough, you know. We just**

don't like it. We don't like war.

George added:

It's, you know... It's just war is wrong, and it's obvious it's wrong. and that's all that needs to be said about it.

McCartney then added:

We can elaborate in England.

Another question was to John and Paul.

It's been said that Lennon and McCartney may someday replace the names Rogers and Hammerstein. Have you ever considered discontinuing performing and instead just keep on writing?

To which Lennon replied: **No.**

They were then asked:

Would you rather perform, then?

McCartney replied:

I mean, you know... When we're eighty we won't be performing. We may be writing.

Lennon added:

and we don't want to be Rogers and Hart, either.

McCartney was then asked about his farm:

> **Paul, I believe you have just recently purchased a farm in Scotland. Have you any intention of purchasing any further, being in the United States?**

He replied:

> **No. I just bought that farm because it was very cheap. and, uhh, I always wanted a farm, and it's a nice place. But that's as far as it goes.**

Then another strange question about McCartney's health.

> **Paul, according to wire reports you became a little ill after you got off the plane last night. What happened? Air sickness?**

McCartney replied:

> **Yeah, something. You know, I haven't been too well on the tour. I just felt a bit ill, that's all, and I was sick.**

If McCartney was ill on the tour it would make sense for *The Beatles'* management to have procured a lookalike to take his place at concerts. Most of the young girls were coming to see James Paul McCartney. It's not unreasonable to assume that the management didn't want to disappoint them. If they used a lookalike on the tour it does not amount to evidence that he died or was replaced at this time. McCartney was said to be suffering from a severe form of IRS which caused him to have to wear a nappy because of acute diarrhoea explosion a condition which was then treated by opiates due to the severe pain. A further press conference took place in Seattle on the 27 August and the following day Epstein and Natt Weiss met Dizz Gillepsie at a Beverly Hills house.

Not to be confused with the iconic black jazz trumpeter, band leader and composer, Dizzy Gillespie, who died in 1969, Dizz Gillespie was an up and coming, aspiring actor and singer with whom Epstein was having a tempestuous on-off affair, one which he would later bitterly regret. That night would become a turning point in the life of Brian Epstein. On the 28 August they attended a press conference in Los Angeles and were asked about the cover of *Yesterday and Today*.

Photographer Robert Whitaker shot the cover for *Yesterday And Today* (1966) which featured a photograph of *The Beatles* in butcher smocks covered in slabs of raw meat and a beheaded baby doll perched on McCartney's shoulder.

It caused such controversy that the album was immediately pulled from the marketplace by Capitol Records when distributors complained that it was offensive. 750,000 copies of the record were in warehouses ready to be shipped but it's estimated that only 25,000 copies of the album were actually sold with the original cover, ultimately making it one of the most collectible albums in rock history.

Whitaker proudly took credit for the cover concept

saying that the idea was entirely his own though he was never consistent in explaining it. Sometimes he said he was not sure why he had posed *The Beatles* that way; other times he said the butcher theme was meant to suggest that *The Beatles*, so worshipped by their fans, were real flesh-and-blood people. On another occasion he said the image was to be one of three that would tell a story.

The question asked was:

> **On the album cover that was banned here, the one with the dolls and meat. Who's idea was it?**

Lennon:

> **The photographers who took it.**

Question:

> **And what was it supposed to mean?**

Lennon:

> **We never asked him, you know.**

Later on a journalist tried to answer a question about doubles but was cut short:

> **Have you ever used or trained Beatle doubles as decoys on a...**

Both Ringo and John cut him off by saying No. Paul said:

> **We tried to get Brian Epstein to do it... he wouldn't do it.** [Laughter]

Harrison said nothing. Questions were then asked about their personal safety:

> **Gentlemen, what do you think would happen to you four if you came to an appearance without the armoured truck and without police?**

Ringo: **We'd get in a lot easier.** (laughter)

John: **We couldn't do it.**

Paul:

> **It depends, you know. Sometimes we could have easily made it much better without the armoured truck. But today, probably we wouldn't have.**

A journalist then asked if they thought they would be physically harmed?

Paul: **Oh... yeah. Probably.**

John: **What do you think?**

Journalist: **Yes, I think so.**

Paul: **Could be.**

The following morning Dizz Gillepsie disappeared with the personal briefcases of Brian Epstein and Natt Weiss. He was later blackmailed over its contents.

At the end of the tour Harrison had had enough and decided he was leaving the group. This brings us up to the 30 August 1966. Immediately after the tour, the band took a three-month break from one another to follow individual pursuits.

I've learnt to compartmentalize. There's me and there's famous Him. I don't want to sound schizophrenic, but probably I'm two people.

Sir Paul McCartney

SGT. PEPPER'S LONELY HEARTS CLUB BAND

On the 24 November 1966 the *Fab Four*, weary of ever touring again, met up in Abbey Road, Studio 2 to commence work on their eight studio album, *Sgt.*

Pepper's Lonely Hearts Club Band. It was to mark the ascendancy of Paul McCartney as the main creative force of the group. They began by working on three songs *Strawberry Fields Forever, When I'm Sixty Four,* and *Penny Lane.*

But EMI wanted a single release and pressurized Epstein to release *Strawberry Fields Forever* and *Penny Lane* as a double A-side. It was released in February 1967 and when it failed to reach number one in the UK, the British media began to speculate that the group's popularity was finally on the wane.

Newspapers and print media carried headlines like "Beatles Fail to Reach the Top", "First Time in Four Years" and "Has the Bubble Burst?"

Following the single's release the childhood concept which was to be the theme of the new album was abandoned in favour of *Sgt. Pepper*, and despite the fact that *Strawberry Fields Forever* took an unprecedented 55 hours of studio time to record Epstein insisted it be dropped from the album.

Following the media criticism of the group at its declining popularity, McCartney vowed that they were going to make the best album ever. On the 6 December 1966 the group began working on *When I'm Sixty-Four*, which was the first track to be included on the album.

On the 18 December McCartney and Jane Asher attended the Warner Theatre, in London for the world premiere of the film *The Family Way.*

On the evening of the 20 December 1966, *The Beatles* arrived separately for their scheduled recording session. Each was interviewed by ITN-TV just outside of EMI's Abbey Road Studios. The evening's session included Lennon, McCartney, and Harrison overdubbing the background harmonies for the song *When I'm Sixty Four*.

Ringo also added the large "bell" percussion to the recording. All of the group denied that they were splitting up and confirmed they would continue to work together.

The album was made on pot and was all about pot according to McCartney who in *Rolling Stone* said:

> **When [Martin] was doing his TV programme on Pepper ... he asked me, "Do you know what caused Pepper?" I said, "In one word, George, drugs. Pot." And George said, "No, no. But you weren't on it all the time." "Yes, we were." Sgt. Pepper was a drug album.**

The BBC also thought so. They banned several songs from the radio such as *A Day in the Life* because they felt that the line "I'd love to turn you on" might be regarded as referring to recreational drug use.

At the time both Lennon and McCartney denied that such an interpretation was intended but later McCartney admitted that that the line was deliberately written to ambiguously refer to either illicit drugs or sexual activity.

The BBC also banned *Lucy in the Sky with Diamonds* because they thought it referred to LSD. *Being for the Benefit of Mr. Kite!* was banned because of the lyric, which mentions *Henry the Horse*. The phrase contains two common slang terms for heroin in the 1960s. In fact, many *Beatles*' fans believed that *Henry the Horse* was a drug dealer and *Fixing a Hole* was a reference to heroin use.

Other lyrics contained obvious drug taking references such as "I get high" from *With a Little Help from My Friends;* "take some tea" which was, at the time slang for cannabis use contained in *Lovely Rita* and "digging the weeds" from *When I'm Sixty-Four*.

The album begins with the title track, starting with ten seconds of the combined sounds of a pit orchestra warming up and an audience waiting for a concert. The idea was to give the illusion of the album as a live performance.

McCartney acts as the master of ceremonies near the end of the *Sgt. Pepper's Lonely Hearts Club* Band track, introducing Starr as an alter ego named Billy Shears.

The lyrics to *She's Leaving Home* is believed by critics to address the problem of alienation between disagreeing peoples, particularly those distanced from each other by the generation gap. McCartney said he was inspired by a piece about teenage runaways published by the *Daily Mail*.

Sgt. Pepper's was the first *Beatles'* album to be released with identical track listings in Britain and America. All of the songs were written and composed by Lennon and McCartney with the exception of *Within You Without You*, which was written by George Harrison.

The cover of the album is hugely important in the context of the conspiracy theory and deserves special mention, particularly because of the extensive interpretations given to it by conspiracy theorists. The Grammy Award-winning album cover was reported to be designed by the pop artists Peter Blake and Jann Haworth and inspired by an ink drawing sketch by McCartney.

This is the official story about the cover. The art director was Robert Fraser and it was photographed by Michael Cooper. The front includes a Technicolor collage of the group dressed in costume as the *Sgt. Pepper's Lonely Hearts Club Band*. They stand beside a group of life-sized cardboard cut-outs of famous people including themselves.

The centre of the cover depicts the *Beatles* standing behind a drum skin, on which a fairground artist allegedly called Joe Ephgrave (a man who doesn't exist) painted the words of the album's title. In front of the drum skin is an arrangement of flowers that spell out the word "Beatles". For the first time ever on a rock and roll album the lyrics were printed in full on the back cover.

The following is the official list of people on the cover in order of their appearance. On the top row are Sri Yukteswar Giri (Hindu guru); Aleister Crowley (Satanist); Mae West (actress); Lenny Bruce (comedian); Karlheinz Stockhausen (composer); W. C. Fields (comedian/actor); Carl Gustav Jung (psychiatrist); Edgar Allan Poe (writer); Fred Astaire (actor/dancer); Richard Merkin (artist); The Vargas Girl (by artist Alberto Vargas); Huntz Hall (actor); Simon Rodia (designer and builder of the Watts Towers) and Bob Dylan (singer/songwriter).

The second row contains Aubrey Beardsley (illustrator); Sir Robert Peel (19th century British Prime Minister); Aldous Huxley (writer); Dylan Thomas (poet); Terry Southern (writer); Dion Dimucci (singer/songwriter); Tony Curtis (actor); Wallace Berman (artist); Tommy Handley (comedian); Marilyn Monroe (actress); William S. Burroughs (writer); Sri Mahavatar Babaji (Hindu guru); Stan Laurel (actor/comedian); Richard Lindner (artist); Oliver Hardy (actor/comedian); Karl Marx (political philosopher); H. G. Wells (writer); Sri Paramahansa Yogananda (Hindu guru); James Joyce (Irish poet and novelist) who is barely visible below Bob Dylan; and an anonymous hairdresser's wax dummy.

The third row contains Stuart Sutcliffe (artist/former Beatle); another anonymous hairdresser's wax dummy; Max Miller (comedian); A "Petty Girl" by artist George Petty; Marlon Brando (actor); Tom Mix (actor); Oscar Wilde (writer); Tyrone Power (actor); Larry Bell (artist); Dr. David Livingstone (missionary/explorer); Johnny Weissmuller (Olympic swimmer/Tarzan actor); Stephen Crane (writer) who is barely visible between Issy Bonn's head and raised arm; Issy Bonn (comedian); George Bernard Shaw (playwright); H. C. Westermann (sculptor); Albert

Stubbins (English footballer); Sri Lahiri Mahasaya (guru); Lewis Carroll (writer) and T. E. Lawrence (Lawrence of Arabia).

In the front row there is a wax model of Sonny Liston (boxer); a "Petty Girl" (by George Petty); a wax model of George Harrison; a wax model of John Lennon; Shirley Temple (child actress) who is barely visible behind the wax models of John and Ringo, which is the first of three appearances on the cover; then a wax model of Ringo Starr; a wax model of Paul McCartney; Albert Einstein (physicist) somewhat obscured; John Lennon holding a Wagner tuba; Ringo Starr holding a trumpet; Paul McCartney holding a *cor anglais*; George Harrison holding a piccolo; Bobby Breen (singer); Marlene Dietrich (actress/singer); an American legionnaire; a wax model of Diana Dors (actress); Shirley Temple (child actress) this is her second appearance on the cover.

Reference should also be made to the props as they also hold an important significance for conspiracy theorists.

The official list of props and their origins are as follows: a cloth grandmother-figure by Jann Haworth; a cloth doll by Haworth of Shirley Temple wearing a sweater that reads "Welcome The Rolling Stones Good Guys"; a ceramic Mexican craft known as a Tree of Life from Metepec; a 9-inch Sony television set, apparently owned by Paul McCartney.

I say this because the actual receipt, bearing McCartney's signature, is exhibited in a museum dedicated to *The Beatles* in Japan; a stone figure of a girl; another stone figure; a statue brought over from John Lennon's house; a trophy; a doll of the Hindu goddess Lakshmi; a drum skin, designed by fairground artist Joe Ephgrave; a hookah (water pipe); a velvet snake; a Fukusuke (Japanese china figure); a stone figure of Snow White; a garden gnome; a euphonium (a baritone-voiced brass musical instrument); and a three-stringed flower guitar. In the album's inner gatefold, McCartney can be seen wearing a badge on his left sleeve that bears the initials O.P.P.

According to Martin the badge was a gift from a Canadian fan; the initials apparently stand for "Ontario Provincial Police." However, the original badge with the letters OPP has been digitally altered to read OPD meaning "officially pronounced dead." Why would anyone do this?

The photo session took place in March 1967. The album's inner sleeve featured artwork by the Dutch design team the Fool. They eschewed the usual standard white paper in favour of an abstract pattern of waves of maroon, red, pink and white.

The actual collage includes fifty seven photographs and nine waxworks that depict a diversity of famous people, including actors, sportsmen, scientists and at George Harrison's request, Mahavatar Babaji, Lahiri Mahasaya, Sri Yukteswar and Paramahansa Yogananda who are all Self-Realization Fellowship gurus.

Also included are film stars Marilyn Munroe, James Dean and Marlon Brando, artist Aubrey Beardsley; boxer Sonny Liston, footballer Albert Stubbins, comedians Stan Laurel and Oliver Hardy and the writers H. G. Wells, Oscar Wilde and Dylan Thomas.

Lennon wanted to have Adolf Hitler and Jesus Christ but management refused his request on the basis that they would be too controversial. Elvis was deliberately excluded because he was considered to be "too important." The cover cost £3,000, a hugely extravagant sum considering that the average cover at the time cost a mere £50.

There was a mixed reaction to the album with the majority of critics praising the new direction taken by the band. The influential *Time* magazine declared it "a historic departure in the progress of music, any music" while Jack Kroll from *Newsweek* called it "a masterpiece".

However, one of the leading music critics of the time, Richard Goldstein, wrote a scathing review in *The New York Times* saying the album was spoiled and reeked of "special effects, dazzling but ultimately fraudulent". After a backlash from fans he was forced to write a defence of his review and in it claimed that the album was still 60% better than any other music around.

The album won numerous awards and honours. At the 10th Annual Grammy Awards in 1968, it picked up best in the categories of Best Album Cover, Graphic Arts, Best Engineered Recording, Non-

Classical and Best Contemporary Album. It also won Album of the Year, the first rock LP to receive this honour. In 2003 *Rolling Stone* magazine ranked it number one in its list of the "500 Greatest Albums of All Time". As of 2014 it has sold more than 30 million copies worldwide, making it one of the best-selling albums in history.

On the 18 May 1967 *The Beatles* signed a contract to represent the BBC, and Britain, on *Our World*, the world's first live television satellite link-up to be seen by approximately 400 million people across five continents. John Lennon wrote the song especially for the occasion, to a specific brief provided by the BBC. The song had to be simple so that viewers around the world would understand it. But it was not strictly speaking a live performance as they used several backing tracks for instruments and vocals to avoid playing live together.

The *Beatles* released *Sgt. Pepper's Lonely Hearts Club Band* on the 1 June and *Our World* took place on 25 June. The satellite link-up was devised by the BBC, and personalities, including Maria Callas and Pablo Picasso, from 19 nations performed in separate items from their respective countries.

The event, which lasted two-and-a-half hours, had the largest television audience to date. No politicians were allowed take part and everything was live. It was a massive television event with an estimated audience of 350 million and huge publicity for the group. *The Beatles* then performed *All You Need Is Love*, surrounded by an assortment of British musicians, flowers, balloons and placards. On the 24 August 1967 the group met Maharishi Mahesh Yogi the world's authority on Transcendental Meditation. They decided along with Cynthia Lennon, Pattie Harrison, her sister Jenny, Alexis Mardas, Mick Jagger and Marianne Faithfull, to travel to Bangor, North Wales, to take part in a ten day conference on Transcendental Meditation. They travelled on the same train as Maharishi and his party. Cynthia Lennon missed the train and was driven to Bangor by Neil Aspinall. Aspinall went to see friends staying in a caravan in north Wales, and didn't attend any of Maharishi's lectures.

Meanwhile, the group were in a first class compartment, travelling for the first time in many years without their manager Brian Epstein or their assistants Neil Aspinall and Mal Evans. Maharishi was in another first class compartment. McCartney later said that despite the dormitories and canteen food they were interested enough to learn the system and they did.

But their sojourn in Wales was rudely interrupted when they received the shocking news on the 27 August 1967. Brian Epstein died of an overdose of *Carbitral*, in the bedroom of his London house. He was discovered by his butler. When news filtered through to the group in Bangor they were stunned, shocked and deeply saddened.

The Beatles did not attend the funeral not because they didn't want to but out of respect to his family so that it would afford them more privacy. But on the 17

October all four *Beatles* attended a memorial service for Epstein at the New London Synagogue in St John's Wood near Abbey Road Studios.

Brian Epstein was never awarded the MBE although he quite clearly should have been. In a BBC documentary interview in 1967 Paul McCartney spoke eloquently about the importance of Epstein adding:

If anyone was the Fifth Beatle, it was Brian.

In 1970 John Lennon told *Rolling Stone* that Epstein's death marked the beginning of the end for the group:

I knew that we were in trouble then. I thought, 'We've fuckin' had it now.

Perhaps the *Daily Mirror* heading of his death summed it up well when they wrote:

Epstein, the Beatle-making Prince of Pop, dies at 32.

The death of their manager was a huge blow to *The Beatles* and for a period of time they were rudderless. But the live concerts were long gone and they were now under the influence of various music producers. They were a different group, in more ways than one. We discuss the truth about Brian's death later on.

MAGICAL MYSTERY TOUR – THE MOVIE

The idea for the movie is attributed to Paul

McCartney who was at the time greatly interested in home movies. He himself later said:

> **I'm not sure whose idea Magical Mystery Tour was. It could have been mine, but I'm not sure whether I want to take the blame for it! We were all in on it, but a lot of the material at that time could have been my idea.**

In fact, not only was it McCartney's home movies that inspired the movie but he also provided most of the script or "scrupt" as he affectionately called it. The movie was shot over two weeks and produced over ten hours of film which was eventually edited down to 52 minutes. They began on the 11 and finished on the 25 September 1967. Filming was centred around the RAF station in West Malling, Kent while the mystery tour itself was shot throughout Devon and Cornwall. The sequence for *The Fool on the Hill* was shot around Nice in France. The script itself was daft and looked as if it was made up as they went along. Needless to say the critics hated it, the public hated it and even their loyal fans were hugely disappointed. Producer George Martin called it a "disaster." Because it was only 52 minutes long it never received a theatrical release until 1974 when New Line Cinema acquired the rights for limited theatrical and non-theatrical distribution in America.

MAGICAL MYSTERY TOUR – THE ALBUM

While the movie may have been a flop the subsequent

album certainly wasn't. *The Beatles* released *Magical Mystery Tour* as a double EP in Britain and as an LP in America. Both versions include the six-song soundtrack to the movie.

The record was released in the UK on the 8 December 1967 as a six-track double EP on the Parlophone label, and in the United States on the 27 November 1967, as an eleven-track LP compiled by Capitol Records, adding the group's 1967 single releases.

The soundtrack was nominated for a Grammy Award for Album of the Year in 1968. It also reached number 1 in America for eight weeks. But music critic Robert Christgau of *Esquire* found three of the album's five new songs disappointing.

He also said that *The Fool on the Hill* might be the worst song the *Beatles* ever recorded. However, he still recommended the album and believed that Harrison's *Blue Jay Way* was excellent.

THE WHITE ALBUM (1968)

The Beatles was a double LP commonly known as the *White Album* because of its virtually featureless white cover. With Epstein gone the group had briefly turned to Maharishi Mahesh Yogi as their guru. They had attended at his ashram in Rishikesh, India, and some were there for three months. This period marked one of their most prolific periods during which 30 songs were written. But India and Yogi wasn't for everyone and Ringo Starr left after only ten days. He hated the heat and hated the food. He arrived with a suitcase full of baked beans and had Mal Evans cook him eggs every day. Starr said the place reminded him of *Butlin's*. Lennon and Harrison became sceptical of the entire trip when it was suggested to them by an electronics technician known as Magic Alex that the Maharishi was attempting to exploit them. When it became known that the Maharishi had made sexual advances to some of the women, Lennon and Harrison then left. The unpublished story was that he tried to rape Mia Farrow. PID Conspirators claim that the Maharishi had promised to bring back the spirit of James Paul McCartney and had tricked them in a séance. McCartney was later to say of the trip:

We made a mistake. We thought there was more to him than there was.

Recording sessions for the *White Album* ran from late May to mid-October 1968. During this period relations between members of the group reached rock bottom and there were several divisive arguments. When Ringo Starr quit for two weeks McCartney took over the drum kit for *Back in the U.S.S.R.* In fact, Lennon and Harrison also drummed on this track and *Dear Prudence*. Meanwhile relations between Lennon and McCartney became so bad that Lennon refused to work with him and mocked him over the track *Ob-La-Di, Ob-La-Da* which he called "granny music shit".

Tensions were further aggravated by Lennon insisting

on bringing his new love interest, Japanese artist Yoko Ono to the recording studio. There had always been a well-established understanding that girlfriends would not attend recording sessions. Her presence caused great friction within the group.

Lennon later said about the album:

> **Every track is an individual track; there isn't any Beatles music on it. It's John and the band, Paul and the band, George and the band.**

It was, in fact, the beginning of the end for the group.

Side one began with McCartney's *Back in the U.S.S.R* with vocals from Lennon and Harrison in the style of the *Beach Boys* at the request of Mike Love. The track became widely bootlegged in the Soviet Union and became an underground hit.

Dear Prudence was written by Lennon and was about Mia Farrow's sister Prudence.

Glass Onion was written by Lennon who according to *Beatles'* insiders wrote it to mock fans who claimed to find "hidden messages" in their music. The songs references other songs in *The Beatles'* catalogue, e.g. *the Walrus was Paul* refers back to *I Am The Walrus* (which itself refers to *Lucy in the Sky with Diamonds*).

The truly awful *Ob-La-Di, Ob-La-Da* was all McCartney's own work although it was credited to Lennon and McCartney. The official story is that the title was suggested by Jimmy Scott-Emuakpor, a friend of McCartney, who later sued him over the rights. McCartney demanded perfection for the track which took over three days to complete much to the growing annoyance of his colleagues.

The song went to number one in singles charts in Austria, Switzerland, Australia and Japan. In the UK and Norway (where it had not been released as a single by *The Beatles*), a cover version by the *Marmalade* also made number one. In 2004, an online poll by Mars ranked the song as the worst ever.

The Continuing Story of Bungalow Bill was written by Lennon and recorded as an *audio vérité* exercise featuring vocal performances from almost everyone who was in the studio at the time including Yoko Ono.

George Harrison wrote *While My Guitar Gently Weeps* while on a visit to his parents' home in Cheshire. Eric Clapton plays on the track. *Happiness Is A Warm Gun*, one of Lennon's favourites, evolved out of song fragments that he wrote in Rishikesh. On side two, *Martha My Dear* refers to McCartney's sheepdog. He plays the entire track backed by session musicians. The song *I'm So Tired* was written by Lennon when he was in India and had difficulty sleeping. The lyrics make reference to Walter Raleigh, calling him a "stupid git" for introducing tobacco to Europe. The song ends with Lennon mumbling "Monsieur, monsieur, how about another one?"

Blackbird features a McCartney solo, accompanying himself on acoustic guitar with a metronome ticking in the background while *Piggies* written by Harrison with a little help from his mum, Louise. *Rocky Raccoon* evolved from a jam session between Lennon and Donovan in Rishikesh. The song was taped in a single session and George Martin only put it on the album as a "filler".

Don't Pass Me By is special as it was Ringo Starr's first solo composition for the band. He had been working on the song for some time but was never given the opportunity to record it as a solo. The basic track consisted of Starr drumming while McCartney played piano. George Martin composed an orchestral introduction to the song but it was rejected as being "too bizarre" and left off the album.

McCartney wrote *Why Don't We Do It in the Road?* in India after seeing two monkeys copulating in the street. He played all the instruments except drums, which were contributed by Starr. McCartney also wrote and sung *I Will* with Lennon and Starr accompanying on percussion.

Julia was the last track to be recorded for the album and features Lennon on solo acoustic guitar. This is the only *Beatles'* recording on which Lennon performs alone. The song is about the loss of his mother and his relationship with Ono, who is the "ocean child" referred to in the lyrics. Although Ono contributes to the lyrics the song was still credited to Lennon and McCartney.

On side three *Birthday* was the only real Lennon and McCartney co-write on the album. Ono, and

Harrison's wife Pattie, added backing vocals to the track. *Yer Blues* was written by Lennon in India and influenced by the British Blues Boom of 1968 which included groups like *Fleetwood Mac* and *Chicken Shack*. Maharishi Mahesh Yogi was the inspiration for both *Everybody's Got Something to Hide Except Me and My Monkey* and *Sexy Sadie*. The former evolved from a jam session. Harrison claimed the title came from one of the Maharishi's sayings with the words "and my monkey" added later on.

Sexy Sadie was initially written as *Maharishi* by Lennon, shortly after he decided to leave Rishikesh. In a 1980 interview, he acknowledged that the Maharishi was the inspiration for the song: "I just called him Sexy Sadie."

It is probably a huge coincidence but I should point out that Sexy Sadie was the nickname given to Charles Manson disciple Susan Atkins long before this song emerged. Atkins was one of the killers of Roman Polanski's pregnant wife Sharon Tate who stated that they wanted to remove the baby from her but they ran out of time and had to flee the murder scene.

McCartney wrote *Mother Nature's Son* in India, and worked on it in isolation from the other members of the band.

The credit for *Helter Skelter* was claimed by Sir Paul McCartney. It was initially recorded in July as a blues number. The official line is that mass murderer Charles Manson was unaware that *Helter Skelter* is the British name for a spiral slide found on a playground and assumed the track had something to do with hell. This was one of the key tracks that led Manson to believe the album had coded messages referring to apocalyptic war, and led to his movement of the same name.

According to Barry Miles who some say believed everything McCartney told him, McCartney was inspired to write the song after reading a 1967 *Guitar Player* magazine interview with *The Who's* Pete Townshend where he described their latest single, *I Can See for Miles*, as the loudest, rawest, dirtiest song *The Who* had ever recorded.

McCartney then wrote *Helter Skelter* to be the most raucous vocal, the loudest drums, et cetera and said he was using the symbol of a helter skelter as a ride from the top to the bottom; the rise and fall of the Roman Empire, and this was the fall, the demise. The final song on side three is Harrison's *Long, Long, Long*. Side four begins with *Revolution 1* written by Lennon. McCartney's *Honey Pie* was a pastiche of the flapper dance style from the 1920s. Although Lennon played the guitar solo on the track he later said he hated the song, calling it "beyond redemption".

In relation to *Savoy Truffle* Harrison later said that Derek Taylor helped him finish the lyrics. The track *Cry Baby Cry* was written by Lennon in India, and the lyrics were partly derived from a tagline for an old television commercial.

Revolution 9 evolved from the overdubs from the *Revolution 1* coda. Lennon, Harrison and Ono added further tape collages and spoken word extracts, in the style of Karlheinz Stockhausen. The song begins with an extract from a *Royal School of Music* examination tape. It ends with Ono's infamous comment, "you become naked".

Yoko Ono was heavily involved in the production, and advised Lennon on what tape loops to use. McCartney did not contribute to the track, and was reportedly unhappy on it being included.

Lennon wrote *Good Night* as a lullaby for his son Julian, and he specifically wanted Starr to sing it. The early takes featured just Lennon on acoustic guitar and Starr singing. Martin scored an orchestral and choral arrangement that replaced the guitar in the final mix, and also played the celesta.

The Beatles album was issued in November and was the group's first album for Apple Records although EMI continued to own their recordings. Apple Records was a subsidiary of Apple Corps, the company Epstein created as part of his plan to create a tax-effective business structure.

The music was commercially successful attracting in excess of two million advance orders. In America it sold almost four million copies in the first month. But critics were not impressed. It lagged way behind *Sgt. Peppers* and signalled the end of the band as a cohesive creative force.

Nevertheless, in 2003 *Rolling Stone* ranked it as the tenth greatest album of all time. *Pitchfork's* critic Mark

Richardson said it was

> **large and sprawling, overflowing with ideas but also with indulgences, and filled with a hugely variable array of material. Its failings are as essential to its character as its triumphs.**

In January 1969 the *Yellow Submarine* LP, contained only the four previously unreleased songs that had debuted in the film of the same name, along with the title track which had already issued on *Revolver*, the track *All You Need Is Love* which was already issued as a single and on the US *Magical Mystery* Tour LP and seven instrumental pieces composed by George Martin. Except for Harrison's *It's All Too Much* the entire venture was largely forgettable. They would record two more albums *Abbey Road* and *Let It Be* before finally disbanding.

It is not my music. I hear what it relates. It says 'Rise.'
It says 'Kill.' Why blame it on me?
I didn't write the music.

CHARLES MANSON

How well did McCartney know Manson?

Some theorists would have you believe that Sir Paul McCartney and John Lennon were, in some way, associated with mass murderer Charles Manson in that they met him in the USA and that he inspired them or helped them to write some of the lyrics for their songs. The author has had difficulty finding any evidence to corroborate any of these claims. However, I did uncover some extraordinary coincidences.

For those of you too young to remember Charles Manson, born in 1934, is an American criminal and leader of what became known as the Manson Family. They were a quasi-commune that hung out in the California desert, in the late 1960s.

In 1971 Manson was found guilty of conspiracy to commit the murders of seven people, Roman Polanski's eight month pregnant actress wife Sharon Tate and four other people at Tate's home, and the following day, a married couple, Leno and Rosemary LaBianca.

One popular but incredible conspiracy theory is that Manson and his family were professional actors working as CIA operatives; that none of the Tate murders actually happened, the murders were staged; that Sharon Tate's father was a high ranking intelligence agent in the US Army; that Tate is still alive and living in South America; that Manson has spent less than 12 months in prison and that the LaBianca murders were carried out by copycat criminals.

Yet, believe it or not, many believe that there is an element of truth to some of these claims!

The official story is that all the murders were carried

out by members of the Family on his express orders. He was convicted of the murders and remains in prison. His Family also murdered several other people at other times and locations, and Manson was also convicted of two of these other murders.

Born into a dysfunctional family, his mother was an alcoholic and he never knew who his father was. Manson spent most of his adolescence in and out of correctional institutions where he was sexually abused. As an adult he was imprisoned for different offences ranging from sodomy to fraud. On his release from prison Manson established himself as something of a guru in San Francisco's hippy Haight-Ashbury area. Although he claimed his religion was *Scientology* he borrowed philosophically from the *Process Church* whose members worshiped Satan.

He established a commune of mostly young attractive women calling them the Manson Family. Among members of the family were Susan "Sexy Sadie" Atkins, Patricia Krenwinkel, Charles Watson, Linda Kasabian, Leslie Van Houten, Lynette Fromme, Bobby Beausoleil, Mary Brunner, Catherine Share and Barbara Hoyt

In late spring 1968, Dennis Wilson of *The Beach Boys* picked up two hitchhiking Manson women, Patricia Krenwinkel and Ella Jo Bailey and brought them to his Pacific Palisades house for a few hours.

The following day Charlie turned up with twelve of his Family. Over the next few months the commune grew to twenty four. Wilson considered that Charlie was actually a talented musician and both of them would sing and talk together while the women were treated as servants to them both. Wilson paid for studio time to record songs written and performed by Charlie, as well as introducing him to various acquaintances in the entertainment business including Gregg Jakobson, Terry Melcher, and Rudi Altobelli.

Jakobson was introduced to Manson at an all-night party at Dennis Wilson's house. He was impressed by "the whole Charlie Manson package" of artist, lifestylist, philosopher and musician. Although he didn't think he had a musical note in his body he thought he had rhythm and was a good rapper.

Dennis was attracted to Charlie's female groupies and invited them to meet his brother Brian. Soon Charlie was part of an inner circle that included singer songwriter Van Dyke Parks and musician Mike Vosse.

Charlie participated in the all night parties where he met people like Mike Jagger, and groups like *The Beach Boys*, *The Mamas and Papas*, *The Byrds* and possibly *The Beatles*. Dennis was very impressed with Charlie's musical abilities and talked him up to everyone he met. He also invited him to everyone else's parties and introduced him to anyone who was anyone.

Months later Charlie offered to work with *The Beach Boys* on their new album *Smile*. He had thematic ideas he wanted to explore with them and showed Brian Wilson a rough sketch of his idea for the album cover "Open Your Mind and Smile".

Brian told him to work away on the cover. Charlie produced a mock up, expanded Brian's original subtle theme of Americana-Religion-Humour and added himself as a character in the theme as well as including a few songs of his own like *Mechanical Man*, *People Say I'm No Good*, *Garbage Dump* and *Cease To Exist*.

But when *The Beach Boys* returned from their European tour and saw Charlie's concept they recoiled in horror. They couldn't advocate an anti-establishment theme as suggested by Charlie. They were America's most popular band. Their management urged them to cut ties with Charlie and he was banned from their studio and from Dennis' house.

Brian struggled to re-write the album, now simply entitled, *SMiLE*. He re-designed the cover. He took off all the hippie, anti-establishment references, but it was to no avail. The rest of the band still vetoed the album, it was still too uncommercial.

SMiLE was dead but Charlie's music ambitions were only beginning.

There are even reports that Charlie, armed with a selection of demo tapes, went to London in February 1968 to meet his favourite group *The Beatles* and get signed on their label. He called and then visited Apple Records in London. Apple had been advertising that they would sign anyone with talent. Charlie reckoned he had talent so they would sign him.

Charlie may have been a big noise in Hollywood but no one knew him in London and he failed to get an audience with any of the *Fab Four* but he did, apparently, meet Yoko Ono and gave her some of the demo tapes for John Lennon. He dropped as many names as he could including the fact that he had worked with *The Beach Boys* and showed her some of *The Beach Boys*' gold discs that he had brought from California.

Charlie hung around Apple for the next few days chatting with the staff and smoking dope with "house hippie" Richard DiLello. Soon he discovered that McCartney was a big *Beach Boys* fan so he left a *Beach Boys'* gold disc in his office as a "gift."

His perseverance paid off and it is said that Charlie was actually assigned studio time at Abbey Road studios to make a demo of two songs for a possible 45 single. Charlie picked his own song *Cease To Exist* as the A-side and a cover of the recently released *Helter Skelter* as the B-side. Charlie's single was assigned an Apple number and some promo pictures were taken before he returned for California.

However, before the record could be released, Allen Klein became the new manager of *The Beatles* and Charlie's music ambitions with Apple were shelved. It is believed that a few test pressings of Charlie's single survive and fetch very high prices at rock auctions.

But maybe McCartney didn't forget the man who left him *The Beach Boys* gold disk when he was back in California? According to an unidentified source, Terry

Melcher told friends that he introduced Paul McCartney to Manson on the 22 June 1968 at the home of *The Mamas and Papas'* John Phillips and that the two talked all night. But today no one is willing to admit that McCartney ever met Manson. Geoff Baker was McCartney's press officer for fifteen years. When I asked him if Paul McCartney ever met Charles Manson he replied: "No, of course not." We do know that on that particular date, the 22 June 1968, McCartney was in Los Angeles. According to the *Beatles' Bible*, the official Gospel according to their management:

> **On this day Paul McCartney addressed a sales conference attended by executives from Capitol Records, where he announced that all future Beatles records would be released through the group's Apple Records label. The conference took place at the Beverly Hills Hilton hotel. McCartney gave a brief address before playing a promotional film which had been made on 11 June.**

The site goes on to say:

> **Following the event, McCartney and his companions – Apple's Ron Kass and Tony Bramwell, plus childhood friend Ivan Vaughan - returned to the Beverly Hills Hotel, where they were staying for the duration of their US trip…..In the evening the party - now including Linda Eastman - went to LA's Whiskey-A-Go-Go, where they watched BB King and the Chicago Transit Authority (later Chicago) perform.**

The site says McCartney and Linda Eastman returned to the hotel in "*the small hours.*" If McCartney did meet Manson it might go some way to explaining an extraordinary coincidence. In May and August 1969 Paul McCartney recorded a track called *You Never Give Me Your Money* for the *Abbey Road* album released on the 26 September 1969.

One verse of that song is as follows:

> **One sweet dream**
> **Pick up the bags and get in the limousine**
> **Soon we'll be away from here**
> **Step on the gas and wipe that tear away**
> **One sweet dream came true... today**
> **Came true... today**
> **Came true... today...yes it did**
> **One two three four five six seven,**
> **All good children go to Heaven**

The coincidence is that almost a year earlier the last two lines were written as follows on the door of the Manson ranch: "1234567 All good Children go to heaven."

Now that's what I call a coincidence. The *Beatles Bible* say:

> **On 25 November police raided the Spahn Ranch used as a base by the Family. They confiscated a door on which was written "Helter Skelter is coming down fast", and the words "1, 2, 3, 4, 5, 6, 7, all good children (go to heaven?)" - the latter words are heard in You Never Give Me Your Money.**

No source is given for the date. But maybe Manson's Family wrote the lyrics on the door after the release of the track? In any event, by the end of 1968 Charlie's attempt to become a rock star were beginning to fade. *The Beach Boys* had dumped him. *The Beatles'* management weren't returning his calls. Gary Stromberg from Universal had rejected him. Brother Records weren't impressed. Gregg Jakobson was only interested in making a movie about him. There was no one else to turn to except Terry Melcher.

Melcher was the most successful music producer in town. He had not only worked with *The Beach Boys* but also *The Beatles* and had worked with Paul McCartney in the past. They had even stayed at his home. Melcher knew him through Dennis Wilson and he had attended parties at Melcher's home at 10050 Cielo Drive a mansion in Benedict Canyon, north of Beverly Hills, Los Angeles, California.

Melcher hadn't auditioned him and hadn't even listened to his tapes but there again he hadn't been asked. Melcher had been to the ranch a few times to enjoy the company of the girls and Ruth Ann in particular according to *Manson: The Life and Times of Charles Manson* (2013) by Jeff Guinn

Charlie knew that if Melcher said so, he could cut him a record deal at Columbia, the best label in town, so he set about wooing him. It wasn't until mid-March that Melcher agreed to come to the ranch to hear Charlie sing his songs.

Charlie was certain Melcher was going to give him a record deal. But that particular day, after Charlie and the Family, had spent the entire day preparing for the arrival of Hollywood's top producer. Melcher never turned up.

Charlie was hugely embarrassed in front of his Family and later called to Melcher's house at Cielo Drive but was met by actress Sharon Tate who explained that Melcher didn't live there anymore.

Charlie finally caught up with Terry Melcher in the second week of May. Melcher didn't apologize for the recent no show but promised that he would turn up without fail at the ranch on the 18 May to hear Charlie sing.

This time he did come and a nervous Charlie gave his best at the audition. In fairness to Melcher he listened intently. Charlie presumed he was going to get a contract there and then but Melcher didn't do business that way. He said he'd think it over and get back to him.

He called his music "interesting" and told him he would hook him up with another musician and recording agent called Mike Deasy. In fact, he agreed to come back with Deasy and gave Charlie $50 for the Family.

He then left, knowing that musically Charles Manson had nothing to offer. But that wasn't the story Charlie gave to his commune. He told them Melcher wanted to sign him up immediately and gave him the money as a down-payment and that he was coming back with a session musician to record. Melcher later stated about Manson:

> **His songs were below average nothing. As far as I was concerned Manson was like every other starving hippie songwriter who was jamming on Sunset Boulevard, a hundred thousand every day who looked, dressed, talked and sang exactly like Charles Manson, sang about the same topics of peace and revolution, about the themes that were in the Beatles' albums.**

Melcher thought Deasy might be able to help Charlie in a much smaller niche market. He spoke to Deasy and they agreed to go back to Manson's ranch on the 6 June. Charlie was now sure that this was it, he was on the cusp of greatness.

He envisaged that he would become as famous as his idols *The Beatles*. Sure enough they returned on the specified date but this time Melcher made it clear he wasn't interested in giving him a record deal. Needless to say, Charlie was not a happy bunny.

Charles Watson whom Manson had met at Dennis Wilson's house soon joined the commune. No later than December, Manson and Watson visited a Topanga Canyon acquaintance who played them *The Beatles' White Album*, as a result of which Manson now became obsessed with the group.

If he wasn't talking to the Family about the Bible he was talking to them about *The Beatles*. For some time,

Manson had told his commune that racial tension between blacks and whites was growing and that blacks would soon rise up in rebellion in America's cities. That New Year's Eve Manson told his followers that the social turmoil he had been predicting had also been predicted by *The Beatles*. The *White Album* songs, he declared, told it all, although in code.

Manson heard secret messages in many of the two-disc set's thirty tracks and convinced himself that the songs were a confirmation by *The Beatles* that a sweeping race war was looming.

He thought that if he could orchestrate a string of grisly murders that could be blamed on black activists, Armageddon would happen and he would rise to power in the void left behind.

In fact, he maintained that the album was directed at the Family itself, an elite group that was being instructed to preserve the worthy from the impending disaster, which he called Helter Skelter, after the song of that name.

By February, Manson's vision was complete. The Family would create an album whose songs, as subtle as those of *The Beatles*, would trigger the predicted chaos. The triumph of blacks over whites would be met with retaliation, and a split between racist and non-racist whites would yield whites' self-annihilation.

But blacks' triumph would be short lived and would merely precede their being ruled by the Family. They would then ride out the conflict in "the bottomless pit", a secret city beneath Death Valley. And so, it came to pass, that on the 9 August 1969, Manson instructed his disciples to go to the Los Angeles home of director Roman Polanski and actress Sharon Tate.

This was the house at Cielo Drive in which Terry Melcher used to live. Polanski was now renting it. He instructed them to kill everyone in the house. Polanski was in Europe making a film but the Family led by Charles "Tex" Watson brutally stabbed to death the five occupants including eight month pregnant Tate.

The word "Pig" was written on the front door in Tate's blood. On Manson's orders the next night, Family members killed Leno and Rosemary LaBianca in their home.

Police found "Rise" and "Death to Pigs" written on the living room walls and "Helter Skelter" misspelled in blood on the refrigerator. The inscriptions were gruesome references to songs from the *White Album*.

The trial of Charles Manson is one of the most bizarre trials ever held in America with complete disregard to the principles of law and natural justice. The evidence against him was minimal. He was set to be convicted even before the trial began with American President Richard Nixon declaring his guilt during the trial.

The *Los Angeles Times* carried the story on its front page with the headline "Manson Guilty, Nixon

Declares." When this was exposed to the jury he was denied a re-trial, the judge accepting that the jury would not be influenced by the President's declaration. At his trial in 1970, Manson addressed the Court in the absence of the jury, providing an insight into the connection Manson made between *The Beatles'* music and the brutal murders of seven innocent people. Manson had a sinister interpretation of McCartney's lines "It's coming down fast".

He told the court:

> **Helter Skelter is confusion. Confusion is coming down fast. If you can't see the confusion coming down around you fast, you can call it what you wish. It is not my conspiracy. It is not my music. I hear what it relates. It says 'Rise.' It says 'Kill.' Why blame it on me? I didn't write the music.**

According to Family member Catherin Share in the documentary *Manson*:

> **When the Beatles' 'White Album' came out, Charlie listened to it over and over and over and over again. It wasn't that Charlie listened to the 'White Album' and started following what he thought the Beatles were saying. It was the other way around. He thought that the Beatles were talking about what he had been expounding for years. Every single song on the 'White Album,' he felt that they were singing about us.**

Revolution 9 which contains a disturbing montage of screams, explosions, grunting pigs and machine gun fire, also resonated with Manson. The instruction

"Rise!" is shouted on the track. "Rise!" was written in blood on the walls of the LaBianca home on the second night of the killing spree. The phrase "Number nine" is repeated throughout, which Manson interpreted as a reference to the ninth chapter of the Bible's Book of Revelation. Manson made a connection between the verses of *Revelation 9, The Beatles* and himself. Here are some examples of how he interpreted the lyrics. Where *The Beatles* sang

> **And the four angels were loosed, which were prepared for an hour, and a day, and a month, and a year, for to slay the third part of men**

Manson interpreted the four angels as *The Beatles*, who would help him destroy the white race. Where the *Beatles* sang

> **And their faces were as the faces of men. And they had hair as the hair of women**

Manson believed this referred to *The Beatles'* long hair. Manson saw himself as the fifth angel which is what he thought was meant by the line

> **And the fifth angel sounded, and I saw a star fall from heaven unto the earth: and to him was given the key of the bottomless pit**

with the bottomless pit being the desert hideout where the Family would wait out Helter Skelter. He also figured that in the words

> **I saw the horses in the vision, and them that sat on them, having breastplates of fire… and out of**

their mouths issued fire and smoke and brimstone the words breastplates of fire

represented *The Beatles'* electric guitars while the "fire and smoke and brimstone" were the band's incendiary lyrics that would incite Helter Skelter. Then when *The Beatles* released the hard-rocking *Revolution* as the B-side to *Hey Jude* in August 1968, it included the lyrics:

**But when you're talking 'bout destruction
Don't you know that you can count me out.**

But when a slower version was released on the *White Album* three months later, the line sung by John Lennon became slightly different:

Don't you know that you can count me out, in.

Manson took this change as an indication that the *Beatles* now sanctioned his plan for a race war.

Although the image of pigs was used to portray greedy people in George Harrison's 'Piggies,' Charlie Manson took the imagery many steps further. Family member Susan Atkins used a towel, saturated in Tate's blood to write the word "Pig" on the front door of Tate's house.

Leno LaBianca was found with a knife in his throat and a fork in his stomach, which was believed to be a reference to the song's last line, that the pigs were "clutching forks and knives to eat their bacon." Paul McCartney told KCRW radio how he came to write the song *Blackbird* in 1968:

> **I was in Scotland just playing on my guitar, and I remembered this whole idea of 'you were only waiting for this moment to arise' was about, you know, the black people's struggle in the Southern states, and I was using the symbolism of a black bird.**
>
> **It's not really about a blackbird whose wings are broken, you know, it's a bit more symbolic.**

Charlie Manson saw it differently. He believed that the track was an emphatic statement that this was the time for black people to revolt against the white power structure.

As George Harrison said in *Anthology*:

> **Everybody was getting on the big Beatle bandwagon. The police and the promoters and the Lord Mayors, and murderers too. The Beatles were topical and they were the main thing that was written about in the world, so everybody attached themselves to us, whether it was our fault or not. It was upsetting to be associated with something so sleazy as Charles Manson.**

While in a *Rolling Stone* interview John Lennon said:

> **A lot of the things he says are true: he is a child of the state, made by us, and he took their children in when nobody else would. He's barmy, like any other Beatle-kind of fan who reads mysticism into it. I don't know what 'Helter Skelter' has to do with knifing somebody.**

While Paul McCartney had this to say:

> It was terrible. You can't associate yourself with a thing like that. Some guy in the States had done it, I've no idea why. It was frightening, because you don't write songs for those reasons. Maybe some heavy metal groups do nowadays, but we certainly never did.

Ringo Starr was actually acquainted with Polanski and Tate:

> It was upsetting. I mean, I knew Roman Polanski and Sharon Tate and, God, it was a rough time. It stopped everyone in their tracks, because suddenly all this violence came out in the midst of all this love and peace and psychedelia. It was pretty miserable, actually, and everyone got really insecure, not just us, not just the rockers, but everyone in L.A. felt: 'Oh God, it can happen to anybody.' Thank God they caught the bugger.

It's possible that *The Beatles* or some of them did, at some stage, meet Charlie Manson at one of the parties held by Terry Melcher in his house at Cielo Drive or elsewhere in Hollywood. In the 1970 *Rolling Stone* interview, Lennon suggested that he, George Harrison and Ringo Starr took their second LSD trip at Doris Day's house in California while touring with *The Beatles*. Could this have been 10050 Cielo Drive, Bel Air, Los Angeles, California, the house where Sharon Tate and four others were murdered? Terry Melcher was Doris Day's son and the house was called the Doris Day house. Here is what Lennon said about his first and second experiences with LSD

> **A dentist in London...laid it on George, me and our wives without telling us at a dinner party at his house ... And then, well, we just decided to take it again in California...We were on tour, in one of those houses, like Doris Day's house or wherever it was we used to stay.**
>
> **And the three of us took it. Ringo, George and I. I think maybe Neil. And a couple of the Byrds...Crosby and the other guy, who used to be the leader...McGuinn. I think they came round, I'm not sure, on a few trips.**

Redwel Trabant wrote in *The Beatles Book of Revelations* (2014) :

> **As far as the world is aware Manson did not meet any members of the Beatles, however, in an interview with Uncut magazine American record producer and impresario, Kim Fowley, claims that Manson was at a recording session in 1967 for the Beach Boys song Vegetable at which McCartney was present, and appears on the track, apparently recorded chewing a piece of celery.**

So, maybe, *The Beatles* did, cross paths with Charles Manson. They met a lot of people, the good, the bad and the ugly. But they can't be held responsible for the actions of everyone they meet, can they?

Baa...Baa...Baa

Sir Paul McCartney to Russian journalists

LET IT BE (1970)

There is an on-going debate as to whether *Let It Be* or *Abbey Road* was the last *Beatles'* album. Although *Let It Be* was released on the 8 May 1970 shortly after the group announced their break-up most of it was actually recorded in January 1969, before the recording and release of the album *Abbey Road*. Because of this some argue that *Abbey Road* should be considered the group's final album. Initially, *Let It Be* was to be released before *Abbey Road* during mid-1969 as *Get Back*. However, *The Beatles* were unhappy with this version, which was mixed and compiled by Glyn Johns, and it was put on hold. Phil Spector who was spectacularly convicted in 2009 of second-degree murder, created a new version of the album in 1970.

The album was eventually released as *Let It Be*, serving as the album for the 1970 movie of the same name. Three songs from the sessions were released as singles before the album's release, namely *Get Back*, *Don't Let Me Down* and *Let It Be*.

The whole idea came from McCartney who wanted to record an album of new material and rehearse it, then perform it before a live audience for the very first time, on record and on film.

The original idea was to produce a one hour television documentary filmed by director Michael Lindsay-Hogg at Twickenham Film Studios in January 1969. But the sessions were not a happy time for the group. Lennon called them "hell". While Harrison, annoyed by the antics of both Lennon and McCartney, walked out and threatened to leave the group. After getting his way he returned after a week.

But the group still couldn't agree on the venue for their concert which would be their final live performance. Eventually, it was filmed on the rooftop of the Apple Corps building at 3 Saville Row, London, on the 30 January 1969. Again, strictly speaking it wasn't live as it involved a complicated set of backing tracks and vocals to ensure they didn't play live together. Five weeks later, engineer Glyn Johns, was given *carte blanche* to assemble an album, the group members having washed their hands of the entire project. It was during this period that serious disagreements developed between the band members regarding the appointment of a new financial adviser following the death of Brian Epstein.

Lennon, Harrison and Starr wanted Allen Klein who had managed the *Rolling Stones* but McCartney wanted his father in law Lee Eastman. When they couldn't agree both were temporarily appointed only for Eastman to take over on his own on the 8 May.

Klein had become the co-manager of the *Rolling Stones* in 1965. The following year he bought Andrew Loog Oldham's share of the *Rolling Stones'* management. Mick Jagger initially recommended him to *The Beatles* but later began to doubt Klein's honesty, integrity and trustworthiness. They fired him in 1970.

However, Klein had already secured himself ownership of all the *Rolling Stones'* song copyrights while under contract with Decca by surreptitiously forming Nanker Phelge (US) and exhorting the band to sign-over all their material.

The band members willingly obliged as they were majority owners in a U.K. company of the same name. In reality, the *Stones* unwittingly signed-away their musical catalogue to Klein, sole owner of Nanker Phelge US.

A seventeen-year legal battle ensued and the eventual settlement meant forfeiting to Klein the rights to most of their songs recorded before 1971.

The story of the *Beatles'* replacement of their manager is quite interesting. After Brian Epstein's death *The Beatles* considered several people to replace him including, Lord Beeching, Lee Eastman, and Allen Klein. Commonly known as Dr. Beeching, Beeching was chairman of British Railways and a physicist and engineer. He became a household name in Britain in the early 1960s for his report "The Reshaping of British Railways", commonly referred to as "The Beeching Report", which led to far-reaching changes in the railway network, popularly known as the Beeching Axe.

Eastman, McCartney's father in law, was a New York show business attorney. Curiously enough he was born Leopold Vail Epstein.

Klein was a controversial figure. In 1979, he was sentenced to two months in jail for tax evasion after it was discovered that he defrauded the Concert For Bangladesh and UNICEF.

Klein contacted Lennon after reading his press comment that he expected *The Beatles* to "be broke in six months" if they didn't get someone to properly manage their affairs.

After a meeting between Lennon and Klein at the Dorchester Hotel, Lennon convinced Harrison and Starr that Klein should take over their affairs. McCartney was staunchly opposed to Klein and did not sign the contract, but Klein was still technically *The Beatles'* manager. This fundamental disagreement over Klein was one of the key factors in the eventual break-up of *The Beatles*.

In 1969, Klein proceeded to re-negotiate *The Beatles'* contract with EMI, and secured for them the highest royalties ever paid to an artist at that time which was 69 cents per $6–7 album. But despite Klein's original assurance that he would only take a commission on increased royalties, it was later disclosed that Klein was taking 20 percent of the entire royalty.

It was during this period that Klein hired Phil Spector to re-produce and release songs that would comprise the album *Let It Be*, a decision that he made without the authorization of all four *Beatles*.

On the 30 December, 1970, John Eastman on behalf of his brother in law, Paul McCartney, filed a lawsuit against Lennon, Harrison, Starr, and Apple Corps, Ltd.

As a result of the lawsuit, a receiver was appointed to manage *The Beatles'* affairs, and Allen Klein was forced to leave Apple. Following the departure of Klein, Neil Aspinall was appointed CEO of Apple, a position which he held until April 2007.

Aspinall, a school friend of McCartney and Harrison,

began working for *The Beatles* as their roadie which included driving his old Commer van to and from shows, both day and night.

ABBEY ROAD (1970)

George Martin said he was surprised when McCartney asked him to produce one more final album for the group. The sessions for *Abbey Road* began on the 2 July 1969. At this stage the divisions were so obvious in that Lennon wanted his and McCartney's songs to occupy separate sides of the album.

Eventually, they compromised with individually composed songs on the first side and the second consisting largely of a medley. On the 4 July the very first solo single by a *Beatle*, John Lennon's *Give Peace a Chance* was released with credit being given to the *Plastic Ono Band*.

The 20 August 1969 is a significant date in the history of *The Beatles* as it was the very last time the group were together in the same studio. That was for the production of *I Want You (She's So Heavy)*.

Exactly a month later John Lennon informed McCartney, Harrison and Starr of his intention to leave the group. He agreed to withhold a public announcement to avoid undermining sales of the forthcoming album. When *Abbey Road* was released it sold four million copies within three months. It topped the UK charts for a total of seventeen weeks.

The second track, the Harrison composition

Something, was issued as a single. It was the only Harrison track ever to appear as a *Beatles* A-side. Despite its flaws, the album itself was a surprise hit.

The front cover design for the album was a photograph of the group on a zebra crossing. It was, apparently, based on an idea sketched by McCartney and was taken at 11.30 a.m. on the 8 August 1969 outside EMI Studios in Abbey Road by photographer Iain Macmillan. He was given only ten minutes to take the photograph while a policeman held up traffic.

In the photograph the four *Beatles* walk across the street in single file from left to right, with Lennon leading, followed by Starr, McCartney, and Harrison. Although he came to the shoot wearing sandals McCartney is barefoot in the photograph selected for the cover. He is also out of step with the other members. Lennon, McCartney and Starr wore suits designed by Tommy Nutter. Harrison wore denim.

The white Volkswagen seen on the left of the picture belonged to one of the people living in the block of flats across from the recording studio. The owner said that after the album was released fans repeatedly stole the car's number plate (LMW 281F). The gentleman standing on the right was an American tourist called Paul Cole who was unaware he had been photographed until he saw the album cover months later. Conspiracy theorists claim that the cover and lyrics present significant clues to the fact that the real *Beatle*, James Paul McCartney, was long since dead by this time.

Abbey Road received mixed reviews, from being

described "as some of the greatest harmonies to be heard on any rock record" to being called "erratic and often hollow." Even Lennon said it was competent but lifeless. On the 3 January 1970 three of the group worked on Harrison's *I, Me Mine*. Lennon refused to return from Denmark to help out. McCartney, who was seriously unhappy with Spector's production work on the album, publicly announced his retirement from the group on the 10 April 1970 just a week before the release of his first, self-titled solo album.

The *Let It Be* documentary film won the 1970 Academy Award for Best Original Song Score. *Sunday Telegraph* critic Penelope Gilliatt described the movie as:

> **a very bad film and a touching one ... about the breaking apart of this reassuring, geometrically perfect, once apparently ageless family of siblings.**

Following several lengthy legal disputes the dissolution of *The Beatles* was formalized on the 29 December 1974.

John Lennon was shot dead outside his apartment in Manhattan on the 8 December 1980. George Harrison survived an attempt on his life on the 30 December 1999 only to succumb to metastatic non-small cell lung cancer on the 29 November 2001. Ringo Starr and his wife, Barbara Bach, still reside together in England.

The man who is known as Sir Paul McCartney has a

farm in Kintyre in Scotland; a London home at 7 Cavendish Avenue, St. Johns Wood; and further homes in Hollywood, New York and the Bahamas. Those close to him say he often has trouble sleeping at night. He is an habitual cannabis user. Is he the original *Beatle* James Paul McCartney?

Only the Good Die Young

Billy Joel (1977)

Many people had heard the rumour.

But most mistakenly believe that the rumour of the death of *Beatle* James Paul McCartney began in America in 1969. They are wrong. The rumour was actually started by *The Beatles'* organization themselves in 1967.

On the 7 January 1967 McCartney's Mini Cooper was involved in an accident on the M1 motorway outside London, as a result of which it was written off. However, the car was not driven by McCartney but by a Moroccan student named Mohammed Hadjij who was an assistant to London art gallery owner Robert Fraser.

The following is the official leaked version of the crash. Robert Hugh Fraser was the son of a wealthy Scots banker. He was privileged, rich, good-looking and knew everyone who was anyone in the swinging London of the sixties. He owned the *Robert Fraser Gallery*, one of the best known art galleries in London.

By 1964, the gallery at 69 Duke Street was recognized worldwide as one of the sharpest and hippest galleries around. It exhibited the latest and most important artists of the period. Fraser included among his friends many well know film stars, TV personalities, music producers, musicians and pop stars. He was friends with Paul McCartney, John Lennon, Mick Jagger, Keith Richards, and Brian Jones.

They were regular fixtures at both his gallery, and at his nearby Mount Street apartment. Fraser offered them an entrée into London's high society. He also provided them and others with hookers, rent boys and drugs, especially drugs. Mohammed Hadjij also called Chtaibi was a young Moroccan student who first met Robert Hugh Fraser in the early 1960s.

The ward of Mark Gilbey, the multimillionaire heir to

the Gilbeys' drinks fortune, the pair soon became very good friends. Hadjij helped him out in the Gallery, and in between collecting and delivering art, he also assisted him in booking hookers and collecting drugs.

He lived in an adjoining penthouse apartment which Fraser was minding for a famous American actor. Sometimes Fraser would bring Hadjij along with him to the many parties he attended. On Saturday the 7 January he invited him to join him in McCartney's house where they were going to have a party.

They arrived that Saturday afternoon by taxi. At first the twenty or so young fans outside the house thought the attractive looking dark haired Hadjij was McCartney but they soon realized their mistake. McCartney buzzed the pair into the house where he was listening to some rock music.

At one stage he left the room and came back a few minutes later with a large book which he placed on the table. Hadjij and Fraser looked on as McCartney opened the book which was hollowed out providing a secret container packed with a variety of hard and soft drugs including acid, hashish, cocaine and heroin.

After a few Benson & Hashish B-52 Bombers joints made from a mixture of dope and tobacco, McCartney and the pair were joined by Mick Jagger, Keith Richards, Brian Jones and Chris Gibbs whose uncle was the former British Governor of Rhodesia.

The party graduated from soft to hard drugs and after

several hours they decided to make a weekender out of it and drive to Richard's house in the country. Richards lived in a secluded thatched-roofed country mansion in West Wittering, Sussex. But Jagger wanted to stop off at his house in Hertfordshire.

High on drugs they ran out into the stillness of the icy night and proceeded to pack into Jagger's Mini Cooper. Realizing that they couldn't all fit in it McCartney instructed Hadjij to take the stash of drugs and drive behind them in McCartney's Mini Cooper.

The car was specially made for McCartney and contained arm chairs, a wet bar, tinted glass, a racing-style steering wheel about 12-inches wide and oversized tyres. It was the only one in England and easily recognizable. The two cars sped off at high speed.

Although he had driven McCartney's Mini many times, it was usually for short trips during the day to places he was familiar with. This evening he was slightly stoned, driving in the dark and trying to follow the car in front because he didn't know the way to Jagger's house. Leaving the bright city lights behind he was soon well up the M1 motorway travelling at 70 mph.

Halfway there he ran out of cigarettes so pulled his car up alongside Jaggers', opened the window and asked them to "chuck him across some fags". They managed to toss a few cigarettes through the open window. Hadjij then slowed down to light his cigarette while Jagger motored on ahead.

As he slowed down another car came up behind him and proceeded to overtake him. Hadjij, unaware of the passing car until the last minute, overreacted and skidded off the road at high speed, flying through the air, and crashing headlong into a concrete pylon.

The car was split in two and completely written off. Meanwhile, Hadjij lay unconscious and bleeding for several minutes before coming too and realizing his predicament. His main concern was not the state of his health or the wreck he'd made of the car but the drugs given to him by the partygoers. Realizing the difficulties that would arise if the police found the drugs in McCartney's car he managed to find the drug box, pull himself out of the wreckage, hobble across the motorway, scale a barrier fence and fling the box down a ravine before returning to the scene of the accident.

Within minutes he was surrounded by rubberneckers and shortly afterwards by police. Some of the onlookers recognized the car as belonging to Paul McCartney and mistakenly believed that the dark haired young man driving it was the *Beatle* himself. Hadjij was put into an ambulance which sped off in the direction of London. Within hours, the word on the street was that McCartney had been in a serious accident.

He was taken to a local hospital where they took the shattered tinted glass out of his face and checked him for head injuries and broken bones. Bolstered by the drugs he assured them he was fine and he signed himself out and returned back to London where he anxiously waited for the partygoers to call him. They never rang and he fell asleep. The following morning an irate Fraser called him and demanded to know what happened. Fraser related the story to McCartney and asked him if his insurance would cover the car. The following Monday a furious McCartney turned up at Hadjij's apartment in Mount Street and lashed into him about the write-off of his prized car. When McCartney asked him how he was going to pay for the damage Hadjij suggested that McCartney's insurance company would surely pay.

But, McCartney explained, his policy only covered him, his designated named driver, Jane Asher, and Jane Asher's mother, Margaret. Hadjij asked Fraser to intercede between him and McCartney. No claim was ever made on the insurers. Hadjij was never compensated for his injuries and McCartney was never compensated for his car.

Despite several assurances from the group's press officers media from all over the world continued to call them seeking confirmation that McCartney was still alive.

The following month a paragraph appeared in the February 1967 edition of the *Beatles Book* Monthly magazine, headed FALSE RUMOUR:

> **Stories about the Beatles are always flying around Fleet Street. The 7th January was very icy, with dangerous conditions on the M1 motorway, linking London with the Midlands, and towards**

the end of the day, a rumour swept London that Paul McCartney had been killed in a car crash on the M1. But, of course, there was absolutely no truth in it at all, as the Beatles' Press Officer found out when he telephoned Paul's St John's Wood home and was answered by Paul himself who had been at home all day with his black Mini Cooper safely locked up in the garage.

Many people believe that this incident provided the inspiration for the Paul is Dead theory.

The rumour later died down when McCartney was seen out and about.

But it was to resurface, with a vengeance, two years later in America. By 1969 many clues and hidden messages, that James Paul McCartney had died and been replaced, had been inserted in *The Beatles'* albums, in lyrics, on tracks (by way of backward masking) and on album covers and sleeves. But the fact was that very few fans had realized that they were there. A *Beatles'* insider then set about ensuring that the fans discover them.

It started as a prank.

The first known print reference to the rumour in America was in an article written by Tim Harper which appeared in the 17 September edition of the *Times-Delphic*, the student newspaper of the Drake University in Des Moines, Iowa. The headline for the story was "Is Beatle Paul McCartney Dead?"

The article questioned the existence of the "real" bassist and singer of *The Beatles*, James Paul McCartney. The theory itself wasn't new. It had been explored and debated for several years among diehard *Beatles'* fans and conspiracy theorists all over the world. But, the nineteen year old author of the article, Tim Harper wasn't a conspiracy theorist or even a hardcore *Beatles'* fan.

He had heard the rumour from fellow *Times-Delphic* Editor Dartanyan Brown. But, unlike Brown, Harper decided to dig deeper into the rumour. His investigation led him to "evidence" proving McCartney's death.

The article revealed that the group's album covers, beginning with *Sgt. Pepper's*, had cryptic symbols hinting at the front man's absence:

> **On the front cover, a mysterious hand is raised over his head, a sign many believe is an ancient death symbol of either the Greeks or the American Indians.**

The article also referenced other "proofs" including a left-handed guitar lying on the grave before them and, on the back cover, George Harrison pointing towards lyrics from the Lennon-penned song *A Day in the Life* the lyrics of which are:

> **He blew his mind out in a car**
> **He hadn't noticed that the lights had changed.**

According to the article the next two albums held

even more clues. The cover of the *Magical Mystery Tour's* album cover pictured *The Beatles* in grey walrus suits with Paul being the only one in black. The article stated that the walrus was supposedly the Viking symbol of death. The next *Beatles'* album dubbed the *White Album* contained two tracks which according to Harper held the most substantial testaments to the scandal.

Glass Onion contained the confessional lyrics:

> **Here is another clue for you all**
> **The Walrus was Paul.**

The article went on to state that the track *Revolution No. 9* screamed with many sound effects, including the noise of a spectacular auto crash and comments from spectators, including:

> **People ride, people ride. Ride, ride, ride, ride. He hit a pole. He'd better go to see a surgeon. In my broken chair, my wings are broken and so is my hair. It's a fine chemical imbalance. Must've got it between his shoulder blades.**

Strangely, if played backward, a voice whispers the words:

> **Turn me on dead man.**

It didn't take long for Harper's article to grab the attention of radio and television stations across the United States. A follow-up article printed by *The Times-Delphic* stated that Harper did interviews with over twelve different radio stations from Los Angeles to Chicago:

> **Maury Leavitt, another editor at the TD, took me in hand and said we could make some money by selling interviews to radio stations. I said 'OK.' He lined up dozens of interviews with radio stations around the country, $10 for five minutes on the phone with Tim Harper. It was surreal.**

Harper later claimed that he wasn't the original source for any of the claims in his articles. He said he was writing for entertainment purposes only, and said he got the information from fellow student, Dartanyan Brown. Brown claimed he got the story from a musician who had heard it on the Californian west coast, and that he also read the story in an underground newspaper.

The rumours gained momentum in October 1969.

On the 12 October 1969, after an on-air phone call to radio presenter Russ Gibb, a DJ on WKNR-FM in Michigan. The caller, identified only as "Tom", claimed that McCartney was dead. The caller turned out to be Eastern Michigan University student Tom Zarski.

Zarski laid out the whole rumour for Gibb and, as proof of its truth, and urged him to play *Revolution Number Nine* from *The Beatles' White Album* backwards. Gibb obliged and, much to his surprise, could distinctly hear the words "Turn me on, dead man" being spoken repeatedly. Gibb was genuinely astounded by what he heard as were many of his listeners.

Listening to the show that night was Fred LaBour, the arts reviewer for student newspaper *The Michigan Daily*. The *Michigan Daily* published the article on the 14 October, under the title "McCartney Dead; New Evidence Brought To Light". Although LaBour intended it as a joke, it had an impact far wider than the writer and his editor expected.

The article began:

> **Paul McCartney was killed in an automobile accident in early November, 1966 after leaving EMI recording studios tired, sad, and dejected. McCartney was found four hours later, pinned under his car in a culvert with the top of his head sheared off. He was deader than a doornail.**

He related in detail how the accident had been covered up and a look-alike found to replace the dead musician but not as a rumour, but as if it were fact. The mysterious clues were held to be part of a strange and disturbing plot orchestrated by John Lennon, who had it in mind to found a new religion with himself as god and the "reborn" McCartney a Christ-like figure at his side.

LaBour's article electrified its readers and the paper sold out its entire run by mid-morning, and a second printing was ordered to meet demand. LaBour was later to comment:

> **I remember walking down Ann Arbor streets**

hearing Beatles music from every single apartment and house.

He also recalls occasionally hearing someone trying to play a record backwards, listening for clues. In fact, it was the enigmatic clues that seemed to draw most people into the rumour's web. The PIA (Paul is Alive) theorists claim that Fred LaBour's article presented more than two-dozen clues, some of which he originated himself.

Of those, many went on to become an integral part of the rumour. But there were many other real and significant clues and hidden messages which he missed because they had yet to be discovered.

One significant clue he actually missed was at the end of the track *I'm So Tired* on the *White Album*. When you reverse it you can actually hear Lennon say

Paul is dead, miss him, miss him.

LaBour used clues from Gibb's program along with several other "clues" he had actually invented himself, including the name of William Campbell, the alleged replacement for McCartney. This is what LaBour later said:

I made the guy up. It was originally going to be Glenn Campbell, with two Ns, and then I said 'that's too close, nobody'll buy that'. So I made it William Campbell.

But one point that is seldom discussed is the real origin of LaBour's story. He received information from an unidentified source who had inside information on where exactly the clues were:

> **A college student was working on something in the newsroom when the telephone rang and he found himself speaking to a guy who kept insisting that Paul McCartney was dead. 'It was really spooky,' LaBour said recalling how the voice pointed him toward the weird incantation that comes out of the mark at the end of strawberry fields.'**

The caller continue to give clues to LaBour which were contained in *Sgt. Pepper's, Magical Mystery Tour, The White Album* and *Abbey Road*. Even *Rolling Stone* magazine was approached with details of the clues and hidden messages that McCartney was dead. They said that a year before that phone call to Russ Gibb, which would have been October 1968, someone had approached the magazine with the story but they dismissed it. Russ Gibb co-produced a one-hour special called *The Beatle Plot*, giving the rumour greater prominence; by then it was well on its way to become a national, then international, talking point, inspiring fans to pore over their albums for further clues. The mainstream media latched onto it with a fervour.

Meanwhile, back in London, Neil Aspinall met with Brian Epstein to tell him that his hunch had been correct. The rumour, far from being damaging to the group, was a major factor in their increased sales.

Fans were not only buying multiple copies of their albums but were buying different versions of the same album, all the while searching for clues and secret codes.

The PID conspiracy theory was proving to be a major financial cash cow. It was literally the gift that kept on giving. Meanwhile, the media were insistent that the rumour be investigated fully and on the principle that if the mountain won't come to Muhammad then Muhammad must go to the mountain, they sought him out.

Planeloads of journalists, including a journalist and photographer from *Life* magazine, were dispatched to England to find Paul McCartney who, for some inexplicable reason, seemed to be unavailable. For those three weeks McCartney's supposed death was one of the main topics of conversation in America. And then he suddenly appeared at Glasgow airport.

H‌arry Moyes was the first to see him.

Harry, a veteran photographer with the *Glasgow Herald*, received a tip-off that McCartney would be arriving at Glasgow airport on the Wednesday with his family. Off he went and staked the place out.

Sure enough after a couple of hours he spotted Paul, Linda and their two kids Heather and Mary disembarking a private shuttle flight from London. Moyes began taking photographs of the bemused *Beatle* who countered with: "Good evening." As McCartney continued walking Moyes ran after him asking:

Have you heard the rumour spreading about you? That you're dead.

McCartney shook his head and laughed while he and his family were escorted into a waiting car.

Meanwhile, *Life* Magazine dispatched their London correspondent Dorothy Bacon up to Scotland to McCartney's High Park, Campbelltown farmhouse with two staff photographers. They were instructed to try and get an interview but, in any event, not to come back without photographs of McCartney.

The trio trekked by foot through the marshy Scottish countryside until they found the modest ramshackle home of the elusive *Beatle*. They were first spotted by *Martha*, McCartney's ever vigilant sheepdog who began barking furiously. This alerted McCartney who emerged dishevelled and angry from the farmhouse screaming abuse at the journalists:

Bloody hell. You're trespassing, that's what you're doing. Get the hell off my property!

Unperturbed by the abuse the seasoned photographers began snapping away at the unshaven furious *Beatle*. Then as the curious reporter Dorothy Bacon began asking awkward questions McCartney lifted a handy bucket of cold water and flung it over one of the photographers, all of which was caught on camera by the second photographer. In order to diffuse the situation and realizing they would getting nothing more the trio began their retreat down the hill. Five minutes later McCartney intercepted them in his Land-Rover jeep, pulled up and bounded across to them. He then apologized for his behaviour and said he would give them a short interview providing they gave him the photographs they had already taken. A deal was done and McCartney gave a statement and answered a few questions in partial explanation of the so-called mystery of his disappearance.

Life Magazine spoke briefly with him about the various "death clues" including the OPD badge on his *Sgt. Pepper* suit, which fans took to mean Officially Pronounced Dead, his black flower in *Magical Mystery Tour*, and his barefooted appearance on the *Abbey Road* album cover.

The reference to the *Abbey Road* cover was that Lennon wore a white suit to represent the preacher; Ringo Starr wore a black suit to represent the undertaker; Harrison wore jeans and a denim shirt to represent a gravedigger and McCartney was barefoot to represent the corpse.

McCartney's response was as follows:

> **It is all bloody stupid. I picked up that OPD badge in Canada. It was a police badge. Perhaps it means Ontario Police Department or something. I was wearing a black flower because they ran out of red ones. It is John, not me, dressed in black on the cover and inside of Magical Mystery Tour. On Abbey Road we were wearing our ordinary clothes. I was walking barefoot because it was a hot day. The Volkswagen just happened to be parked there.**

> Perhaps the rumour started because I haven't been much in the press lately. I have done enough press for a lifetime, and I don't have anything to say these days. I am happy to be with my family and I will work when I work. I was switched on for ten years and I never switched off. Now I am switching off whenever I can. I would rather be a little less famous these days.
>
> I would rather do what I began by doing, which is making music. We make good music and we want to go on making good music. But the Beatle thing is over. It has been exploded, partly by what we have done, and partly by other people. We are individuals, all different. John married Yoko, I married Linda. We didn't marry the same girl. The people who are making up these rumours should look to themselves a little more. There is not enough time in life. They should worry about themselves instead of worrying whether I am dead or not.
>
> What I have to say is all in the music. If I want to say anything I write a song. Can you spread it around that I am just an ordinary person and want to live in peace? We have to go now. We have two children at home.

But the only people making up rumours were *The Beatles* themselves who were providing dozens of hidden messages in each of their albums suggesting that McCartney was dead. Why were they doing this? No one asked him that question possibly because some of the backward masking messages had yet to be discovered.

But McCartney knew they were there because he was directly involved in planting some himself. *Life* weren't the only journalists to call up to his house. So did Chris Drake from the *BBC*. McCartney told him:

> **I'm going through a phase now where I don't want to be in the limelight. I just think it ruins our life.**

to which his wife Linda added:

> **I don't think people realize that to them, it's headlines in the newspapers, but everybody starts bothering us. We came out here on holiday to be left alone.**

McCartney then said:

> **I'm not going to try to spoil people's fantasies, but if the conclusion they reach is that I'm dead, then they're wrong. Because I'm alive and living in Scotland.**

Once again no one asked him the crucial question. It was obvious that he was alive but was he the original *Beatle* known as James Paul McCartney?

Hugh Farmer from *The People* newspaper was one who didn't get an interview.

> **When I approached, John [McCartney's neighbour] shouted and bawled as my car wheels spun in the mud, to make it clear I had to go no further, and that no one was going to get near his**

VIP neighbour.

But the intrepid journalist finally got to McCartney's house only to be told by McCartney:

Tell them how you have found me, very much alive.

Later the *Liverpool Daily Post* managed to get him on the phone. McCartney told them that earlier on he had phoned his dad in Wirral and said:

Don't be surprised if you hear rumours that I am dead.

It didn't end there. When *KOIN* DJ Roger W. Morgan accompanied by a *London Financial Times* journalist caught up with McCartney, the beleaguered *Beatle* emerged from a nearby barn with a loaded rifle and told them to "Piss off."

As for LaBour, he later said he was concerned about his unintentional role in sending the rumour spiralling out of control. In early November he was even invited to Hollywood to participate in an RKO television special that featured celebrity attorney F. Lee Bailey conducting a mock trial in which he examined various expert "witnesses" on the subject of McCartney's alleged death. About the program LaBour later said:

I was a nervous college kid, way out of my league. I told Bailey during our pre-show meeting that I'd made the whole thing up. He sighed, and said, 'Well, we have an hour of

television to do. You're going to have to go along with this.' I said OK.

However, by the time the programme was scheduled for broadcast, public interest had waned. The programme was shown only once on a local television station in New York City on the 30 November, 1969.

Still diehard theorists were not convinced that James Paul McCartney had not been replaced. They pointed out that the voice on the track *Oh! Darling* promoted as belonging to McCartney, sounded very different from the soft dulcet tones they heard on the track *Yesterday* or *Here There and Everywhere*.

Furthermore, *Lady Madonna*, initially mistaken by many *Beatles'* fans to belonging to Ringo Starr, didn't sound anything like McCartney either. They were convinced there was an impostor at large. He may be very talented by the was still an impostor.

Bruce Cook, in the *National Observer* took a very pragmatic approach. He found that the idea that James Paul McCartney had actually been replaced was absurd adding:

> **If Paul McCartney really did die shortly before the group recorded Sgt. Pepper and opened all those new horizons in pop, then they had better stick with this new guy and quit dropping all those dumb hints that he's not genuine. He's better than genuine. He's a distinct improvement.**

Even legal experts were called in to comment. They

pointed out that it would have been very difficult for an impostor to convince the British government that he was James Paul McCartney.

It was pointed out that McCartney had recently received a new passport, which would require his fingerprints, and had been issued a marriage certificate on the 12 March 1969 when he wed Linda Eastman.

But the passport was never offered up for comparison purposes. Not that McCartney was under any obligation to hand it up just as today he is not obliged to produce DNA to prove who he really is but as American broadcaster Alex Bennett noted to AP at the time:

> **The only way McCartney is going to quell the rumours is by coming up with a set of fingerprints from a 1965 passport which can be compared to his current prints. Otherwise, people will suspect either that the story is true, or that the story is being used as promotion by Apple, and that would hurt the Beatles' image.**

McCartney refused to produce any fingerprints. Did he have something to hide? On the 16 January, 1980, McCartney was arrested at Tokyo International Airport having arrived for a week-long Japanese tour with his post-Beatle creation, the overwhelmingly mediocre band he called *Wings*.

The tour was cancelled when a customs officer discovered a fist sized bag of marijuana in his carry-on luggage. He was detained in Tokyo Prison for eight days and faced a sentence of eight years imprisonment.

After intense lobbying by the British vice-consul he was deported without charge. Part of the problem was that the fingerprints of inmate #22 did not match those taken by Japanese authorities in 1966 when he toured with *The Beatles*.

Tell people there's an invisible man in the sky who created the universe, and the vast majority will believe you. Tell them the paint is wet, and they have to touch it to be sure.

George Carlin

What is the document called 60IF? The 60IF

document has been introduced to the internet by someone with very inside knowledge who has systematically over the years furnished snippets of information about the true circumstances surrounding McCartney's alleged replacement. When something is changed it is usually because the previous information was found to be false. According to intelligence sources a lot of what has been written could possibly be true.

60IF is a compilation of evidential documentation, including over 10,000 original EMI photos, narratives and more which claims to tell the true story behind *The Beatles,* in general, and the deaths of James Paul McCartney and Brian Epstein in 1966 in particular while in the hands of kidnappers, and the subsequent cover up and replacement with impersonators. The internet version is a summary of the story.

The main author is thought to have been *Beatle* George Harrison. He related the story to his Eastern friends who wrote it down in their own Eastern language. He also gave them documentation to hold for safekeeping. Harrison left them specific instructions that the story was to be published on a specific date on the internet after he died.

That date was the 18 June 2002, the exact day that Paul would've been 60 had he been alive; hence the name 60IF. Those in control of the document admit that it has been modified and added to as more details have been uncovered but that it is still essentially Harrison's story and that he was determined that one day the truth would come out.

What does 60IF say?

On the evening of Sunday, the 11 September, 1966, Brian Epstein and Paul McCartney were returning from their trip in good spirits. It had been a wonderful time. After John's notorious phrase which had instigated the storm in the world against *The Beatles*, everything seemed to be finally returning to normal. Paul had had a sudden burst of extraordinary creativity over a very short period of time, and things were looking up.

It had been a typically seasonal rainy day. At a normally quiet intersection, a van suddenly cut across the street, blocking the car Brian and Paul were in. The car didn't quite stop in time and hit the van, but not seriously enough to do any real damage.

They expected to discuss what had happened with the occupants of the other vehicle, but instead men dressed in black appeared from the van and grabbed Epstein, McCartney and one of the girls who happened to be with them at the time and forced them into another car that had turned up in the meantime. The second girl who was with them, however, had the presence of mind to run away.

The morning afterwards, not knowing what had happened, Harrison tried to call Epstein and McCartney but strangely they couldn't get hold of them. They retraced their steps through their common friends but nobody had seen or heard from them. Harrison and others were on the telephone all day looking for them.

The following day on the 12 September the police phoned to tell Harrison that they had a girl with them confirming that Epstein and McCartney had been kidnapped. Ringo Starr was the first one to arrive where the kidnapping had taken place; the vehicles were empty. The girl told them what had happened.

Harrison, Lennon and Starr began to panic. Lennon became hysterical and they didn't know what to think or what to do. But they were able to suppress the story from the Wednesday newspapers.

This was thanks to some acquaintances they had. They then directly contacted the intelligence service who understood the gravity of the situation and the social ramifications if word got out.

MI5 or a group associated with it told them that they would take care of everything. All they had to do was to continue their daily routine and keep all their previously appointed business engagements.

Lennon, Harrison and Starr waited for the kidnappers to contact them with a ransom demand of some sort. Time passed and nothing happened. As more days passed, their apprehension grew.

It wasn't until Tuesday of the following week, the 20 September 1966, when they received the call, but not the one they had been waiting for. They were called out in order to identify McCartney's body.

At the time Lennon was in Paris and Harrison was in India. They immediately returned home. McCartney was found at the foot of a hill, a little distance from a white Volkswagen. He was in a ghastly state. He had been dead for a while and beasts had begun to eat at him; his lips looked as if they had been torn by some animal. The left side of his face had also been torn to pieces and the whole of his ear had been bitten off.

The kidnappers had tried to burn him to eliminate the evidence, but only the legs had managed to be burnt before the rain extinguished the fire.

When they arrived there was a line of police officers blocking them while a crowd of men in shirts were retrieving material for further investigation. They were so oblivious to the grief the other group members felt that one of them exclaimed right in front of the dead body: "Look ...it seems like a walrus!"

With his teeth hanging outside of his eaten-up lips and with a shiny swollen ear and dripping wet Harrison says that he really did look like a walrus. Lennon confronted the man who had spoken so insensitively and they began to brawl. He had to be pulled away as he howled: "I.., I am the walrus ..not him, I.., I am the walrus!"

Epstein was found, two days later, in a car which had been pushed over a cliff and set alight. The remaining *Beatles* were desperately aware that McCartney, Epstein and *The Beatles* were finished. But their anger made them think: they would not stop, they would not give up.

McCartney had left a lot of material that was yet to be published. The surviving members met up and decided that nobody had to know and Paul McCartney could still be kept alive. The only question was how.

It was announced to the press *The Beatles'* wished not to play any more concerts and only work in the recording studio, which gave them a bit of breathing space.

Harrison says that it was suggested to them from the same intelligence service department what to do: they had in their secret labs at their disposal cosmetic surgeons with the technical skills to recreate perfect doubles but in exchange for their help the surviving members had to keep quiet about what had happened; the penalty for refusing to remain silent was death.

They found a look-alike for Epstein and a few contenders for McCartney but the main problem was to find one with the most similar voice possible. They had to check out a number of imitators and find one with a face compatible with McCartney's. They found a boy with a beautiful voice that was able to imitate McCartney in a cogent manner but his face presented problems that would not be compliant with the cosmetic surgery needed.

They decided however to use him to complete the songs for the album that was in current preparation so it could be released as quickly as possible in order to divert the suspicions and rumours that had begun to hound them.

They had all but given up when the right man was found. His name was William Shepherd and he had formerly been an Ontario police officer. He was also a musician who was familiar with, and fond of, the music of *The Beatles*.

He had a beautiful voice but the quality of his McCartney voice imitation was not as good as that of the boy who had already been working with them. However his face as presented was wonderfully compatible as regards to the profile and jaw, two key factors in determining the correct candidate that the cosmetic surgeons could use.

Despite this, there were a number of differences: Paul was far-sighted while Bill was near-sighted. Paul had hair that naturally went from left to right while Bill had hair that went naturally from right to left. Paul had a round face but Bill had a long face. Paul was left handed and Bill was right handed.

In an irony of fate the "substitutes" had inverted heights: The substitute for Paul was taller and the counterpart of Brian was smaller. For this, tricks were suggested to them that to adopt when they filmed together.

When Bill Shepherd was in the police he was nicknamed Sgt. Pepper because he liked to drink and his nose, a bit rounded, was often red. After plastic surgery Lennon gave Bill the nickname of "Faul".

The Beatles' introduction to Faul was the French national hymn at the start of *All You Need Is Love*, and *Sgt.Pepper* was the first album with the photos of Faul even though they needed to be retouched.

According to Harrison this album cover is full of messages. Many of those that have been discovered are true, while others are not, and some have been wrongly interpreted. One of the most important is *Welcome The Rolling Stones* written with blood. Harrison said they hadn't had news about who it was that had killed Epstein and McCartney and Lennon was sure that his murder had been commissioned by associates of the *Rolling Stones* as they were well-known as delinquents. (This is probably a reference to the notorious London gangsters, the Kray twins.) The crowd on the cover of the album is made up of those that McCartney would have wanted at his funeral.

Harrison goes on to say what clues are true. In the lowest row of flowers the word "Paul" is written. The band had its name changed; they were no longer called "The Beatles" but only "Beatles". Most effectively in the bass drum there are mirrored words: it's the date of Brian and Paul's disappearance:

1ONE IX (September 11).

The references that fans found on the back of the cover are all correct; Harrison points out the last completed song sung by Paul: *She's Leaving Home*.

Faul had an older appearance than Paul and so to confuse the issue they all grew beards and moustaches so that they would all seem a bit older. Faul also wore contact lenses to darken his natural green colour eyes. They were quite discreet but someone noticed that something had changed: the surgeons had forgotten to duplicate the small ditching that Paul had on his chin. This was retouched in the photos. Also Faul had to endure other plastic surgery sessions with some improvement although the result still wasn't perfect.

The surgeons altered his mouth again: his teeth and his chin were fully rebuilt, his nose was made shorter and thinner, even his hands were reshaped and the cheeks and chin had to be increased with time-limited botuline injections when they were in public or when any photos were taken because his face was also a lot thinner than Paul's.

In spite of these operations today's traces of the old scar can still be seen on Faul's chin. The nose does not look the same overall: Faul's is smaller and is not shaped the same. But above all the distance between the eyes is completely different: Paul's were much wider.

And the old Faul, what happened to him? Well, according to the 60IF document he's the one in the photo in the left bottom side of the *White Album* poster. To divert suspicion the photo was mirror printed. Faul slowly learned to play left handed and to sing better.

The counterpart of Brian Epstein could not hold up

the role for very long so they had to get him out of the picture as quickly as possible while they worked on the legal aspects of how to manage the musical material that McCartney had left to them. This is the reason why Apple was born. Lennon also wanted to leave a strong reference to Paul McCartney: for "Apple Corp Ltd" you can read "A Paul Corp Ltd".

The trip in India was their attempt to put McCartney's soul into Faul's body but of course it didn't succeed. Harrison admits it was a crazy idea, but says they were almost going out of our heads with grief.

After some time Harrison says that they discovered that it was Brian Epstein and not Paul McCartney who was the main target of the kidnappers.

Although Lennon initially favoured the plan, as time went by the memory of McCartney replaced his happiness. But he was determined not to let *The Beatles* die or allow those who had killed him and Brian Epstein to win.

Harrison says that without discussing it with them first, Lennon began to insert phrases into the tracks which whispered the truth. He risked wrecking everything but the phrases were replaced in the next copies of the albums. In spite of this Lennon succeeded with a maximum amount of astuteness to publish the *White Album* poster which actually is the White Book of the whole matter.

When the material left by McCartney was all

published Lennon did not find any reason to continue *The Beatles*. However, he didn't want them to fold completely until he had inserted all the clues in the songs so that everything that had happened could be reconstructed. Also, the end of Faul's role was supposed to coincide with the end of *The Beatles* but according to Harrison Faul didn't respect the contract that had been made. He believed he would be strongly protected by the secret service and so he published his first solo album which had actually been prepared by other musicians.

Harrison says that the remaining *Beatles* were so annoyed that they were tempted in the last album to reveal the truth but corporate managers and lawyers prevented it. The reference "28IF" on the Volkswagen plate in the *Abbey Road* cover is correct because the album was to supposed to come out a year later than it actually did, but there was a fear that some of the truth would come out prematurely so it was released earlier.

The document goes on to say that there are references in places other than *Beatles*' albums or songs; there were a few friends in the music business and entertainment industry in general who were aware of their dilemma, and wrote disguised songs of support and condolence.

The document specifically mentions the track *Mrs. Robinson* written by Paul Simon as a poetic to Jane Asher, in 1968. The document adds that if you listen closely to the popular music of that era, the musicians of the world who knew were sympathetic.

After *The Beatles* disbanded John Lennon went to America to find the people responsible. During the second half of 1967 he had discovered they were members of the KKK. After years of personal investigation Lennon was getting very close to the truth. He left Yoko Ono and a few months later he was assassinated because he had requested not to have daily body guards with him anymore. The document ends by saying that in spite of his betrayal, fans should give Faul an immense thank you, because he sacrificed his life for *The Beatles*. While this ruse has been financially successful to him, he has felt out of place quite a bit. He himself inserted several clues into the albums.

But after *The Beatles* he merely became a puppet in Linda Eastwood's hands because she wanted to become a rock star at any cost. In the end, despite it all, he became a very small Paul McCartney or perhaps slightly better than small. That is essentially the summarized version of what 60IF, allegedly written by George Harrison, says.

But is this far-fetched story actually true?

In fact, is any of it true or is the entire PID urban legend a complete hoax accidentally started by Fred LaBour or deliberately started by *The Beatles* themselves to sell more records at a time when their sales were plummeting?

What else do we know about 60IF? We know that the "document" has changed over the years as additional pieces of news were added or subtracted from it. It was later said that McCartney's body was found at the bottom of a hill in France horribly disfigured. Some theorists speculated that it was found at *Bourlonge-sur-Mer,* an important fishing port and a terminus of cross-channel ferry service. It was either discovered or first seen by the other *Beatles* on the 28 September 1966. The differences of opinion all seem to relate to how Paul died but not the fact that he did die.

How much of the 60IF scenario is true? How much can we say is definitely untrue? Like nearly all information on *The Beatles* fact is mixed with fiction, sometimes deliberately, to disseminate misinformation about the real facts. Before examining it in detail let's look at another source of information about what happened from a fascinating film released in 2010.

Then along came Joel Gilbert.

The "Paul is Dead" theory gained a new generation of fans with Los Angeles film director Joel Gilbert's 2010 release of *Paul McCartney Really is Dead,* a full length feature film. Though billed as a "mockumentary," the film's chilling narrative by way of an alleged confessional by George Harrison himself made *Beatles'* fans wonder if in fact Paul was really dead.

Paul McCartney Really is Dead is available on DVD and iTunes, where the reviews vary from "I laughed the whole time" to "it must be true." Gilbert's film is a parody which outlines what might have happened to McCartney told through the eyes of fellow *Beatle* George Harrison. The film clearly sets out the main clues left by *The Beatles* indicating the death of McCartney. Although the film has received mixed reviews it is a highly entertaining watch and a must see for any real *Beatles'* fan. The film is also an excellent source for clues left by *The Beatles* concerning the alleged death of James Paul McCartney.

On the 1 July 2005, music and video producer Joel Gilbert informed the world that an unsolicited package arrived at the Hollywood offices of his Highway 61 Entertainment in California. There was no return address but the package was postmarked in London.

Inside there was a mini cassette player accompanied by two mini-cassette audio tapes. The words "The Last Testament of George Harrison" were written on each of the two tapes. Gilbert says that over a period of five years his company endeavoured to authenticate the tapes but as he himself says: "Each test proved inconclusive."

A voice purporting to be that of *Beatle* George Harrison's related an incredible and shocking story: James Paul McCartney was killed in a car crash in November of 1966 and replaced with a double! The voice on the tape which sounds nothing like that of George Harrison begins his story by saying the date is the 30 December 1999. The voice says he is making the tape while in the Royal Berkshire Hospital in Reading England. The date is the day after an attempt had been made on his life by a man called Michael Abrahm who broke into his mansion in Henley on Thames and stabbed him several times in an attempt to kill him. Harrison says he doesn't know why he was attacked but he has his suspicions. He said he asked his wife Olivia to bring him in a cassette so he could make the tapes in the hope that they would protect him. He recounts that John Lennon was killed almost exactly twenty years ago by deranged fan Mark Chapman and calls Lennon "reckless." But, says Harrison, "there's much more to the story."

He claims that in or around the 1 December 1980 John Lennon rang him and told him he was "going to go public and tell everything about Paul." Eight days later John Lennon was shot dead.

Harrison says that two weeks before his attack he met and spoke with Sir Paul McCartney and told him that he "couldn't keep up the deception any longer." He says that in 1966 the four *Beatles* promised never to tell the story that he was now about to reveal. He talks about the burden of guilt he feels over the "deception" but explains that there were important reasons for it. Harrison says that he loved Paul, that they all loved Paul, the real James Paul McCartney.

Harrison met McCartney in school when he was 14 and Paul was 16. He recounts how he was eventually allowed to join the group, then called *The Quarrymen* and talks about their early success and phenomenal popularity. He says it wasn't all fun and joy and that there was a great amount of anger directed at them and controversy surrounding them.

In 1966 Lennon took their popularity too far by telling a journalist that they were more popular than Jesus. The comment caused a backlash against them in America. They were boycotted, fans burned their records and they were universally condemned.

Despite several explanations and apologies by both John Lennon and Brian Epstein the resentment and anger became ingrained. The KKK nailed their photograph to a cross and burned it, vowing vengeance against the group.

Memphis City Council voted to ban their concerts saying that they would not support any group who were disrespectful to anyone's religion. Harrison refers to American DJ Tom Charles who organized for fans to publicly burn their records as a "red neck wanker." Harrison, obviously annoyed by Lennon continued "If that wasn't enough he managed to get the Jews mad at us too."

This is a reference to Lennon's quote to English journalist and former lover Maureen Cleave which was carried in the *New York Times* Magazine on the 3 July 1966 in which Lennon said: "Show business is an extension of the Jewish religion."

Asked to explain the comment at a news conference John Lennon replied: "I said that to her as well, no comment. I mean, you can read into it what you like." Harrison says that luckily by November 1966 the storm in the world against *The Beatles* instigated by Lennon's notorious comments had subsided.

Harrison says that on the 9 November 1966 they began a recording session at Abbey Road Recording Studios around midnight. Paul became more and more agitated as he and John disagreed over song lyrics. Paul wanted the chorus to be kitschy while John wanted it to be vague more "Bob Dylanesque!" Paul was screaming at him: "We're the Beatles. We make radio hits."

John was shouting back: "We have the public's ear. We need to say something for a change." After more heated words, Paul stormed out of the studio just before 5.00 a.m.

It was raining heavily as Paul drove off in his white Austin Healey. At about 6:00 a.m. the three remaining *Beatles* decided to leave the studio, still shaking from the row between Paul and John. As they exited the building an official looking black van pulled up in front of them. A man wearing an officer's uniform emerged. He flashed an official badge and said that there had been a terrible accident involving Paul McCartney. He said they must come with them and identified himself only as Maxwell.

Maxwell said he had been dispatched from MI5, the British Intelligence Service, because it was a high profile situation. He said his officers were at the scene of a fatal accident involving a white Austin Healey and that a woman named Rita was insisting that the dead man was Paul McCartney.

They were needed to verify if, in fact, the corpse was Paul McCartney. Harrison says there were in absolute shock. They drove three miles with Maxwell where they saw the mangled white car. Maxwell pointed to a girl sitting in the rain wearing a light blue dress who was crying hysterically and informed them that that was Rita. She claimed she was walking on the pavement in the cold rain and Paul offered her a lift.

She accepted and quickly realized he was the *Beatle* and became hysterical, grabbing at him causing him to lose control of the car. The car smashed into a lorry and turned over. Rita said McCartney was strapped inside. She escaped from the vehicle and ran for help. When she returned the car had exploded and Paul was decapitated. Maxwell led them to the draped body of the deceased and slowly lifted the cover as John, George and Ringo looked on. John was sobbing uncontrollably. They saw a body with a decapitated head next to it in a pool of blood. It was an horrific sight. The head was split open and had one eye missing. Paul's hair was burnt off. The head had no teeth except for two molars sticking through the cheeks. Maxwell asked them if it was Paul McCartney.

They each confirmed that it was him. Maxwell then commented flippantly that he kind of looked like a walrus. Lennon lost his composure completely and began thumbing Maxwell screaming: "No, I am the walrus. I am the walrus."

They were walked back to the van in a state of total shock and utter disbelief. Maxwell then drove them to an MI5 safe house. He left them in the sitting room and went to another room and made a number of phone calls. Eventually, according to Harrison, Maxwell finally emerged and announced that Her Majesty's Government believed that if Paul's death was made public a rash of suicides would quickly follow. Therefore it had to be kept a secret for as long as possible. They spent two days in the safe house initially believing that *The Beatles* were finished but in their despair they realized that the group were at the top of their creative peak. Lennon said he had a backlog of songs that he and McCartney had written as well as unfinished ideas.

Lennon believed he could complete as many as fifty songs written by Lennon and McCartney which would keep *The Beatles* going for a long time. They had a meeting and agreed that they would not disband, that no one had to know what had happened to Paul. The only problem was how they would be able to keep it a secret.

Having discussed the idea with their MI5 handler, Maxwell suggested that since MI5 had expert plastic surgeons at their disposal they could create a double of McCartney from a person of close resemblance. But they had to promise never to reveal MI5's involvement in the plan, the penalty for disclosure would be death.

They all agreed and the deal was done. The next day their manager confirmed to the media that *The Beatles* were going to stop touring and work only in the recording studio. The idea was that this would give them breathing space to find a double. Next, at their behest, the American teen magazine *Tiger Beat* in conjunction with Dick Clarke's *American Bandstand* TV program held a Paul lookalike contest. The judges were unaware of the seriousness of their task. Harrison says that no winner was ever announced but there was a winner. His name was William Campbell and he was chosen to become the new Paul McCartney.

Although he was told that it would take several operations William Campbell was thrilled with the opportunity to become *Beatle* Paul McCartney.

He literally couldn't believe his good fortune. Although he bore a good resemblance to McCartney there were a number of imperfections in his features that required surgery to his upper lip, eyebrows, jaw, ears and finally chin. Campbell also required speech therapy to acquire the trademark Liverpool accent.

Another problem was that Campbell or Bill as he came to be known was right handed but since he would be playing bass guitar only in the studio no one would be the wiser. After the first plastic surgery Lennon began calling Bill "False Paul" later shortened to "Faul." The other three members were worried that if it was ever found out that they had deceived their fans so completely that they would become hate figures all over the world.

Lennon then told them about a book by Arthur Stephen Crane called the *Open Boat*. The story concerned four men who were trapped in a lifeboat at sea. One died. When the three remaining reached land they covered up the death but wrote about it in poetry.

So, according to Harrison, Lennon suggested that they place visual clues on their album covers and write hints about Paul's accident in song lyrics. The reason for this was that if the truth ever did emerge they could say that they were forced into silence by MI5 under the threat of death but they had tried to tell their fans by hiding clues in their work.

Bill was hired on a salary basis only as the other three members did not wish to share royalty payments with him. A new publishing company was formed by Lennon, Harrison and Starkey. Lennon proposed it be called A Paul Corporation in memory of their friend but it was considered too close to the bone so the name was changed to Apple Corporation.

Although they accepted Bill as McCartney's replacement they never forgot the real Paul. Ringo began calling Bill "Rubber Paul" because of all the plastic surgery he had to undertake. Lennon thought it was the perfect name for their first album without the real Paul McCartney but Harrison said that his name would be way too obvious so they settled on *Rubber Soul*.

The album cover for *Rubber Soul* was of the four Beatles taken from the perspective of Paul looking up at them from the grave. Because they were afraid people would recognize that Bill was not Paul McCartney they decided to contort all the faces. The hairstyles adopted by the group of long mops of hair were only continued so that they could cover up the scars of Bill's surgery. On the back of the cover there is a photograph of Bill smoking a cigarette. Back in the sixties in Britain cigarettes were called coffin nails so they thought this would be an appropriate clue.

Shortly afterwards Bill began smoking marijuana which he claimed eased the pain he suffered as a result of the surgeries. For the cover of the single *Nowhere Man* and in order to distinguish Bill from the other three, Bill is looking in a different direction from the other three *Beatles*. The *Nowhere Man* in the lyrics refers to Bill.

> **He's a real Nowhere man,**
> **Sitting in his Nowhere land.**
> **Nowhere man,**
> **can you see me at all?**

The song *Girl* was about Paul's girlfriend at the time, Jane Asher. They had Bill break up with her by way of a typed written letter because they thought she couldn't be trusted to keep the secret. A third song was about Bill:

> **I'm looking through you,**
> **You don't look different,**
> **but you have changed.**
> **I'm looking through you,**
> **you're not the same.**

They named the next album *Revolver* to represent the revolving door through which Paul left the *Beatles* and Bill Campbell had entered the band. Because Bill had just undergone his second major plastic surgery a photograph of the group was deemed to be too risky for the cover of the album. Instead they decided to use a drawing.

Bill is the only *Beatle* facing away symbolizing his separateness from the others. His drawing only shows one eye because this was the way he appeared the last time they saw him.

They also placed a photograph of Paul screaming in agony as they imagined him in the car accident. Harrison goes on to say that while Bill was improving all the time he still didn't sound exactly like Paul so he suggested that they add new effects and experimental sounds to their music to disguise Bill's contribution on bass and vocals. Because Lennon and McCartney had written most of the group's songs to date, now that Paul was dead, Lennon asked Harrison to try and contribute more.

Harrison added Indian music backwards to the songs while Lennon added sound effects. Harrison also wrote a new song called *Taxidermist* but Ringo felt that the song title was too obvious a clue and so the title was change to *Taxman*. They shout the word "Paul" at the end of each phrase.

> **If you drive a car [Paul];**
> **If you get too cold [Paul];**
> **In the end you have to see the taxidermist**
> **to preserve your remains for the funeral.**
> **My advice to those who die, Taxman.**

By this time Lennon was becoming increasing more guilty about their deception and began to insist on stronger clues for their album covers. So, for the album, *Yesterday and Today*, he used bloody meat and baby doll parts to represent the horrific nature of Paul's accident. John placed two decapitated dolls on Paul's shoulders pointing towards his head as a reference to Paul's decapitation.

On Paul's right arm he placed Paul's teeth knocked out by the car crash and Lennon told Bill not to smile since his teeth were on his arm.

Another doll held by Harrison had burnt off hair and no teeth. The cover photo was submitted to Capitol records.

The very next day Lennon burst into the studio screaming "that wanker Maxwell" had showed up in his flat that morning with one of his goons. He punched him in the side and put his head in a headlock and told him he's snap off his head and he'd just look like Paul if they didn't change the album cover. Harrison says he told Lennon that they should change the cover as it was going a bit far. Harrison then rang Capitol Records and withdrew the cover.

A new photo session was quickly arranged for later that day. This time they put Bill inside a trunk representing a casket. In fact, when the cover is turned on its side it appears that Bill is lying in a grave. Lennon was seething with anger that they were forced to change the cover. In the photograph you can see him holding his right side where he was punched. Campbell has a scar on his upper lip from recent plastic surgery. Harrison suggested to Lennon that they use the song names as clues to Paul's death and Lennon readily agreed.

Drive My Car was what Paul was doing when he died. *I'm Only Sleeping* is what Paul looked like dead. *Dr. Robert* was the plastic surgeon who turned Bill into Paul. *Yesterday* was about Lennon's sorrow.

Act Naturally was what they all tried to do so Bill could pass as Paul. *We Can Work It Out* was about their decision not to give up. The film goes on to indicate the other clues placed by the group. It was all working to plan except that Lennon was becoming increasingly depressed and concerned about the deception.

Also, McCartney's absence in his life as a creative force left Lennon incredibly lonely. Even after a year, he was clearly still affected by the death of McCartney and vowed to make what amends he could – hence the next album *Sgt. Pepper's Lonely Hearts Club Band* – the album which would provide the most number of clues as to McCartney's untimely death.

In the tapes the narrator, allegedly George Harrison, then begins to talk about India, *The Beatles'* trip there and the reason for it. He says that they missed Paul so much that they decided to try something "desperate".

They decided to seek the help of Maharishi Mahesh Yogi, a leader in the world of Transcendental Meditation. "They wanted him to direct Paul's soul to enter into and take over Faul's body." By "Faul" he is referring to Bill Campbell. Yogi agreed to try if they came to him in India. They agreed. Here they met Mia Farrow who had just left Frank Sinatra.

As the narrator says:

> **Of course the idea to put Paul's soul into Faul didn't succeed. Yes, I know it was a crazy idea. But we were going out of our heads with grief. Faul enjoyed the trip. I remember Faul smiled and picked his nose a lot. We never told him why we went because if it had worked William Campbell would have ceased to exist. He thought we were there to learn Transcendental Meditation or something like that. He was so stupid. He really had no idea.**

When they realized it didn't work, they flew back to England, disappointed, never to return. While working in the recording studio Harrison received a call from Maxwell who told him that having seen the *Sgt. Pepper's* cover it was obviously meant to indicate a funeral for McCartney. He warned him to be careful.

Harrison pleaded with Lennon to stop giving out clues to McCartney death, that Maxwell was on to them, and had warned him of the consequences. But Lennon's inspiration for writing was driven by inserting these clues. Harrison regarded the practice as reckless and felt it was only a matter of time before they would be caught out.

The problems were adding up when Bill began taking LSD and then stupidly admitted to the media that he was taking it. Harrison says that Bill was naive and didn't know how the media worked. The rest of the mockumentary goes on to talk about other clues. Many people seem to misinterpret this film. They don't seem to realize that it's a parody. One of my favourite reviews of the film is from a Brian Uecker on Amazon.com:

> **Do not watch this chilling and disturbing documentary late at night, or you may find yourself running screaming through your house in a state of panic, making calls to the police and friends. Yes, it is that scary.**

Gilbert told me an interesting story about the film after it was released:

> **I received an angry letter from George Harrison's estate attorney who complained about the use of Harrison's voice and likeness in the film.**
>
> **According to copyright law, a celebrity's voice and likeness can be used without permission if a film is a parody , but not if it's a depiction of real events (a regular commercial film). So, if the story of "Paul is Dead" were true, the law is clear that I would, in fact, need permission to use Harrison's voice and likeness.**
>
> **I responded to Harrison's estate attorney in a letter that he was welcome to sue me in court and prove that Paul McCartney really was dead, meaning the film was a true story (and therefore I needed to get permission) and that I would argue in court that McCartney was in fact alive, meaning this was a parody and I did not need**

permission. I also wrote that I would call McCartney himself to testify as to whether he was dead or alive. I never heard back from Harrison's estate again after that letter.

So, what do all these clues mean? What is their significance or do they have any significance?

And what of the core story that McCartney died in 1966 and *The Beatles* replaced him with a double? Remember this film is a parody. It presents a version of events that might have happened. Of course, we know that William Campbell did not exist but what about Billy Shears or Billy Shepherd?

One thing for certain is that there are a lot of gaps and contradictions in the official story about *The Beatles* in late 1966. In fact, it would neither be unreasonable nor untrue to submit to you that there is a serious level of mis-information. It is the amount of mis-information which is so disconcerting. The clear implication is that they had something to hide, some dark secret that they dare not disclose. Let's examine that story and ascertain what we can prove to be false and then see what we end up with.

It is quite possible that societies - much like individuals - collectively repress information, concepts, and ideas which would produce high anxiety levels if dealt with consciously.

Wilson Bryan Key

Let's imagine a crazy scenario for a moment: Imagine someone tried in a court of law to disprove this ridiculous conspiracy theory. How would that pan out?

INT. ROYAL COURTS OF JUSTICE, LONDON
MR.JUSTICE SOLOMAN:

> Members of the jury, let me remind you what this extraordinary case is about and what your role in it is. In this case, music impresario, Sir Paul McCartney, a knight of the realm and one of the world's most renown and respected musicians, has sued the author of the book *The Beatles Controversy: John, Paul, George, Ringo and Bill* for libel and substantial damages because the author has claimed and or implied that Sir Paul is an impostor and that he is not the original *Beatle* James Paul McCartney who was born on the 18 June 1942.
>
> Sir Paul is represented by Lord Walrus, Lord Outreau, and Sir William Campbell instructed by three firms of solicitors and lawyers, the London firm of Mason, Ick, Order and Co., the Scottish firm of Argue and Phibbs, and American law firm of Diamond, Silverstein, and Brassneck. The author is representing himself.
>
> Sir Paul is in court, but, on the advice of his legal team, has declined to give evidence. He has also, on the advice of his legal team, refused to call any witnesses. His counsel, Lord Walrus states that the allegations are baseless, completely without merit, malicious, ridiculous and

preposterous. Lord Walrus, has also already told us that it is quite clear that Sir Paul is alive because he is here; that he does not have to offer any explanations for gaps or contradictions in his life history and that he is not obliged to give produce his fingerprints pre and post 1966 nor a DNA sample to prove who he is.

I, as the Judge of this matter, have determined that in all three respects he is correct and it is up to the author to prove to this court and to you, the members of the jury, that there was a *Beatles'* conspiracy in one or more forms and that the following occurred:

That James Paul McCartney died in 1966, and/or

That Sir Paul McCartney is not the original *Beatle*, and/or

That *The Beatles* conspired between themselves and with other to plant clues in the form of hidden messages in their album covers and interiors, song lyrics, interviews and films to fraudulently induce their millions of fans that James Paul McCartney died in 1966 and was replaced by someone else so as to capitalize on additional record sales.

Because this is not a criminal case the author does not have to prove any of these allegations *beyond a reasonable doubt.* But he does have to prove that, *on the balance of probabilities,* it is more likely that these statements are correct rather than being incorrect, an extraordinary difficult task, I would imagine.

And so, dear reader, indulge me for a moment.

Pretend that you are a member of this fictitious jury and you have to decide, not so much if any of these conspiracy theories are true, but if, far from being preposterous, they are, in fact, quite plausible. And are even more plausible by the continued reluctance of the individuals involved to clarify the discrepancies and fill in the obvious gaps in their story.

This chapter will deal with the circumstances surrounding the death of James Paul McCartney. The proof that *The Beatles* placed hidden messages in their work to say he died is dealt with elsewhere. The third part of the evidence to prove a conspiracy is contained in a chapter which outlines scientific forensic evidence that the person calling himself Sir Paul McCartney is more than likely not the same person as the original *Beatle*, James Paul McCartney.
Other evidence that will be submitted will include the following:

The behaviour of the three remaining *Beatles*, particularly Lennon, immediately after McCartney's death;

The inability of the Lennon and the new McCartney partnership to produce any music together;

Their sudden decision never to play live together again and why this was never publicly announced;

The ostracization of McCartney by the remaining *Beatles* after he dishonoured the agreement between them and, last but not least,

The mysterious deaths of the main protagonists. Taken together PID theorists will submit that the evidence that McCartney died and that Sir Paul McCartney is an impostor is actually overwhelming.

If James Paul McCartney died...

If McCartney died or became so incapacitated that he retired from the group, then the only period in which it is possible that this happened is sometime between the 31 August 1966 after their last American concert and the 24 November 1966 when the four *Beatles* came together to resume recording.

Now you all know *The Beatles*. The group was made up of John, Paul, George and Ringo. You all know at least some of their music. They were, at the time, the biggest band in the world. Even today they are regarded as the most influential and successful rock and roll group ever. Countless books have been written about them.

Their every movement has been recorded in print and on film. There are hundreds of websites dedicated to them on which you can ascertain what they were doing at any time. The *Beatles Bible* and *Anthology* are two such sources.

Enter a date and it will spew out what each of the *Fab Four* were doing on that date. It may not always be the truth and sometime most certainly isn't but it is the official line and covers every stage of their lives. Every year, every month, every week and almost every day is covered. But someone, sometime, tore out one chapter in this detailed biographical history.

Someone tore out the chapter that told us exactly what James Paul McCartney was doing from the 31 July 1966 until the 24 November 1966.

In fact, there has been a feeble attempt to rewrite this period of time in relation to McCartney. It is feeble because it was hastily assembled. The result is that it is contradictory. In the entire ten year period that this group existed this is the only period about which they have nothing or very little to say.

Why is this? Because, dear reader, sometime within this particular period, James Paul McCartney died or became so incapacitated that he was replaced in the group by an imposter and this fact was never disclosed to the public.

The Beatles began their third and final tour of America in August 1966. It began on the 12 August and ended on the 30 August. The group then returned to the United Kingdom on the 31 August. During some of those concerts a lookalike took the place of Paul McCartney. The reason for this was that either Paul was unwilling or unable to perform.

He may have been unwilling to perform live because he feared for his personal safety. After John Lennon's statement that *The Beatles* were bigger than Jesus various threats had been made on their lives. For example, the Klu Klux Klan vowed vengeance against them. McCartney was intelligent enough to take the threat seriously. He may have declined to perform live because he was frightened or he may have been unable to perform because he was ill. McCartney suffered from a severe form of IBS – Irritable Bowel Syndrome. The condition was so bad that he was obliged to wear nappies or what the American's call diapers in case of emergencies.

The Beatles have always denied that they ever used doubles but the author has uncovered two independent sources from each side of the Atlantic that confirm that this is untrue. Not only did James Paul McCartney have a double but the likelihood is that he had at least two.

In 1965, Pat Conroy worked as a rent boy. Pat worked as a waiter in one of London's best known restaurants in the 1960s. He supplemented his income by working as a rent boy (a young male prostitute). He was on intimate terms with *The Beatles'* manager Brian Epstein. Brian was a homosexual who paid Pat on a regular basis for "companionship." Pat was a frequent visitor to Epstein's homes at Kingsley Hill, Warbleton, Sussex and 24 Chapel Street, Belgravia, London.

Sometime at the beginning of August 1966 before *The Beatles* embarked on their third American tour Pat called around to Brian's London house. Just before entering the house he met "Paul McCartney" coming out, on his way down the steps. Except it wasn't Paul McCartney. It was a lookalike. Pat knew there was something strange about the man.

> **Well he had a house in the country, you know, but it was his London house, 24 Chapel Street in Belgravia. I got there a bit earlier than I should have….about 15 minutes and as I was walking up the steps who comes out of the house only Paul McCartney on his own. He was smiling and he just walked straight past me without saying a word. It was strange.**

When I asked Pat why was it strange he said:

> **Because he knew me, he knew I was a rent boy and he often saw me with Brian and though he wouldn't have a conversation with me, you know, but he'd always say "hello" or nod….like acknowledge my presence. He wasn't stuck up his own arse like George or anything. But that's not all that was strange. He looked different to Paul.**

I then asked him in what way did he look different to James Paul McCartney:

> **It's hard to say really, like he looked like him but he didn't look like him. His demeanour was different. He didn't know me. He was taller than Paul and he had a different nose, you know, like a beak nose but having said that he looked very like Paul. I didn't think much of it at the time….like that he just ignored me…like he didn't have to say hello…I just thought why would he do**

> that…particularly when he was in a good mood. I rang the bell and Brian came out straight away. I said to him: "What's wrong with your man? He just blanked me." Brian said "Who? I said Paul McCartney. And then Brian said: "That's not Paul. He's a lookalike. We're bringing him on tour with us to America."
>
> One of the reasons why Brian paid me so much money for my time was that he trusted me to keep my mouth shut about what I saw and heard so I knew he trusted me so I knew never to ask questions but this time I was really curious and I said "Why are you using a lookalike". He gave me that look that said "don't ask" but then said: "Paul isn't always well and if he can't perform for any of the concerts we use Bill."

When I asked Pat if he ever saw Bill again he replied:

> Not in person but I saw him in photographs when he was covering for Paul.

I enquired if this was after 1967?

> No I never saw the same fella in photos after 1967.

When I asked him if he thought that this Bill or Billy was Sir Paul McCartney he said:

> To be honest. I don't think so. I know that's not what you want to hear because you're writing your book and all…

I told him that my situation was simply that I wanted to know the truth and again asked him if he was sure that he saw a man who looked like Paul McCartney and Brian Epstein told him he was a lookalike that they were going to use on the America tour?

Absolutely...swear on me mother's grave.

He also said that Brian Epstein never spoke of the lookalike again. This is the first source I have that *The Beatles* were using a double for McCartney in 1966.

Joey Armato also saw a McCartney double. Armato was working security with his father at the San Francisco concert in Candlestick Park on the 29 August 1966. His father was in charge of security at the stadium. Joey was positioned outside the door of the group's dressing room and witnessed the following scene:

> **They was having a huge argument inside and I put my ear to the door......First of all I hears one guy saying: 'For fucks sake just strom it, it's not as if anyone is gonna know.' Just then the door opens and Jeez I got such a fright. It was George Harrison and he says "What the fuck do you want"...you know that kinda English accent like they have 'Wot du fuck du you wont' [laughing] So I just says 'Just minding the door for you Sir make sure you're not disturbed'. 'Good man', he says and shuts the door but just before he does I see that its John Lennon putting the guitar on Paul McCartney. McCartney looks really nervous man he's shitting himself like it's the first time he ever played a friggin concert. Then Harrison**

closed the door. It was weird man.

I then asked him if the musician looked like Paul McCartney?

> That's the thing man. About ten minutes later the four of them come out and it's like a friggin funeral man. They ain't talking; they ain't smiling and McCartney just keeps looking at the guitar as if he doesn't know what it is that's around his neck. Me and Pops walk behind them, like escorting them to the stage with the stage manager in front. He tells them to wait and they're just standing there in a row when this photographer comes up and starts taking photos and then Lennon yells at him 'Oi no fucking photos'. So, Pops stand in front of the photographer and then makes him move on.

When I asked him if the photographer managed to take any photographs he answered:

> Yes he got about five or six away. Lennon was really pissed. I mean really pissed. But here's the thing. This guy didn't look like McCartney. He looked like a bad double.
>
> He was much taller than Lennon and he was really worried. The four of them just stood there for four or five minutes. They never spoke to each other not one word. McCartney, if that was him, was smoking furiously. Then after the stage manager called them Lennon says to McCartney – 'Don't worry it'll be over in half an hour and no one will know'.

Then I asked him if he was sure that was what he

said.

> **Man I was five feet away from them. Anyways the following day I sees this press conference and I'm looking at it thinking to myself Hey that's not the same guy as last night. That's the real Paul McCartney.**

I then asked him to confirm that what he was saying was that the McCartney who played at the concert was different to the McCartney who spoke at the press conference.

> **Yeah man. I don't remember if it was before or after that concert but I didn't see the press conference until after the concert.**

He goes on to say that he mentioned this fact to his father.

> **That's the thing man. I says to Pops that it wasn't the real McCartney at the concert and all he says is 'It was probably a double. They're always doing that'. You know man it was no big deal.**

Brian Epstein was a great believer in holding press conferences. He regarded it as free publicity and he encouraged it for every event. Every concert had to have a corresponding press conference. Everything they did had to have a press conference. It was all publicity. The more publicity they got the more famous they became. The more famous they became the more sales they made.

As stated in Part One of the book the issue of Paul McCartney's illness and the question of whether or not *The Beatles* ever used a double came up during these American press conferences.

Let's revisit the press conference held in New York on the 22 August 1966. Here a journalist asked the following question:

> **Paul, according to wire reports you became a little ill after you got off the plane last night. What happened? Air sickness?**

McCartney replied:

> **Yeah, something. You know, I haven't been too well on the tour. I just felt a bit ill, that's all, and I was sick**

Then at a later press conference on the 28 August in Los Angeles a very strange question was asked:

> **Have you ever used or trained Beatle doubles as decoys on a...**

Before he could finish the question Ringo Starr cut him short with a curt No. John Lennon also said No. George Harrison said nothing and McCartney made the following comment:

> **We tried to get Brian Epstein to do it. He wouldn't do it.**

The point to be made here is not that *The Beatles* were lying. Although never officially acknowledged, everyone knew they used a double for McCartney, at least, in this American tour.

The fact is that there was, at this time, already in place, someone who could immediately act as a double for James Paul McCartney if the need ever arose.

Beatles' assistant Peter Brown made an admission which angered *The Beatles* in his controversial book *The Love You Make: An Insider's Story of The Beatles* (1983) indicating how easy it would have been for the group to get away with using a double:

> **For some of the concerts the Beatles didn't even bother to sing. They mouthed the words and played the music as fast as they could so they could get the hell off stage.**

However, the need for a permanent double was to arise much earlier than expected.

In the 1964 film *A Hard Day's Night* there is a particular scene where George Harrison is sitting in a room when an old man walks in an hands him a bunch of clothes. He says to Harrison:

> **Put these clothes on.**

But Harrison is reluctant to put them on and replies:

> **And what happens if I don't want to?**

To which the old man replies:

You know something? You can be replaced.

Robert Spitz is an accomplished author and *Beatles'* historian. In his opinion there has been an attempt to cover-up a period of *Beatles'* history and an attempt to erase it to such an extent that you will never find the truth of what happened to James Paul McCartney between leaving America on the 31 August 1966 and turning up again in London on the 24 November 1966, at least not in any official biography.

He writes about

A stunning lack of reliable source material

He claims that

Accuracy remains suspect

Circumstances were fabricated or obscured

Misinformation was also a key element of the Beatles' legend.

The question we must ask ourselves is why?

What did they have to hide?

The cover of a 1967 album might hold the key.

Sometimes referred to as the Death Album *Sgt. Pepper's Lonely Hearts Club Band* is said to conceal numerous important clues and hidden messages as to what exactly happened to James Paul McCartney in the period September to November 1966.

The most obvious and significant clue is contained on the drum skin. If you take a mirror and split the words *Lonely Hearts* you will discover a code which reads 1 ONE 1 X HE DIES. This is the date that James Paul McCartney died. It is not, as our American friends believe, the 9 November 1966. Rather, because of the different way we write dates in the United Kingdom, the date he died was the 11 September 1966. The entire album, from cover to inserts, from lyrics to backwards masking is riddled with clues and hidden messages that James Paul McCartney died in a car crash in 1966. If he didn't die then why did they go to so much trouble to make their fans believe that he had died? Here are the alleged "facts" of this conspiracy theory.

Fact One
In September 1966 James Paul McCartney was alone while on holidays in France.

Fact Two
He was driving his dark blue Aston Martin DB5 sport car which he had flown over by air cargo from Lydd Airport, (then called Ferryfield) Ashford, Kent, in England.

Fact Three
He and the car arrived safely on the same day at Le Touquet in France a coastal port approximately 45 miles from Calais.

Fact Four
On the 11 September he was involved in a road accident between Outreau and Boulogne Sur Mer approximately one half hour from his arrival port.

Fact Five
Due to the severity of the crash he was either decapitated, or seriously disfigured, or concussed to such an extent that although he walked away from the crash he later fell over a cliff.

Fact Six
An orchestrated effort was made to conceal McCartney's death.

Fact Seven
Whether by design or compulsion the three remaining *Beatles* never spoke publicly of the death but left hidden messages in their work.

Fact Eight
A replacement was found shortly afterwards from one of the session musicians they had worked with before.

Fact Nine
That session musician was not the only Paul McCartney lookalike used by them.

Fact Ten
The three remaining *Beatles* agreed to allow him become a replacement for a limited time only in order to complete two albums but, in deference to their friend, they made a solemn pact between them that they would never publicly perform with his

replacement.

Fact Eleven
Those who threatened to expose this cover up were eliminated.

Fact Twelve
Sir Paul McCartney is not the original *Beatle*.

On the 12 September 1966 when word of the crash seeped through to Fleet Street journalists from their French counterparts Tony Barrow the NEMS spokesman received more than one dozen calls asking if Paul McCartney was still among the living. These were serious enquiries. Barrow had no idea where they came from because he wasn't part of the inner circle – the cradlers of secrets.

The Beatles and their management made a deliberate attempt to misinform the public about the circumstances surrounding McCartney's holiday and eventual death in France.

The following is a timeline of events from the 31 August 1966 which is the day the *Fab Four* arrived back in England from their American tour.

Ten days earlier Paul McCartney's girlfriend Jane Asher had begun working in the play *A Winter's Tale* at the Edinburgh Festival.

The play finished on the 10 September. There are no reports of McCartney ever going to see her perform during that period or in October when she was performing in London. On the 5 September John Lennon accompanied by Brian Epstein flew to Hanover, Germany for the filming of *How I Won the War*.

On Tuesday the 13 September it was announced that Paul McCartney and Ringo Starr attended at the Melody Maker Awards at lunchtime at the Post Office Tower Restaurant in London. A fake photograph of them with Melody Maker plaques magically attached to their hands is widely available on the internet.

A photograph of the pair with Dusty Springfield and Tom Jones was distributed to the Press. The story appears in the *Beatles Bible* but it is not true. It is obvious from the available photographs that *The Beatles'* management used a lookalike for the photograph. If the pair actually did attend the launch then their presence there was completely ignored by the national press.

The only stories the following day concerned Dusty Springfield throwing a roll or a tart at a fellow guest because of his rudeness to a waiter. The same day Epstein cancelled his Star Scene 66 promotional tour. On the 14 September 1966 George Harrison and his wife Pattie flew from London to Bombay (Mumbai) in India so that George could take sitar lessons from Ravi Shankar, and for the couple to study yoga. The Harrisons stayed at the Taj Mahal hotel in Bombay, under the names Mr. and Mrs. Sam Wells.

In *Anthology* Harrison says:

> **First I flew to Bombay and hung out there. Again, because of the mania, people soon found out I was there. I stayed in a Victorian hotel, the Taj Mahal, and was starting to learn the sitar. We travelled all over and eventually went up to Kashmir and stayed on a houseboat in the middle of the Himalayas.**

The couple would not return to England until the 22 October 1966.

On Thursday the 15 September 1966 McCartney is alleged to have attended a performance of experimental music at the Royal College of Art in London. There are no photographs available of this visit. The performers were the group AMM, who at the time were joined by composer Cornelius Cardew.

The audience, which numbered fewer than 20 people, was invited to participate, and McCartney made occasional sounds using a radiator and beer mug. If McCartney did attend it was not the real Paul McCartney.

We then learn that Neil Aspinall has joined John Lennon in Germany because according to the *Beatles Bible*, Lennon accompanied by Aspinall left Celle, in Germany on the 15 September to travel to Paris. No reason is given for the trip other than it was for a "break."

This is confirmed by Mark Lewisohn who says they travelled to Paris by train. The question remains: Why would Lennon need a break? He had only been in Germany ten days. On Friday the 16 September the

Beatles Bible tell us that Lennon and Aspinall were joined by McCartney and Brian Epstein. We are told that the four men had a weekend break in the city and on Sunday the 18 September Lennon and Aspinall travelled to Spain to continue the filming.

No explanation is given as to why they had to meet in Paris other than they wanted a "break." However, it is more than likely that only three of them went to Paris, Lennon, Aspinall and Epstein.

Was this because they had just received word that McCartney had died in a car crash in northern France and the authorities needed someone to identify the body? If they needed to link up to have a business meeting why not do so in Celle where Lennon and Aspinall were already? Was this when they decided never to tour again? If so, why wasn't Ringo Starr and George Harrison invited to such a meeting? Why did Aspinall return to Spain with Lennon?

We know that Lennon then travelled to Almería in Spain on the 18 September 1966 to take part in the film *How I Won The War*, the Richard Lester film which featured him in the minor role of Private Gripweed. Principal photography took place on the 19 September 1966. Lennon was there for seven weeks during which he wrote *Strawberry Fields Forever*. David Sheff quoted Lennon as saying:

> **Dick Lester offered me the part in this movie, which gave me time to think without going home. We were in, and it took me six weeks to write the song. I was writing it all the time I was**

making the film. And as anybody knows about film work, there's a lot of hanging around. I have an original tape of it somewhere. Of how it sounded before it became the sort of psychedelic-sounding song it became on record.

On the Sunday Lennon travelled on to southern Spain to continue filming. He made this comment.

I was always waiting for a reason to get out of The Beatles from the day I made How I Won the War in 1966. I just didn't have the guts to do it, you see. Because I didn't know where to go. I remember why I made the movie. I did it because The Beatles had stopped touring and I didn't know what to do. Instead of going home and being with the family, I immediately went to Spain with Dick Lester because I couldn't deal with not being continually onstage.

That was the first time I thought, 'My God, what do you do if this isn't going on? What is there? There's no life without it.' And that's when the seed was planted that I had to somehow get out of this, without being thrown out by the others.

But I could never step out of the palace because it was too frightening. I was really too scared to walk away. I was thinking, 'Well, this is the end, really. There's no more touring. That means there's going to be a blank space in the future.' At some time or other that's when I started considering life without The Beatles - what would it be?

And I spent that six weeks thinking about that: 'What am I going to do? Am I going to be doing Vegas? But cabaret?' I mean, where do you go? So

> that's when I started thinking about it. But I could not think what it would be, or how I could do it. I didn't even consider forming my own group or anything, because it didn't enter my mind. Just what would I do when it stopped?

This statement is interesting in several respects. It appears to be the first indication we have that *The Beatles* had decided not to tour anymore. Lennon says:

> I did it [made the movie] because The Beatles had stopped touring and I didn't know what to do.

He then says:

> Well, this is the end, really. There's no more touring.

And finally:

> Just what would I do when it stopped?

Just when was this huge decision made that *The Beatles* would stop touring?

There isn't a single piece of documentation in existence that we have been shown that explains when and where and by whom and for what reason this momentous decision was taken. Why isn't it documented? Why hasn't a press conference been called to announce it? I mean this is the biggest decision they ever made. What prompted it?

There was no statement made at their last press

conference which took place in California at the end of August that they were no longer going to tour. In fact, it wouldn't be until 9 November that Brian Epstein telephoned UK promoter Arthur Howles to inform him that there would be no more live performances.

You might remember this exchange between journalists and Lennon and McCartney in New York on the 22 August 1966:

> **Have you ever considered dis-continuing performing and instead just keep on writing?**

To which Lennon replied: **No.**

They were then asked:

> **Would you rather perform, then?**

McCartney replied:

> **I mean, you know... When we're eighty we won't be performing. We may be writing.**

Furthermore, it should be noted that they already had concerts books all throughout 1967, including another Shea Stadium concert in New York so it is clear that they had every intention of continuing to tour. So, the most probable reason for the Paris summit was to visit the morgue where McCartney was, identify him and collect his belongings. They then telephoned Ringo Starr and George Harrison to tell them. Harrison was in India so there was nothing he could do but Starr, on hearing the news made his way with his wife Maureen to meet Lennon in Spain. Starr and his wife stayed with Lennon until the 9 October 1966. The official reason for visiting Lennon was because he thought Lennon was "lonely." Of course, Lennon was not lonely. He was there with his wife Cynthia, Neil Aspinall and even Michael Crawford and his family. This is what Starr said:

> **Towards the end of 1966, with John being in Spain filming How I Won the War, I went and hung out with him because he was lonely. We really supported each other a lot.**
>
> **Maureen and I decided to go out and stay with Michael Crawford, who was with John in the film, and every five or six days we would move house. All of us were living in the same house and there was always something wrong with it - that was the most boring part about it, and it was damn hot.**

One can only surmise that when he says "We really supported each other a lot" he was talking in relation to McCartney's death. While Lennon and Starr really needed to support each other McCartney's death was too much for Brian Epstein to handle. A week later, on Monday the 26 September, he checked himself into the Priory, an addiction clinic.

The official line is presented in the *Beatles Bible* under the heading "Brian Epstein is hospitalized in London" and dated the 26 September 1966. It reads:

> **The Beatles' manager Brian Epstein had been suffering from depression and anxiety for some**

time, a condition exacerbated by his use of drugs - both prescribed and illegal.

His anxiety had heightened following The Beatles decision to stop touring, which left Epstein with less involvement in their careers. Each member was undertaking individual projects in the late summer of 1966, and he had intended to join John Lennon in Spain on the set of How I Won The War. On this day, however, Epstein was hospitalised in a London clinic. The official given reason was that it was a check-up, although it later transpired that he had overdosed on prescribed drugs. As a result, he was forced to cancel his visit to Spain in order to recuperate.

Although Epstein is known to have made later suicide attempts, it is believed that this overdose was accidental.

It is claimed that this left Epstein with less involvement in their careers but this is not the case. He was also busy with his other clients.

In fact, he had never been busier or happier. He told close friends that he had intended to join John Lennon in Spain on the set of *How I Won The War*.

It is also interesting that continuing with their policy of revisionism and misinformation *The Beatles* refer to their decision to stop touring:

> **His anxiety had heightened following The Beatles decision to stop touring.**

But, of course, no one knew this at the time.

Writing about this period in the *Beatles Monthly* magazine Neil Aspinall wrote:

> **On the night of Thursday September 15 we travelled by train from Hamburg to Paris, met up with Paul there for a couple of days and then flew from France to Spain the following Sunday, while Paul and Brian Epstein returned to London.**

Nowhere in the article does he mention that *The Beatles* have decided to stop touring. Meanwhile, suspicions must have been raised about McCartney's death because a week after entering the Priory Brian Epstein was forced to emerge to deny reports that Paul McCartney was leaving the band.

Sometime between the 11 September and the 3 October 1966 Epstein, Aspinall, Evans, Harrison and Starr had come to a decision. The decision was that in view of the very real possibility that they would be sued for not completing their contracts that they would stop touring and record two more albums with a lookalike Paul McCartney. If they were to continue to tour the fans would clearly see that the lookalike was not the genuine James Paul McCartney. The fact that they kept this a secret from everyone is corroborated by the evidence of one of the sound engineers. Why would they do this?

In fact, the decision to stop touring was kept secret from all of their staff including their chief sound engineer Geoff Emerick until they returned to the studio to begin recording on the 24 November 1966.

Emerick writes in *Here, There and Everywhere* (2007):

> **It was our first night back in the studio and we were huddled around the mixing console, discussing how we wanted to approach the new album. I'd had no inkling of their decision to stop touring, there had been no announcement in the press because Epstein was anxious to keep it quiet.**

So, here is the crucial evidence that there was no public announcement that they had decided to stop touring. Epstein had told Arthur Howles on the 9 November 1966 in a telephone call but no one else. Why was Epstein "anxious to keep it quiet?"

Why didn't he even trust his own staff with the announcement? Even after telling Howles on the 9 November he still didn't tell the staff. It was a complete shock to Emerick. Even George Martin the man who put them on the rock map, wasn't told. This is what Epstein's assistant Peter Brown said about Epstein's call to Howles on the 9 November 1966:

> **On November 9th I could no longer put off the worried phone calls from our English tour promoter, Arthur Howles about booking future Beatles concerts. Brian, who couldn't bear to admit the truth, finally called Howles and told him that the Beatles would no longer accept any booking.**

What was the truth he couldn't bear to admit? Why was he anxious to keep it quiet? It was because one of the *Fab Four*, James Paul McCartney, had died on the

11 September 1966 which is the reason why Epstein had a nervous breakdown and was admitted to the Priory on the 26 September, two weeks later.

When they eventually found a musician who resembled McCartney they persuaded him to undergo plastic surgery. They also engaged another McCartney lookalike who didn't play, possibly the same one as appeared in San Francisco at the end of August 1966.

They secured the agreement of James Paul McCartney's father and brother and his "girlfriend" Jane Asher. It was only meant to be a stop gap measure and not a permanent deal. Lennon, Harrison and Starr agreed to it subject to a number of conditions:

1. That it would be only for a limited time until they announced the breakup of *The Beatles*.

2. That the three remaining *Beatles* would never, under any circumstances, perform live with McCartney's replacement. This was out of respect to the memory of the original *Beatle*.

3. That the family of James Paul McCartney would be looked after.

4. That the remainder of the music composed by James Paul McCartney would be published under the name Lennon and McCartney.

We must then ask ourselves an important question. Who initially knew and agreed to this short term strategy?

1. John and much later his wife Cynthia

2. Ringo and his wife Maureen

3. George and his wife Pattie

4. Brian Epstein

5. Neil Aspinall

6. Jane Asher

7. Jimmy McCartney, Paul's father

8. Mike McCartney, Paul's brother

Who had to be informed to make the plan work?

9. Mal Evans, Beatles' roadie

10. Dr. John Riley, London Society Cosmetic Dentist

11. Dr. Richard Asher, Jane's father

12. Tara Browne, Paul's best friend

13. David Jacobs, Paul's lawyer

14. Kevin MacDonald, the replacement's agent

15. Brian Epstein, the manager.

Who enforced the plan?

16. MI5, The British Intelligence Agency

17. CIA, The American Intelligence Agency

Several session musicians had already been used that could replicate McCartney's guitar playing and to a lesser extent his voice. But they needed to get his replacement out of London and as far away as possible to give him time to assimilate himself into McCartney's persona and to undergo plastic surgery.

Once they found a willing partner they formulated a plan. Mal Evans would take him to France and then to Kenya where he would undergo treatment in a specialized treatment used by MI5 and the CIA. Dr. Richard Asher, was the intelligence agencies' contact.

Fanciful?

Perhaps, but bear with me and everything will be explained to your complete satisfaction.

Forget everything you have read elsewhere.

Immediately after the American tour James Paul McCartney had decided on a short touring holiday in France. Or so, his friend and biographer, Barry Miles in *Paul McCartney: Many Years From Now* (1997) would have us believe:

Back home, that September, Paul still found wound up from their tour and decided to take a driving holiday in France.

But strangely enough Miles mentions nothing more about the September trip. So, is this what really happened? James Paul McCartney travelled to France on his own in early September and died on the 11 September 1966 as a result of injuries he sustained while driving his Aston Martin between the French towns of Outreau and Boulogne Sur Mer. McCartney was under the influence of alcohol and or drugs at the time and was, while driving, filming the French landscape.

He was alone in the car. The injuries he received were such that it was not immediately possible to recognize him. The French police connected him to *The Beatles* by virtue of documentation found in the car. This led them to Brian Epstein who was the first to be informed.

Epstein then phoned Lennon in Germany. Lennon was with Aspinall. Epstein, Lennon and Aspinall met in Paris and drove north to identify the body.

Once they were sure it was Paul, Lennon phoned Starr who was in England and Harrison who was in India. Starr immediately left England to meet up with Lennon. Starr met Lennon and Aspinall in Spain. This brings us up to the 16 September 1966.

Between the 16 September and the 30 October the plan was put in place. It would involve a monumental betrayal to their fans but they felt they had no choice. By this time they had found a replacement who from now on would only ever be called "Faul" by John Lennon. "Faul" was short for False Paul. Others would know the replacement as "Bill." It was decided to proceed as normally as possible.

One session musician who was used to cover some of James Paul McCartney's guitar playing and may be the actual replacement is a man called Billy Pepper from the Liverpool Merseybeat group from 1963 called *Billy Pepper and the Pepperpots*. Billy Pepper vanished without trace in 1966 and has never resurfaced since. Pepper may have been a stage name and his real name was probably Billy Shepherd.

Very little is documented about *The Beatles* in this period. Check the biographies, the *Beatles Bible*, the *Beatles'* monthly magazine. There is nothing documented. Nothing. People began to talk. The talk turned into gossip. The gossip soon became speculation. Journalists began probing.

Something was seriously amiss with *The Beatles* and Paul McCartney. Had they split up? And where was he?

When news got out that *The Beatles* were looking for a replacement for McCartney, one outsider put two and two together. Kevin MacDonald was a shareholder in London's top club at the time, *Sybillas*. He also worked for impresario Charlie Kray. Charlie was a legitimate show business agent who owned the *Charles Kray Agency*. He was also the older brother of twins

Charlie and Reggie Kray. The twins were the most notorious of all London gangsters who were, for a short period of time, interested in taking over *The Beatles*. George Harrison was alleged to have been a partner in the club but he only ever gave his name to it. Tara Browne was a partner as was Kevin MacDonald, Sir William Piggott-Brown and DJ Alan "Fluff" Freeman.

When MacDonald began to spread the rumour that McCartney had died and that *The Beatles* were looking for a replacement it looked as if the whole plan would unravel. It was decided he had to be taken care of. Brian Epstein knew the Kray twins well and one of them intimately. He asked him to talk to MacDonald and to request him to stop spreading the rumours which were now spreading like wildfire.

On the 15 October 1966 as Brian Epstein sat next to Georgie Fame in first class on their flight from London to New York sipping glasses of chilled *Moet et Chandon* Champagne, Kevin MacDonald inexplicably threw himself off the top of a London building. It was classified as a suicide. But few believed that. It was murder and it was a message to all others out there who felt like talking.

In fact, of the seven people listed above, (those numbered 9 to 15) who may have been involved in the replacement of James Paul McCartney all seven would die, either by accident or suicide, within a very short period.

Mal Evans RIP

John Reilly RIP
Dr. Richard Asher RIP
Tara Brown RIP
David Jacobs RIP
Kevin Mac Donald RIP
Brian Epstein RIP

This is a fact, not speculation, but documented fact.

It may be a coincidence, but think about it, all seven of them?

And this doesn't include the later murder of John Lennon or the attempted assassination of George Harrison.

Immediate action was needed to dispel the rumours.

On the 16 October United Artists announced that their next film would be retitled *All In Good Time* and that John Lennon and Paul McCartney would be writing the soundtrack together. This was complete news to Lennon but he knew it was an effort to counteract the death rumours. The film was eventually released as *The Family Way* and, of course, John Lennon had no involvement whatsoever in the musical score.

Two days later, Bill aka Paul McCartney went to a party with Jane Asher who had eventually agreed to co-operate but only for a very short period of time. Bill, who had not yet received any plastic surgery, only agreed to go to the party because it was fancy dress. He went disguised as an Arab prince.

Paul McCartney came dressed as an Arab in white robes and head dress and competently was able to blend in with no one recognizing him or Jane Asher.

Lennon also publicized McCartney's appearance in a radio interview he gave Fred Robbins on the 29 October 1966 Lennon joked about McCartney saying he just heard that McCartney was in London recently dressed as an Arab at the Fancy Dress party for the *International Times* on the 15 October.

They (the theorists) say that the situation was highly charged because no one was sure Jane Asher would be able to keep her composure about the death of Paul. But Asher is an actress and played the role perfectly if not a little sullenly. People put it down to a lover's tiff. But those on the inside knew the couple barely spoke.

A devastated George Harrison returned from India on the 22 October. Still shell shocked from the news he boarded himself up in his home and refused to leave or talk to anyone. During this period he became completely and hopelessly dependent on drugs fuelled with alcohol.

On the 27 October Epstein returned to London and the following day he told Sid Bernstein that there were no plans for the next American tour. Between the 28 October and the 6 November Epstein,

Aspinall and Mal Evans met Lennon, Harrison and Starr and described their immediate plans. No one was sure it would work.

But so far, everyone, including Jane Asher was willing to co-operate. If Bill could quickly undergo his plastic surgery and "mental education" no one would be able to tell. And those who would tell, like Kevin MacDonald, would, well, you know, be persuaded otherwise.

Just to be absolutely clear, neither *The Beatles* nor anyone involved in their management were, in any way, involved in MacDonalds's death. In fact, the Coroner held that there was no foul play. Teresa Stokes, a relative, is convinced it was suicide.

In late October a lookalike McCartney visited the *Maximum Sound Studios* in London to play tambourine on a track called *From Head to Toe* for the *Escorts*, a little known Liverpool beat group.

On the 3 November Epstein attended the opening of the review *Way Out In Piccadilly*, starring Cilla Black and Frankie Howerd, at the *Prince Of Wales Theatre* in London. On the 6 November the *Beach Boys* held a concert at the *Astoria Cinema*, Finsbury Park. *Sounds Incorporated* was one of the support acts which is why Epstein attended.

Epstein had the media primed.

He knew the London newspapers would mention that "Paul McCartney" had begun his holiday in France.

The plan was finally in motion and everyone was on board. The new Paul McCartney would now, in November, begin a holiday in France.

On the 6 November 1966 Bill, the Paul McCartney lookalike boarded the Airferry which left Lydd Airport (then called Ferryield) in Kent, England. It was a forty minute flight to *Tourquet* in France. He wore a thinly veiled disguise consisting of a fake moustache and a pair of glasses and carried a British passport which bore the name James Paul McCartney Born 18 June 1942 in Liverpool.

It wasn't him but it was soon to become him.

To make sure that he was recognized he was told to take with him Paul's new Goodwood Green Aston Martin DB6 registration LLO840D with its distinctive black leather upholstery and optional chrome wheels with three-ear spinners.

Paul had taken delivery of the car in March of that year and it had featured in many newspapers and magazine since then. As he watched the other passengers snapping photographs of him and the car he must have wondered if he was the luckiest man alive.

He was just 28 (Bill was born in 1938) and he had, by the most fantastic of all set of circumstances, acquired instant fame, fortune and world celebrity status. His life would never be the same again. He must have also wondered if he could really deceive so many people for so many years to come. At this stage, some of you may be saying, hang on a minute, that's a very interesting story but there is a fatal flaw in it. You see you've just told us that McCartney died on the 11 September 1966 after he crashed his Aston Martin outside Outreau so how come he's now on an Airferry with his Aston Martin that was crashed less than a month ago. That doesn't make sense, I hear you say. And, you're right, it doesn't make sense – if it was the same car. You will have to search very deeply to discover that James Paul McCartney had two Aston Martins. He had a 1966 green DB6 but he also had a 1964 blue DB5, the one he crashed in France on the 11 September 1966. I finally tracked this car down (Chassis no. DB5/1653/R; Engine no. 400/1641)and discovered it was sold by auction on the 31 October, 2012 for £344,400. After some deliberate misinformation I also discovered the car's history.

The car had a 280 horse owner, 3,995 cc dual overhead cam inline six-cylinder engine, three SU carburettors, five-speed manual gearbox, independent front suspension with coil springs, live rear axle suspension with coil springs and Selectaride dampers, and four-wheel disc brakes. Wheelbase: 2,490 mm.

It was the same type of car that was used in the James Bond film *Goldfinger*. The one with the ejector seat. I remember that, as a child, I had a Dinky metal model of the car, complete with ejector seat, and a little plastic man that would be ejected out through the roof at the touch of the button. Every time I think of that like plastic man the words Plastic Macca comes to mind.

Ordered by McCartney prior to his departure for *The Beatles'* world tour in the summer of 1964, the car numbered 1653/R completed assembly on the 3 July 1964. It was finished in Sierra Blue paint and fitted with a black leather interior.

Desirable options included the Armstrong Selectaride rear shock absorbers, chrome wire wheels, a Motorola radio, and an unusual Philips Auto-Mignon record player, which was obviously the perfect amenity for a professional recording star. The interior leather also originally included musical note-styled patterns in the stitching. Though the upholstery had been replaced, an authentic sample of the original material remained with the car, for the owner that might wish to recreate the car in its original McCartney livery.

The car was actually delivered on the 22 September to Bryce, Hanmer, and Isherwood, who were, at the time, McCartney's accountants. It was subsequently registered in the name Paul McCartney. The car was crashed in 1966 and then repaired. Service records indicate that in 1970, when 1653/R was fitted with a new clutch and received some other minor service work, the odometer displayed 40,513 miles.

In 1983 the car was sold to Truebell Stationers in Wandsworth, London. They sold it on to a John Richard Rogers of Ilford, England on the 12 March 1983. Mr. Rogers retained the car for thirteen years before selling it on the 16 July 1996 to a John Hardy Shannon. In 2002, this Aston Martin was completely rebuilt by Walter Baroni, of Corsico, Milan, including bare-metal sanding and repaint in the car's original colour of Sierra Blue. The restoration was completed in early 2011. Signor Baroni, although at first, extraordinarily reluctant to talk about the car said he was aware of the rumours surrounding McCartney's death in 1966.

He also said he was 100% certain that the car was involved in a serious crash in 1966. But he stressed that the car was not written off. This is what he had to say:

> **He said that the car had received a significant blow, but in his opinion, not sufficient to cause the death. As the collision, probably with a pole or something similar size, had caused a recess about a foot wide and as deep. A big crash, in short, but not enough to be fatal. In addition, the windshield was broken but, for example, the steering was intact. This confirms to him that the blow was not strong or the steering wheel, wooden, would snap. That said, anything can happen, too, that you can break your neck falling in the bathtub of the bathroom. I do not mean anything except that the magnitude of impact, by itself, may want to say everything and nothing.**

It is interesting that there are no official reports from *The Beatles* in 1966 that Paul McCartney crashed his Aston Martin. (There are reports that his Mini Cooper was crashed by someone else) Baroni said he was aware of the then recent article in the Italian edition of *Wired* magazine providing forensic evidence that Sir Paul McCartney was not one and the same person as the original *Beatle* James Paul McCartney but he had doubts about the truth of the evidence and suggested that the mystery could easily be solved by McCartney giving a DNA sample.

Perhaps the most significant piece of information Signor Baroni had was that a documentary team from the *Discovery* channel had recently visited him and filmed the car and documentation that was with the car. They said that the documentary was planned to be broadcast only after the death of Sir Paul McCartney and that it would contain "a very outstanding revelation."

Revisionists rewrote *The Beatles'* history and their reports of what happened on the 6 November 1966 are contained in the *Beatles Bible* for that date and also in the book by his friend Barry Miles. Referring to Sunday the 6 November the *Beatles Bible* writes:

> **On this day Paul McCartney flew to France on a plane-ferry from Lydd airport in Kent, England. The intention was to take a driving holiday. In order to escape the attention of The Beatles' fans, McCartney wore a disguise, although his brand new dark green Aston Martin DB5 was enough to attract the attention of even the least observant bystander... McCartney donned his disguise after passing through French customs. Wig Creations, the film cosmetic company used by The Beatles on A Hard Day's Night, had made him a moustache to wear.**

Talking about the wig McCartney told Barry Miles:

> **They measure you and match the colour of your hair, so it was like a genuine moustache with real**

> glue. And I had a couple of pairs of glasses made with clear lenses, which just made me look a bit different. I put a long blue overcoat on and slicked my hair back with Vaseline and just wandered around and of course nobody recognised me at all. It was good, it was quite liberating for me.

According to the *Beatles Bible* McCartney planned to drive to Paris before heading south to Bordeaux, where he had arranged to meet Mal Evans under the clock on the Saint-Eloi church on 12 November 1966. In 1997 he told Barry Miles:

> It made me remember why we all wanted to get famous; to get that thing. Of course, those of us in the Beatles have often thought that, because we wished for this great fame, and then it comes true but it brings with it all these great business pressures or the problems of fame, the problems of money, et cetera. And I just had to check whether I wanted to go back, and I ended up thinking, No, all in all, I'm quite happy with this lot.

They then intended to follow the Loire river from Orleans. He explained his trip in detail to Barry Miles:

> It was an echo of the trip John and I made to Paris for his twenty-first birthday, really. I'd cruise, find a hotel and park. I parked away from the hotel and walked to the hotel. I would sit up in my room and write my journal, or take a little bit of movie film. I'd walk around the town and then in the evening go down to dinner, sit on my own at the table, at the height of all this Beatle

thing, to ease the pressure, to balance the high-key pressure. Having a holiday and also not be recognised. And re-taste anonymity. Just sit on my own and think all sorts of artistic thoughts like, I'm on my own here, I could be writing a novel, easily. What about these characters here?

McCartney goes on to tell us that his journal was later lost, as was his film of his trip. Some of the reels were stolen by fans who broke into his home. He also related this in great technical detail to Barry Miles:

> Kodak 8 mm was the one, because it came on a reel. Once it became Super-8 on a cartridge you couldn't do anything with it, you couldn't control it. I liked to reverse things. I liked to reverse music and I found that you could send a film through the camera backwards. Those very early cameras were great.
>
> If you take a film and run it through a camera once, then you rewind it and run it through again, you get two images, superimposed. But they're very washed out, so I developed this technique where I ran it through once at night and only photographed points of light, like very bright reds, and that would be all that would be on the first pass of the film. It would be like on black velvet, red, very red. I used to do it in my car so it was car headlights and neon signs, the green of a go sign, the red of a stop, the amber
>
> The next day, when it was daylight, I would go and shoot and I had this film that was a combination of these little points of light that were on a 'black velvet' background and daylight. My favourite was a sequence of a leaning cross in a

cemetery. I turned my head and zoomed in on it, so it opened just with a cross, bingo, then as I zoomed back out, you could see the horizon was tilted at a crazy angle. And as I did it, I straightened up. That was the opening shot, then I cut to an old lady, facing away from me, tending the graves.

A fat old French peasant who had stockings halfway down her legs and was revealing a lot of her knickers, turning away, so it was a bit funny or a bit gross maybe. She was just tending a grave so, I mean, I didn't need to judge it. I just filmed it. So the beautiful thing that happened was from the previous night's filming. There she is tending a grave and you just see a point of red light appear in between her legs and it just drifts very slowly like a little fart, or a little spirit or something, in the graves. And then these other lights just start to trickle around, and it's like Disney, it's like animation!

One thing I'd learned was that the best thing was to hold one shot. I was a fan of the Andy Warhol idea, not so much of his films but I liked the cheekiness of Empire, the film of the Empire State Building, I liked the nothingness of it. So I would do a bit of that.

There were some sequences I loved: there was a Ferris wheel going round, but you couldn't quite tell what it was. And I was looking out of the hotel window in one French city and there was a gendarme on traffic duty. There was lot of traffic coming this way, then he'd stop 'em, and let them all go. So the action for ten minutes was a gendarme directing the traffic: lots of gestures and

getting annoyed. I ran it all back and filmed all the cars again, it had been raining so there was quite low light in the street. So in the film he was stopping cars but they were just going through his body like ghosts. It was quite funny. Later, as the soundtrack I had Albert Ayler playing the 'Marseillaise'. It was a great little movie but I don't know what happened to it.

There are several suspicious elements to these tales. The first is the great detail McCartney goes into to convince us that he really was driving around France writing this journal and making this film. Why bother to tell us in such detail? It's almost as if he's desperate to convince us he was there, on his own, and had arranged to meet Mal Evans four days later. So, remember this. The new McCartney says he was in France between the 8-12 November 1966 on his own. Mal Evans was not with him until the 12 November 1966. Presumably then, and there is nothing to suggest directly or indirectly otherwise, Mal Evans was in London on the 8, 9, 10 and at least 11 November 1966. Park that thought for a moment. The third really strange thing about this story is that the *Beatles Bible* says that his journal was "lost" and film was

Some of the reels were stolen by fans who broke into his home on Cavendish Avenue, London

while McCartney adds "It was a great little movie but I don't know what happened to it."

The question is this: Why would someone go to the trouble of breaking into his home, stealing his film and not try and sell it? *Beatles'* memorabilia like that fetch hundreds of thousands of pounds at auction. It is inconceivable that such a journal or reels of his film would not surface somewhere, sometime. They have never re-surfaced. But a little footage from Mal Evans covering the period the 12-19 November is available on a DVD called The *Complete Mal Evans Silent Films*.

It shows the new McCartney and Evans in various places in Spain and Kenya. Two of the reels were sold at auction and purchased by a mystery buyer on behalf of Sir Paul McCartney.

Meanwhile, back in London, Yoko Ono, was to have an Exhibition at the Indica Gallery in Mason's Quay, off Duke Street between the 8 and 18 November. Indica was owned by McCartney's three friends John Dunbar, Peter Asher (Jane's brother) and Barry Miles. His best friend Tara Brown had nothing to do with it. McCartney gave them £8,000 to help them open it. In the *Beatles Bible* they write about the exhibition:

> **On the day before her exhibition Unfinished Paintings And Objects was to open, Japanese artist Yoko Ono was introduced to John Lennon for the first time.**

Ono was, at this time, married to Tony Cox, a jazz musician, film producer and art dealer. Lennon was married to Cynthia.

This would make the date that Lennon met Ono as the 7 November 1966. This is verified by an interview he gave to journalist Jann S. Wenner in Lennon

DAVID ELIO MALOCCO

Remembers in *Rolling Stone* (1971):

There was a sort of underground clique in London; John Dunbar, who was married to Marianne Faithfull, had an art gallery in London called Indica, and I'd been going around to galleries a bit on me off days in between records, also to a few exhibitions in different galleries that showed sort of unknown artists or underground artists.

I got the word that this amazing woman was putting on a show the next week, something about people in bags, in black bags, and it was going to be a bit of a happening and all that. So I went to a preview the night before it opened. I went in - she didn't know who I was or anything - and I was wandering around. There were a couple of artsy-type students who had been helping, lying around there in the gallery, and I was looking at it and was astounded.

There was an apple on sale there for two hundred quid; I thought it was fantastic - I got the humour in her work immediately. I didn't have to have much knowledge about avant-garde or underground art, the humour got me straightaway. There was a fresh apple on a stand - this was before Apple - and it was two hundred quid to watch the apple decompose.

But there was another piece that really decided me for-or-against the artist: a ladder which led to a painting which was hung on the ceiling. It looked like a black canvas with a chain with a spyglass hanging on the end of it. This was near the door when you went in. I climbed the ladder, you look through the spyglass and in tiny little letters it says

> 'yes'. So it was positive. I felt relieved. It's a great relief when you get up the ladder and you look through the spyglass and it doesn't say 'no' or 'fuck you' or something, it said 'yes'.
>
> I was very impressed and John Dunbar introduced us - neither of us knew who the hell we were, she didn't know who I was, she'd only heard of Ringo, I think, it means apple in Japanese. And Dunbar had sort of been hustling her, saying, 'That's a good patron, you must go and talk to him or do something.' John Dunbar insisted she say hello to the millionaire. And she came up and handed me a card which said 'breathe' on it, one of her instructions, so I just went [pant]. This was our first meeting.

Of course if Yoko Ono pretended that she didn't know about *The Beatles* before meeting John Lennon on the 7 November 1966 that would be untrue. For a start Ono "pestered" John Dunbar to invite Lennon to the Exhibition so that she could meet him. She also pestered Paul McCartney a year earlier.

Meanwhile, it was two days later that Epstein told Arthur Howles that there would be no more touring.

On the 11 November Epstein appeared on the David Frost television program for an interview. Before agreeing to appear he made it a condition precedent that the current *Beatles*' situation was not to be raised and if Frost did raise it, Epstein would add nothing to the statements already made. Nothing had been decided about their future activities.

What about Bill?

Bill or Paul McCartney as he was now calling himself, met Mal Evans at the Saint-Eloi Catholic church, on *Rue Saint-James* in Bordeaux on the 12 November. They then intended to follow the Loire river from Orleans. He told his biographer:

> **Then we drove down into Spain but we got to Madrid and we didn't know anyone; the only way would have been to go to a club and start making contacts. So we thought, This is not going to be any fun, and rang the office in London, and booked ourselves a safari trip.**

The *Beatles Bible* tell us that the pair drove from Bordeaux to Spain, making films on their journey. They had hoped to meet Lennon in Almería, but filming for *How I Won The War* had ended and he had returned to England. Instead they decided on a safari holiday and flew to Kenya. McCartney arranged to meet his girlfriend Jane Asher there, and in Seville had someone drive his Aston Martin DB5 back to London.

Nonsense! Why do I call it nonsense? Because if Mal Evans had come from London he would have already known that John Lennon was in London at the Indica Gallery for the Yoko Ono Exhibition on the 7 November. Are they saying that Mal Evans forgot Lennon was in London and still in Spain?

The official version continues. McCartney and Evans flew from Seville to Madrid, and from there to Nairobi. They had a 10-hour stopover in Rome, during which they did some sightseeing.

Upon their arrival in Kenya they toured Ambosali Park, overlooked by Mount Kilimanjaro, and stayed at the Treetop Hotel, the royal family's Kenyan base. The holiday came to a close on 19 November, when McCartney, Asher and Evans flew from Nairobi back to London.

Really? I don't believe it. Why? There are three reasons: Firstly, film of Bill and Mal has surfaced which shows them in Spain and in Kenya. Each film had a few seconds of shots of Bill, and, it must have been before he underwent any surgery because he doesn't look anything like James Paul McCartney.

Secondly, Jane Asher was never in Kenya. How do I know this? Well, it's a winter's tale. Between the 21 August and the 10 September 1966 Asher appeared in *A Winter's Tale* at the *Edinburgh* Festival in Scotland. She reprised the same role in the *Cambridge Theatre* in London beginning on the 30 September and immediately following that she was directed by Frank Dunlop in the film version of the same play all through November with co-star Lawrence Harvey. There's even a photograph of her and Harvey playing around with one of the cameras which was taken on the 13 November 1966.

Thirdly, in the January 1967 edition of *Beatles Monthly* under the column *Mal's Page*, there is a "Special

Report by Mal Evans who went on safari with Paul." He describes in detail what they did in Spain and Kenya. Curiously enough, nowhere in the article is there any mention made of Jane Asher. Did he forget she was there? Meanwhile, back in London, the *Sunday Telegraph* of the 13 November published a front page story that two of *The Beatles* had approached Allen Klein who already managed the *Rolling Stones* through a third party. Klein, in London, did not announce the story himself or make himself available for comment. Epstein dismissed the story as ridiculous. Harrison and Starr were said to be disturbed by the report. Lennon claimed to be annoyed about the suggestion that they were disenchanted with Brian. McCartney was said to be abroad and unavailable for comment. The following Tuesday Epstein issued a statement in response to rumours concerning *The Beatles'* breakup.

On the 24 November John Lennon, George Harrison and Ringo Starr met up with their new bass guitarist, Bill. A published photograph of Bill carrying his guitar appears on the internet. There is a slight resemblance to James Paul McCartney but much more plastic surgery had to be undertaken to make him like the genuine article. This is essentially what the conspiracy theorist believe happened to James Paul McCartney and they ask the vital question – if he didn't die, why bother going to the trouble of placing hidden messages and clues in their albums for several years saying he did die?

And what about John Lennon in September 1966? Following the identification of the body of James Paul McCartney, his friend and partner, John Lennon suffered a nervous breakdown. Epstein, Harrison and Starr were deeply shocked and became reclusive and depressed but Lennon fell completely into a dark hole from which he found it almost impossible to extract himself. After the 11 September he was utterly distraught. Why? What brought him to this dark place?

Normally a fun loving prankster with an acerbic wit he now became clinically depressed almost overnight. Bob Spitz wrote:

> **John and Cynthia had only just returned to London suffering from fatigue and an ominous melancholy. Friends described John's mood as "tense" and "bitter".**

No explanation is given as to why they would be suffering from "fatigue" or "an ominous melancholy" or why Lennon should feel "tense" or "bitter." But the obvious reason is that they had recently learned of the death of James Paul McCartney. Another friend, John Dunbar, recalls Lennon's behaviour at this time:

> **There was so much going on in his head that he couldn't get on top of it.**

What was going on? What could he not get on top of? He had just had three months off. In that three month he had been acting for about ten days. The rest of the time he was relaxing and writing music. It should have been the most restful period in his life since the start of *The Beatles* in 1960. Referring to his conduct at home Spitz also wrote that:

> **John was aloof, uncooperative, disappearing into the music room for hours on end or staring hypnotically at the television – until he passed out from fatigue.**
>
> **Food no longer interested him.**

Concerning the same period another Hunter Davies, biographer recalled:

> **For long periods he chose to be cut off.**

This type of behaviour is completely consistent with someone who is grieving. Epstein was also grieving and attempted suicide ending up in the Priory on the 26 September. Lennon too had resorted to drugs with Spitz telling us.

> **His drug taking and depression ragged on ceaselessly without regard for days or night.**

John Dunbar eventually persuaded Lennon to come to the Indica Gallery on the 7 November 1966 to view an exhibition by Japanese artist Yoko Ono. Lennon had no idea he was going to meet the artist there. The exhibition was to open on the 8 and this was a preview for selected guests only. Lennon was driven to the Gallery by his long time chauffeur Les Anthony who was seriously concerned about his employer's state of health. Spitz described the time immediately before Lennon went into the gallery:

> **Lennon was in such a fragile condition that when his car pulled up to the Indica Gallery, he couldn't get out of it. 'When they pulled up to the kerb outside Mason's Yard, he'd practically lost his nerve. Les Anthony, who'd been John's driver for two years, said they sat in the car for some time, perhaps as much as half an hour, while John debated whether to go inside. 'I'm not ready yet'. He agonized every few minutes. Lennon stated, 'Let's just sit her....Let's see what happens."**

The fact is that John Lennon could not face anyone and still pretend that James Paul McCartney was alive, that nothing had happened. Another source states:

> **When the famous night Monday November 7, 1966 rolled around, John Lennon, was out of his mind....He's been without sleep for three days.**

Lennon's clinical depression continued on into the spring of the following year. Geoff Emerick was to comment:

> **By the spring of 1967 he was becoming increasingly disengaged, and that would more or less continue until the end of the Beatles career.**

And yet another biographer Bob Spitz also wrote:

> **During the winter and early spring of 1967 he reached an apogee of drug taking and self-abuse, unparalleled since Art College....John was in Hell.**

Lennon's depression had a profound effect on his ability to continue to write music. He just didn't have it in him anymore. The toll of James Paul McCartney's death, the deceit in hiding it and the ramifications if it ever got out were too much for him and the others to take. As Albert Goodman wrote in *The Lives of John Lennon* (1988) about the group when they went back into the studio in November 1966:

> **John was not the only Beatle to experience depression during the sessions. All the boys, but Paul, were numbed by this unprecedented ordeal.**

In fact, Harrison was so depressed he only wrote one song on the entire *Sgt. Pepper* album and didn't even participate in making musical suggestions towards any song on the album. Emerick also mentions Harrison's state of mind at the time:

> **Often, the more time we spent on George's songs, the worse they got.**

They were so depressed that they could not even function properly. Barry Miles points out:

> **Once Emerick had helped equalize the Trident sound, Harrison led the band through 'Not Guilty' over two nights, staying until 5.45 a.m. on August 8 to go through over one hundred takes.**

After working on this track for a further two days it was eventually abandoned. Many people noticed Lennon's deterioration during the making of *Sgt.*

Pepper. For example, Goldman wrote:

> The photos of John Lennon taken during the Sgt. Pepper sessions are disquieting. Instead of the typical Lennon pub shot mouth agape, eyes popping, the whole face a clown mask, here is a young man who has suddenly aged about forty years…..The eyes behind his granny glasses look like those of dead fish. His dry, droopy moustache belongs on the face of an old geezer.
>
> His slumped posture is that of an ancient sage door keeper. Miles, a frequent visitor to the sessions explained, 'John set out to destroy his ego. He made a good job of it…ego death, the product of heavy doses of LSD and the Tibetan Book of the Dead could be the reason for Lennon's sudden metamorphosis into the superannuated man. But the two facts make this interpretation untenable.

Goldman then goes on to explain what these two facts were. The first was that Lennon never dropped acid when he was cutting wax, and secondly, as soon as the sessions were over his melancholy mood instantly changed. Goldman put Lennon's mood down to an "intense emotional disturbance." His then wife Cynthia was also concerned about his state of mind and wrote about it in her book *A Twist of Lennon*:

> I, too, was worried about John's health; the drugs had ruined his appetite and he did indeed look terrible. I feared he might kill himself. John had the potential to self-destruct and now he seemed hell bent on fulfilling it….I believe he had turned

to drugs to escape.

Finally, Peter Carlin also commented:

> **John lurked in the sitting room, curled uncomfortably onto a settee. He watched television for days on end, barely eating anything beyond the chemicals that allowed him escape the reality he couldn't bear to face.**

This reality could only have been the recent death of his song writing partner and childhood friend and the dark secret he kept about covering it up. Lennon's fragile condition only worsened in 1968 and 1969, culminating with another breakdown in 1970. In the same period Harrison had become completed addicted to drugs; Starr became a hopeless alcoholic and Epstein eventually succeeded in committing suicide. Meanwhile, the new and revitalized Paul McCartney thrived and prospered. Now let's look at the trouble the group went to in placing clues and hidden messages in their albums about the death of James Paul McCartney in September 1966 in a car crash.

THE BEATLES CONSPIRACY: John, Paul, George, Ringo and Bill

There is nothing hidden that will not be revealed, and there is nothing secret that will not become known and come to light.

Luke 8:17

What about the hidden messages?

When I asked Joel Gilbert if he believed that James Paul McCartney died and was replaced by the man now known as Sir Paul McCartney he refused to answer the question and directed me to a website and suggested I look it up. The website is www.paulreallyisdead.com and is well worth looking up if you believe the theory. PID conspiracy theorists claim that *The Beatles*, racked with guilt and consumed by grief, at the part they played in covering up the death of their beloved Paul, decided to embark on a campaign about what exactly had happened so that when it did eventually come to light their fans would not hate them.

In relation to the clues this is what Joel Gilbert had to say:

It is clear, unmistakable and undeniable that there were in fact numerous intentional "clues" placed by the Beatles in their music that Paul McCartney had died. However, whether it was just dry British humour of bored Beatles messing with their fans, or for some other purpose, is up to Beatles fans to ponder.

According to Andru J. Reeve in *Turn Me On Dead Man: The Beatles and the "Paul is Dead" Hoax* (2004) there are a minimum of 140 visual and audible clues left my *The Beatles* in their albums and films. *The Beatles* persistently denied that there were any clues and said people were reading into the covers and lyrics their own interpretations.

Some of these "clues" are a matter of subjective interpretation. They can signify different meanings to different people. Some may not be referring to the death of Paul McCartney at all, they might be referring to the death of the old style of *Beatles* and the emergence of a new type of music. This is a fair point. But the sheer volume of clues and the fact that they were spread across the lyrics, the music and the printed word should persuade even the most sceptic of believers that these "clues" or what we should more properly call "hidden messages" were deliberately placed there by *The Beatles* for a specific purpose.

And it gets curiouser and curiouser as Alice would say. Why? Because after *The Beatles* broke up and went their separate ways, after John Lennon was assassinated and after George Harrison died, a whole new industry was reborn and the entire Paul Is Dead urban legend was re-ignited. Sales increased, massive free publicity followed and one person, in particular, profited enormously.

Guess who that was? Sir Paul McCartney.

Here is a list of the main clues or messages deliberately inserted by the group.

YESTERDAY AND TODAY

The infamous original sleeve for the US only compilation of leftover *Beatles'* songs is a picture of the *Fab Four* with broken dolls and raw meat strewn around them.

The macabre image screams Paul's death. Here we have blood, raw meat and body parts. Sitting on Paul's arm is a dental ridge and George holds a decapitated doll's head. The controversial and offensive cover was quickly withdrawn and replaced but not before it received massive free publicity. In response to the claim that it represented Paul's death Robert Whitaker the album's photographer said in a 1991 interview in Goldmine magazine:

Rubbish, absolute nonsense.

He went on to say that the image was actually created wholly and totally by him as a comment on celebrity idolatry. Instead of the usual publicity shots he said that they decided to experiment instead. Whitaker even titled this project "A Somnambulant Adventure."

Among the other photographs taken during the day was a shot of George pounding spikes in John's head; a picture of John holding a cardboard box with Ringo peeking out from inside; and a tableau of the *Fab Four*, a woman kneeling down and a sting of bangers.

> **The actual concept was Moses coming down from Mt. Sinai with the Ten Commandments. He comes across people worshipping a golden calf. All over the world I'd watched people worshipping, like idols, like gods, the four Beatles. To me they were just stock standard normal people.**

So, what Mr. Whitaker is saying that the best way he found of portraying the mundane nature of *The Beatles* was to pose them in butchers' coats with decapitated dolls' heads and throw a bit of raw bloody meat around?

> **I was trying to show that the Beatles were flesh**

and blood. Behind the head of each Beatle would have been a golden halo and in the halo would have been placed a semi-precious stone. It was just after John Lennon had said that the Beatles were more popular than Jesus Christ. In a material world that was a very true statement.

But when it was decided to just use the raw photograph everything was taken out of context because Whitaker says:

It made no sense at all. It was just this rather horrific image of four Beatles, which everyone loved, covered in raw meat.

Which was, Mr. Whitaker what was precisely intended! The replacement cover continued with a clue about Paul's death. They replaced the butcher cover with a shot of *The Beatles* positioned around an open trunk. And who was inside the trunk? You've guessed it. None other than Paul McCartney. And if you rotated the photo 90 degrees to the let the trunk becomes Paul McCartney's coffin.

Further clues were inserted into the lyrics. For example, the track *Nowhere Man* has the lines referring to McCartney's replacement:

**He's a real nowhere man
Sitting in his nowhere land.**

The title of the song *Dr. Robert* is a reference to the surgeon who carried out the alleged plastic surgery on William Shepherd. The track also contains the line

You're a new and better man.

The song *Yesterday* is even more telling with the following lines:

**Yesterday,
all my troubles seemed so far away
Now it looks as though they're here to stay
Oh, I believe in yesterday
Suddenly, I'm not half the man I used to be
There's a shadow hanging over me.
Oh, yesterday came suddenly**

Revolver

On the cover of the album the *Beatle* that is singled out, and this occurs time and time again, is Paul McCartney. Out of all the Klaus Voorman sketches of *The Beatles*, only McCartney is depicted in a different way. While all the other band members are looking straight ahead, he is looking away.

In the track *Taxman* George has the line

**Now my advice to those who die
Declare the pennies on your eyes.**

This is an old British custom of placing pennies on dead people's eyes. The song *Eleanor Rigby* is supposedly about McCartney's secret funeral in an abandoned Church graveyard in Blackpool near Liverpool in England:

Ah look at all the lonely people

The fact that no one was there to listen to the sermon is referenced in the lines:

> **Writing the words of a sermon**
> **that no one will hear;**
> **No one comes near.**

The track continues:

> **Fr. McKenzie wiping the dirt from his hands**
> **as he walks from the grave;**
> **no one was saved.**

In the track *For No One* we hear a comment from the perspective of someone who was close to McCartney, probably his girlfriend Jane Asher:

> **she says her love is dead**
> **she says that long ago**
> **she knew someone**
> **but now he's gone.**

The car theme is again replayed in the track *Got To Get You Into My Life*

> **I was alone, I took a ride**
> **I didn't know what I would find there.**

Finally, in the track *Tomorrow Never Knows* Lennon sings the line:

> **Paul played the game**
> **existence to the end.**

Even the cynical Andru J. Reeve admits:

All of the clues from Revolver sit on the cusp of relevance, depending on when it is agreed that Paul's death took place. If the fatal car crash occurred on the earlier cited date, the 26 December 1965, [the moped accident] then these clues are valid.

More clues appeared in *Sgt. Pepper's*. *The Beatles* denied any clued existed.

SGT. PEPPER'S

The album cover was literally flooded with clues that Paul McCartney was dead. The front cover was designed as a funeral scene.

The foreground is a freshly dug piece of earth complete with decorative floral wreaths. A gravestone in the shape of a bass drum faces the grave. The crowd was made up of people that Lennon thought McCartney would have liked to have had at his funeral. Although one wonders if McCartney would really have wanted a Satanist like Aleister Crowley at his funeral. In fact, there are not one but two photographs of Crowley on the cover.

Some theorists have even suggested that McCartney was replaced, at one stage, by Aleister Crowley's son Aleister Attaturk aka Charles Edward d'Arquires aka Randall Gair Doherty aka Aleister Macalpine born in

Newcastle England on the 3 May 1937.

Every figure represented someone who was either dead; had a near death experience; or, had portrayed death.

On the bass rum gravestone, the *Beatles* created a clue that required a mirror. In the middle of Lonely Hearts you get the message

1 One 1 X He Die

According to theorists the three "ones" represented the three live *Beatles*. Paul was the X who was wiped out. The line also showed the date that McCartney died:

11 September 1966

The next two digits are IX the Roman numeral for Nine which American theorists interpret are the date November 9. (The problem with this date is that in the UK people don't write their dates like month, day, year. They write their dates like day, month, year. Would this would mean that 9-11-1966 should really be read as 11-9-1966?)

The last two words read "He Die". The entire line therefore reads November 9 He Die. *Beatles'* management have never been able to explain the significance of what theorists regard as the most deliberate coded clue ever found. The yellow flowers represent McCartney's left handed bass guitar with three wires or strings to signify only three remaining *Beatles*. The flowers also form a capital "P" for Paul when turned on its side. The word "Hear" taken from "Hearts" and the word Lies" [the "I" come from Paul's rugby trophy] from the "les" of the word "*Beatles*" and the yellow bass guitar representing Paul is supposed to signify the words "Here Lies Paul."

On the front cover, on the left, there is a doll on whose lap is the model of a white car representing the Aston Martin McCartney was driving when he died. The doll was placed in the shadow of a deathly looking figure to represent the shadow of death who wore blood stained rider's glove in his left hand.

Just above the "B" they placed another doll and split its head open to symbolize Paul's head injury.

A photograph of Arthur Crane with an out-stretched hand can be seen over the figure of McCartney is a reference to the novel *Open Boat*.

The *Open Boat* is a short story by American author Stephen Crane which was first published in 1897. It was based on Crane's experience of surviving a shipwreck off the coast of Florida earlier that year while travelling to Cuba. Crane was stranded at sea for thirty hours when his ship sank after hitting a sandbar. He and three other men were forced to navigate their way to shore in a small boat; one of the men, an oiler named Billie Higgins, drowned after the boat overturned.

The outstretched hand could not, in any way, be

explained away as a mere coincidence as it appears at least six times on *Beatles'* album covers or interior booklets. The outstretched hand is used all the time in Christian religions.

Theorists claim that Lennon, Harrison and Ringo Starr posed for the cover but for McCartney they used a cardboard cut-out figure which was propped up from behind like in real life. *The Beatles'* management claim that there are numerous outtakes from this photo session which took place on the 30 March 1967 with the group shown in a variety of poses. It is "pure coincidence" and a "matter of aesthetics" that this one was used.

Next to Diana Dors, they placed a mirror image of a walrus to signify McCartney's final state of being.

The inner sleeve looks quite innocent until you realize that it's covered in red blood.

On the back cover the figure of McCartney is taken with his back to the camera to signify that he is not a real *Beatle* and they sure that the lyrics "without you" were printed beside McCartney's head while Harrison is pointing to the lyric "Five o' clock" the supposed time of McCartney's death. Curiously enough, McCartney is quoted as saying in *Musician* magazine in 1980:

> **It was just a goof when we were doing the photos. I turned by back and it was just a joke.**

Some theorists have claimed that the reason why his

back is to the camera is because the figure isn't McCartney but someone else.

Finally, McCartney is wearing a badge on his left arm with the initials "OPD" which mean Officially Pronounced Dead. *The Beatles* have said that the letters really read OPP for the Ontario Provincial Police and that the patch just has a wrinkle in it.

According to Harrison, despite all of these clues, Lennon wanted more and found a new way of hiding clues by inserting audio messages in reverse hidden by the original recording so that they could only be heard by playing the album backwards.

In the title track, the line about Billy Shears is a play on words:

So let me introduce you
To the one and only Billy Shears

For "Billy Shears" read "Billy's here." They were introducing Bill to their fans. They didn't want *The Beatles* to end:

I don't really want to stop the show
But I thought that you might like to know
That the singer's going to sing a song
And he wants you all to sing along
So let me introduce to you
The one and only Billy Shears
And Sgt. Pepper's Lonely Hearts Club Band

Theorists claim that Billy Shears was used instead of the impostor's real name Billy Shepherd as that would have been too obvious. Contrary to popular believe it was not Billy Shepherd who won the Paul McCartney lookalike contest. James Barry Keefer, an America DJ of 98.6 FM fame won the contest.

Of course, it is already established that the name William Campbell was just made up by Fred LaBour. He simply didn't exist. But there is evidence that a Billy Shepherd did exist. He was originally called Billy Pepper and he had a group called *The Pepperpots*.

In the song *It's Getting Better* theorists believe that they were encouraging Bill who was growing in confidence and whose imitation of the real *Beatles* was getting better all the time.

> **I have to admit it's getting better**
> **A little better all the time.**

If the chorus of this song is spun in reverse it will yield the words:

> **Waaaahh…after all Paul's dead, he lost his head.**

Many other clues to McCartney's fatal crash were placed throughout the album, including the following lines:

> **Wednesday morning at five o'clock**
> **As the day begins.**
>
> **When I caught a glimpse of Rita**
>
> **I took her home. I nearly made it.**
> **The news was rather sad.**

> He blew his mind out in a car.
> He didn't notice that the lights had changed.
> A crowd of people stood and stared.
> They' seen his face before.
> No one was really sure if he was
> from the House of Lords
> Nothing to do to save his life.
>
> You are on your own
> You are in the street
>
> Never glimpse the truth.
>
> If they only knew
> we were talking about the love
> that's gone so cold.
>
> And the people who gain the world
> And lose their soul
>
> And life flows on
> Within you and without you

Do these lines refer to the death of James Paul McCartney? There were claims that the song refers to the Hon. Tara Brown but this has since proved to be false. In relation to Brown's death Lennon told Hunter Davies:

> I didn't copy the accident. Tara didn't blow his mind out in a car.

Meanwhile, McCartney told Spitz:

> Paul recalled, as far as he could remember, there was no discussion about Tara Brown.

So, if the song has nothing to do with the death of McCartneys' best friend who is the song about? Whose death were they talking about? Whose motor accident were they talking about?

An insider told me that the song is most certainly about the death of James Paul McCartney and talks about how and when John Lennon found out about the accident and exactly how it happened. Here is how the song is decoded and what John Lennon mean by each line:

I read the news today, oh boy.

I was informed today about what happened to Paul

About a lucky man who made the grade.

About one of the world's most talented songwriters.

And though the news was rather sad, well I just had to laugh.

I was first told he had crashed his Aston Martin and I laughed because this was the second car that had been written off [referring to the Mini Cooper crash]

I saw the photograph

They showed me a photograph of Paul at the scene of the accident.

He blew his mind out in a car.

He died in the car crash.

He didn't notice that the lights had changed.

He went straight through a red light.

A crowd of people stood and stared

A crowd gathered at the horrific scene

Nobody was even sure if he was from the House of Lords

These are the lyrics but actually Lennon sings House of Paul. Some people thought it might be the *Beatle* because there were reported sightings of him in the area. This is also the reason for the confusion that arises in relation to Tara Brown whose father was in the House of Lords.

I saw a film today, oh boy.

The police handed him McCartney's camera on which he had filmed various scenes.

The English army had just won the war.

This refers to the exact time Lennon heard of the death. It was when he was filming how *I Won the War*.

I just had to look....having read the book.

Here Lennon says he that he had to look at the home movies that McCartney had just filmed having read his friend's journal. In other words the film and the journal were never lost. They were handed to John

Lennon by the French authorities. This is the real meaning of this iconic song.

If the words do not refer to McCartney they are evidence of a cynical betrayal by *The Beatles* of all their fans for the sole purpose of making more money from them.

In 1969 they were over the hill and their sales were plummeting. When news of these coded clues came out their sales rocketed. People were buying not one but two albums because they were wrecking their albums by playing them backwards. They were also buying back albums searching for clues. Either James Paul McCarthy really was dead or *The Beatles* were playing a cynical game, which they have kept up to this day, to con their fans into buying more of their records.

The clues and secret messages didn't stop. On the contrary they seemed to be more and more of them.

Magical Mystery Tour

For the next album *The Magical Mystery Tour* Bill or Paul or whoever, was depicted on the cover as a hippopotamus with a gaping hole in his chest. Theorists say it was to signify that Bill had no heart or soul since he wasn't real.

Lennon dressed himself as the walrus to again identify with McCartney. When they designed the name *The*

Beatles it signified a number when you turned the album upside down. The number was 5371038. Someone had secured the number on the London telephone exchange and forwarded it to a funeral home, supposedly the Epping Funeral Home.

In an inside photograph Capitol Records "accidentally" printed a photograph which exposed Bill as looking very little like Paul McCartney.

Inside the sleeve is a photograph of the *Beatles* with McCartneys' figure appearing to be headless.

The inside booklet is full of "clues". Page one begins with the words:

**High above the clouds
there lived four or five musicians.**

On page 3 there is a photograph of McCartney sitting at a desk behind a sign which reads

I was or **I You Was**

On page 4 McCartney holds a magic wand in his right hand. He also uses his right hand at the beginning of the *Fool on the Hill* segment in the film when he takes a cigarette out of his mouth. On the bus when the crew are drunk McCartney holds the bottle of beer in his right hand. There are several other clips of McCartney being right handed in the film.

On page 7 McCartney once again has a hand over his head as if a priest if giving him benediction or blessing the body of a dead person. Page 9 of the booklet is the most revealing. Firstly, the importance of the number 9 is again emphasized. The name "McCartney" contains nine letters. And since he supposedly died on the 9th day themes of birth and rebirth are obvious in the following five panels of the cartoon. After the headline "THE MAGIC BEGINS TO WORK" they insert depictions of McCartney's death and the subsequent cover-ups.

On page 10 McCartney isn't wearing any shoes. Once again this is a symbol of death in many countries including Britain, Greece, Italy and India.

On page 14 McCartney is again behind his desk and on the wall behind him is a poster which reads: God Save the Queen.

The caricature is pointing outward with his hand above McCartney's head. This occurs again on page 24 when the man in the bowler hat has his hand over McCartney's head.

The clues go on and on. Page 23 is very revealing and cannot be regarded as some kind of coincidence. All the *Beatles* are in tuxedos and are all wearing red carnations, except McCartney. He is wearing a black flower. When asked about this Sir Paul McCartney said that there were meant to be four red carnations but they could only find three so he used the black one. Really? Then there are the clues in the lyrics!

When the track *Your Mother Should Know* is spun backwards you can hear the words:

> **Why doesn't she know me dead?**
> **I shed the light.**
> **Why doesn't she ask my mind to be sure.**

At the end of the track *I Am the Walrus* a radio play of Shakespeare's *The Tragedy of King Lear* can be heard. It is a segment from Act IV, Scene VI. It is a death scene and contains the following lines:

> **Bury my body**
> **Oh untimely death**
> **What? Is he dead?**

Author Mark Lewisohn has said that this was purely a coincidence. A live radio feed was mixed onto the master tape and the radio's dial happened upon the BBC1 Third Program where the broadcast originated. That may be so but it is rather stretching our beliefs.

Furthermore, if the chorus of *I Am a Walrus*, the "got one, got one" segment, is played backwards the chorus strangely becomes something else:

> **Ha! Ha! Paul is dead**
> **Ha! Ha! Paul is dead**

In fact, *ABC News* in America presented this clue on national television on the 23 October 1969. At the very end of the song *Strawberry Fields* Lennon says

> **I buried Paul.**

Lennon claims he was saying "cranberry sauce." No one seems to have ever asked him why? But seriously, the last syllable is clearly "Paul".

Something else worth mentioning is that about one minute and fifty one seconds into the film of the same name there is a picture indicating where James Paul McCartney died. The frame contains a single shot of a French town.

The town is Outreau.

Again, ask yourself the question: why would they do this?

THE BEATLES aka THE WHITE ALBUM

If the original version of the *White Album* is placed under an ultra violet light, it will reveal a hidden phone number. This is supposed to have been the number that would connect you with Billy Shepherd. Alex Bennett revealed this clue while in England via the WMCA airwaves. The number is now defunct.

As regard the lyrics, in *Glass Onion,* there is a line

> **I told you about the Fool on the Hill**
> **I tell you man, he living there still.**

The implication is that he is "living" there because he is buried there. Also the same track contains the words

> **Well, here's another clue for you,**
> **The Walrus was Paul.**

As far as theorists are concerned Lennon actually admits that Paul was the walrus and is dead. Lennon later denied this.

In an interview in *Playboy* magazine in September 1980 Lennon said: Well, that was a joke. The line was put in partly because I was feeling guilty I was with Yoko and I was leaving Paul. It's a very perverse way of saying to Paul, you know, "Here, have this crumb, this illusion, this stroke, because I'm leaving."

Ringo Starr laments the loss of Paul in *Don't Pass Me By* in the line
> **You were in a car crash**
> **and you lost your hair.**

At the end of the song *I'm So Tired* there is some mumbling which when played backwards reveals the message.

> **Paul is dead man…**
> **miss him, miss him, miss him.**

In the song *Ob-La-Di, Ob-La-Da* when the chorus is sun in reverse a voice says

> **Ha, ha, I know we did it.**

When the song is played backward you can clearly hear someone state "how are you singing of Satan" and "I Devil, He's Devil."

In fact the title is a Spanish anagram for Diablo La Boda. And what does Diablo La Boda mean? The

Satanic Wedding. For those of you not conversant with Satanic practices a Satanic wedding is an ancient occult ritual of joining a soul with a live or partially dead person, or the wedding of the two. This is said to be their ridiculous attempt to transfer the soul of the dead *Beatle* into Bill.

The track *Yer Blues* contains the line

> **If I ain't dead already,**
> **Girl you know the reason why.**

At the end of the song *While My Guitar Weeps* George Harrison wails
Oh Paul…Oh Paul….Oh Paul

If the chanting on the words "number nine" from *Revolution 9* are played in reverse they come out as

> **Turn me on dead man.**

This is certainly one of the most important clues to surface and is latched onto by theorists as further evidence of McCartney's death. The author's interpretation of this line is that it might refer to a person who is seriously injured and on a life support system which has eventually been turned off.

The crowd audio on *Revolution 9* seems to refer to a car accident

> **He hit a light pole**
> **We better go to see a surgeon**
> **My wings are broke**
> **And so is my hair**

YELLOW SUBMARINE

In the cover of the album Lennon is holding his hand over a cartoon drawing of McCartney's head. This is yet another example of benediction a religious blessing of a person about to be buried.

He shows only three fingers indicating the three genuine *Beatles*.

If you listen carefully to the song *Yellow Submarine* in the middle of it you can hear Lennon say at least twice "Paul is dead, head. Paul is dead, head."

One clue stands out in the lyrics. In the song *Hey, Bulldog* there is a line which is

> **You may think you know me**
> **But you haven't got a clue**

Theorists say that this is Billy Shepherd saying that while he looks like James Paul McCartney he's not really him.

At nineteen minutes 49 seconds into the film we see George Harrison in a car driving by. After he drives by a few times Ringo Starr and John Lennon get into the car. After driving off screen we hear the sound of a horrible car crash which is all happening off-screen. The three *Beatles* come running back into the range of the camera shouting Paul! Paul! Paul! They go in search of Paul by opening some of the doors in the long hallway. Once they find Paul, he steps out of the door and of you listen very carefully you will hear them say "Billy Shears." This indicates that this is the false Paul. But also notice that the three other *Beatles* do not appear happy to see him.

Finally, if you watch the animated film *Yellow Submarine* there is one particular shot which shows five Beatles, John, Paul, George, Ringo and Bill!

ABBEY ROAD

Theorists point out various clues on the cover of the album which all lead them to believe that they are messages from the group that McCartney is dead. In fairness though most of these clues are very subjective and are open to numerous interpretations.

McCartney is wearing no shoes and is the only one out of step. His eyes are closed and although he is supposed to be left handed he holds a cigarette in his right hand. The beetle car on the left hand side has a registration number which they interpret as IF 28 – if McCartney was alive he would be 28. (Actually he would have been 27 but an insider explains that the album was released a year earlier than expected.)

Lennon is dressed in a white suit representing the preacher, McCartney is barefoot representing the corpse, Starr is dressed in black representing the undertaker and Harrison is dressed in jeans representing the gravedigger.

Sir Paul McCartney years later stated on the David Letterman show that he went to the shoot wearing a pair of sandals and the reason why he wore no sandals on the shoot was because it was a very hot day.

If it was a very hot day would the hot tar from the road not burn his feet? Why kick off his sandals? Furthermore, what's the first item of clothing you take off on a hot day? A jacket perhaps? Why kick off your sandals, wear your jacket and walk across hot tar? But actually, it wasn't a particularly hot day in London on the 8 August 1969 when the shot was taken. The highest temperature was 70 F and the lowest was 55 F. It was a warm day, not a very hot day.

Iain MacMillan was the photographer assigned to take the cover photograph on Abbey Road on the 8 August 1969. He said he took five outtakes (all of which can be seen in the book Beatles' *Anthology*).

When you compare the photographs, the one chosen is really the only one worth selecting as all the others (some with McCartney wearing sandals) are flawed. He only had a limited time to take the photos as the police had to stop the traffic on Abbey Road to facilitate the shoot. MacMillan says that they tried to get them to tow away the white Beetle but the owner who lived in a flat across the road was away.

Another clues is in the lyrics of the music. In *Come Together* Lennon sings

One and one and one is three

representing the three remaining *Beatles*.

OTHER SOURCES

In *Lady Madonna* one lyric refers to the news blackout about McCartney's death at five o'clock on the morning of Wednesday the 9 November 1966:

Wednesday morning papers didn't come.

While in the song *Rain* we see the following lines

When the rain comes
They run and hide their heads
They might as well be dead.

It was raining on the morning of the 9 November 1966 in London at 5:00 a.m. (But these contradict the notion he died on the 11 September 1966.)

On the sleeve for the *Plastic Ono Band* single *Cold Turkey* there is an X-ray of a skull supposedly the skull of McCartney after his accident. It should be noted that on the 1 July 1969 Lennon and Ono were involved in a serious car crash of their own. They were both slightly injured. The picture of the skull is actually a composite of both of their skulls according to a source.

On the 1996 *Anthology 1* there is a brand new *Beatles'*

song called *Free As a Bird*. If you play this backwards you will hear two secret messages from John Lennon:

Turned out nice again
I hear that noise again…Paul is dead.

In the next volume *Anthology 2* there is a line on the new song is *Real Love* which says

Paul, he use to sing with me
He used to…

In the reverse of *Real Love* you will find the line

Paul is nowhere at all.

In John Lennon's 1971 album *Imagine* are two none too subtle lines

How do you sleep?
Those freaks were right
when they said you were dead.

These three clues were discovered by Andrew Spooner Jr. who operate a website called Undeniable forensic proof that Paul McCartney really was replaced by a lookalike. Check out www.james-paul-mccartney.150m.com.

Now, dear reader, do you still think that after reading all of the above hidden messages and clues, all relating to the death of James Paul McCarthy that they are still pure coincidences? No, neither do I.

The hardest thing to explain is the glaringly evident which everybody had decided not to see.

Ayn Rand

Where is the music?

We have pointed out how depressed John, George, Ringo and Brain Epstein were following a traumatic event in early September. The only likely event which could have been so traumatic was the sudden death of James Paul McCartney. After a break of three months between September and November 1966, the longest by far, in their musical careers, it would not be unreasonable to expect that on their return to the recording studio on the 24 November 1966 that the *Fab Four* in general, and Lennon and McCartney in particular would be replete with new musical compositions.

If nothing else, Lennon and McCartney were prolific songwriters.

Remember when they recorded their first album *Please Please Me* on the 11 February 1963? The session began at 10:00 a.m. on Monday morning and finished at 10:45 p.m. Essentially, it was a thirteen hour live act with a couple of breaks thrown in between.

In three sessions of three hours each *The Beatles* produced an entire album and even recorded another song *Hold Me Tight* during these sessions but as it was considered to be surplus to requirements it was not included on the album.

Certainly they recorded some cover songs but look how many songs were composed by Lennon and McCartney. On side one we had *I Saw Her Standing There*; *Misery*; *Ask Me Why* and *Please Please Me*. On side two we had *Love Me Do*; *P.S. I Love You*; *Do You Want to Know a Secret?* and *There's a Place*.

The entire album took less than 600 minutes and when released on the 22 March 1963 reached the top of the UK album charts in May 1963 where it remained for thirty weeks before being replaced by their second album *With the Beatles*.

Their second studio album was released on the 22 November 1963 and featured eight original compositions, seven by Lennon and McCartney and one by George Harrison, *Don't Bother Me*, his first recorded solo composition and his first released on a *Beatles'* album. Although the album was recorded over a three month period the only reason for that was because they were performing in between. If you actually break the dates down you will see that the entire album was recorded over seven sessions, i.e. seven days.

So, on their first album, recorded in one day, Lennon and McCartney produced eight original songs. On their second album they produced seven originals and two further ones for a single.

They returned to the recording studios in January 1964 to record their third studio album *A Hard Day's Night*. The album was recorded on the 29 January, the 25, 26 and 27 February, the 1 March an between the 1 and 4 June 1964, at EMI Studios, in London, and Pathé Marconi Studios, in Paris.

After nine sessions they produced an incredible thirteen original Lennon and McCartney songs. This was just three months after their last album was recorded.

And just a month after the release of the film *A Hard Day's Night* they were back in the studio recording their fourth studio album, *Beatles for Sale*.

The first session took place between the 11 and 14

August 1964. The final session was on the 26 October 1964. Not surprisingly they had exhausted their repertoire of songs and their hectic schedule did not allow them the opportunity to replenish their store. But that wasn't the end of their original compositions, far from it.

Their fifth studio album *Help!* released on the 6 August 1965 was recorded over ten sessions between the 15-19 February, the 13 April, the 10 May and between the 14–17 June 1965. Of the fourteen tracks recorded a total of ten were by Lennon and McCartney.

Their sixth studio album, *Rubber Soul*, was recorded at EMI studios in London on the 17 June and between the 12 October to 11 November 1965. It was released on the 3 December 1965 in time for the Christmas market.

According to Lewisohn virtually all of the album's songs were composed immediately after *The Beatles'* return to London following their North American tour. For this album Lennon and McCartney produced twelve original songs.

Revolver, their seventh studio album was recorded between the 6 April and the 21 June 1966, again at EMI Studios, in London. Lennon and McCartney produced eleven of the fourteen songs.

Revolver spent thirty four weeks on the UK Albums Chart, reaching the number one spot on the 13 August 1966. It also reached number one on the

Billboard Top LPs, where it stayed for six weeks. It was ranked first in the hard-cover book All-Time Top 1000 Albums and third in *Rolling Stone* magazine's list of the 500 greatest albums of all time.

So, let me make this clear. Although they never had a full week's break between the making of the first album and their seventh album this is the number of original Lennon and McCartney song recorded in that period:

Please Please Me (22 March 1963) - Eight
With the Beatles (22 November 1963) – Nine
A Hard Day's Night (10 July 1964) - Thirteen
Beatles for Sale (4 December 1964) – Nil
Only cover songs were produced for this album.
Help! (6 August 1965) - Ten
Rubber Soul (3 December 1965) - Twelve
Revolver (5 August 1966) - Eleven

No song writing partnership has ever produced the quality and quantity of original music as Lennon and McCartney did between 1963 and 1966 and no one ever will. No one could disagree with music producer George Martin when he said:

> **There seemed to be a bottomless well of songs, and people have often asked me where that well was dug. Who knows? To begin with, they'd been playing about at writing songs since they were kids and had a large amount of raw material which simply needed shaping.**

So, it would not be unreasonable to expect a lot more new songs. When they walked back into the recording studio on the 24 November 1966, after a total break of three months, everyone expected that they would once again reprise their old partnership and provide another set of new compositions.

But the shocking truth is that the new and revitalized Paul McCartney had absolutely nothing new to offer. And when I say nothing new, I mean nothing, zilch, rien, nada, niente, niets, or wala lang as we say in the Philippines.

What had happened in those three months to so adversely prejudice their song writing abilities? Was it the even same James Paul McCartney?

Something is missing from this jigsaw puzzle but what is it? It's not just a three month vacation period we are talking about here. The last new song was recorded in June 1966. So, between June and November 1966, Paul McCartney had not composed a single new song.

This was the man who claimed he would "dream" a song and write it the following morning. This was the man who told author Bob Spitz:

> **A few hours each day was spent essentially cloistered a hotel room, writing furiously in a journal and thinking all sorts of artistic thoughts.**

So, what happened in the recording studio between the 24 November 1966 and the 1 February 1967? They got together to produce a new album but were unable to finalize one in time for the Christmas market. This was the first time in their history that they didn't have an album ready for the Christmas market.

Let's rework what we've already done! They began the November 1966 session by recording *Strawberry Fields*. Although the song was written by John Lennon it was attributed to the Lennon and McCartney song writing partnership.

It was inspired by Lennon's memories of playing in the garden of Strawberry Field, a Salvation Army children's home near where he lived. He began writing the song when he was filming in Almeria the previous September. The song took 45 hours to record spread over five weeks.

The next song they began working on was McCartney's *When I'm Sixty Four*. This was not a new song. McCartney told his biographer Barry Miles he wrote the song when he was 16.

Lennon told *Anthology*:

> **Paul wrote it in the Cavern days. We just stuck a few more words on it like 'grandchildren on your knee' and 'Vera, Chuck and Dave' ... this was just one that was quite a hit with us.**

The song was recorded between the 6 and the 21 December. They then broke up for Christmas and returned on the 29 December 1966 to record *Penny Lane*. Was this an original McCartney song?

Yes, but it was written months before. The chorus already existed in demo form and already worked out and recorded by James Paul McCartney in 1965. In fact, the idea for *Penny Lane* existed up to 18 months before it was recorded if we are to believe author Ian MacDonald who wrote:

> **Lennon and McCartney had been toying with this title for 18 months when writing songs for Rubber Soul.**

Furthermore Mark Lewisohn also wrote:

> **McCartney mentioned Penny Lane as early as November 1964.**

So, both *When I'm 64* and *Penny Lane* were songs previously worked on my James Paul McCartney and were not new.

Because the record label were concerned at the lack of productivity and the delay in producing a new album they insisted that *Penny Lane* and *Strawberry Fields* be released in February 1967 as a single.

So, what exactly did the new and revitalized Paul McCartney contribute to the album *Sgt. Peppers* that was not previously worked on by James Paul McCartney? He worked on four songs: *Sgt. Pepper's Lonely Hearts Club Band*, *Fixing a Hole*, *She's Leaving Home* and *Lovely Rita*. But Mal Evans in his diaries claims he contributed to *Sgt. Pepper's* and *Fixing a Hole*. On the 27 January 1967 he wrote:

> **Sgt. Pepper. Started writing song with Paul**

> [McCartney] upstairs in his room, he on piano and did a lot more of "where the rain comes in" [a lyric from Fixing a Hole]. Hope people like it. Started Sergeant Pepper.

Then on the 1 February Mal Evans wrote:

> Sergeant Pepper sounds good. Paul tells me that I will get royalties on the song—great news, now perhaps a new home.

And on the 2 February:

> Recording voices on Captain [sic] Pepper. All six of us doing the chorus in the middle, worked until about midnight.

Of course Mal Evans never did receive royalties or even a credit for his efforts and remained on his weekly wage of £38 (£600 in modern day currency).

Keith Badman in *The Beatles Off The Record* (2008) referred to a tape recording of Evans speaking shortly before his death, on which Evans reiterated some of the statements made in the diary.

According to Badman, Evans was asked at the time if it would be a problem that he was not credited as a writer, because the Lennon and McCartney writing name was "a really hot item".

So did Sir Paul McCartney even write *She's Leaving Home* and *Lovely Rita*? Apparently, yes he did, with a little help from his friends. In relation to the former he told Barry Miles:

John and I wrote 'She's Leaving Home' together. It was my inspiration. We'd seen a story in the newspaper about a young girl who'd left home and not been found, there were a lot of those at the time, and that was enough to give us a story line. So I started to get the lyrics: she slips out and leaves a note and then the parents wake up ... It was rather poignant. I like it as a song, and when I showed it to John, he added the long sustained notes, and one of the nice things about the structure of the song is that it stays on those chords endlessly. Before that period in our songwriting we would have changed chords but it stays on the C chord. It really holds you. It's a really nice little trick and I think it worked very well.

While I was showing that to John, he was doing the Greek chorus, the parents' view: 'We gave her most of our lives, we gave her everything money could buy.' I think that may have been in the runaway story, it might have been a quote from the parents.

Lovely Rita was written and performed by Sir Paul McCartney.

McCartney goes on to tell us that the whole concept of *Sgt. Pepper's Lonely Hearts Club Band* was his idea. And who are we to disbelieve him? He told the story many times, and each time he had a different version.

According to Albert Goldman he first came up with the idea in February 1967 after *Penny Lane* and *Strawberry Fields Forever* were released as a single:

> After cutting several sides, including what turned out to be the album's concluding soundtrack, McCartney had a brainstorm. He proposed that they arrange all the music within the format of an old fashioned brass band concert, commencing with an overture and concluding with a reprise. Why, he urged they could even take typical names, like Billy Shears, and present themselves like characters in a play, having a lot of fun with the corny style of such amateurish entertainments.
>
> Paul was fresh from a visit to San Francisco where bands were starting to sport kooky monikers, like Big brother and the Holding company or Country Joe and the Fish. Getting into the same spirit, he came up with a marvellous camp title: Sgt. Pepper and his Lonely Hearts Club Band.

But then it wasn't February that McCartney visited San Francisco. Well, not according to another biographer, Bob Spitz. He says McCartney didn't visit San Fran until April 1967:

> In early April 1967 Paul had slipped in and out of the States. It had been a whirlwind visit. The few days he spent in San Francisco showing up at the Fillmore.

So, when did he come up with the idea, February 1967 or April 1967? And was it really his idea to come up with a reprise? Eh, no. That was the talented Mr. Apsinall.

Well, that is what *Beatles'* historian Ian MacDonald

says:

> Neil Aspinall, the Beatles' factorum, suggested to McCartney that Sgt. Pepper be reprised in abbreviated form to book end the album an segue into a Day in a Life.

Even McCartney's friend Barry Miles wrote:

> Only later in the recording did Neil Aspinall have the idea of repeating the Sgt. Pepper song as a reprise, and the Beatles and George Martin began to use linking tracks and segues to pull it all together, making it more of a concept album.

And McCartney told another biographer, Bob Spitz, that the entire concept for *Sgt. Pepper's* came to him on the 19 November 1966 on his way back from Kenya:

> On the plane home from Nairobi, on November 19th., Paul began formulating an idea for a new Beatles' album. Less about music, it was more about premise.
>
> Paul and Mal kicked around the idea during the in-flight meal. At first they played with names for a band, mimicking the variety of groups that were just coming into vogue: The Bonzo Dog Doo Dah Band, Big Brother and the Holding Company, Lother and the Hand People.
>
> Mal distracted, picked up the little corrugated packets of paper marked "S" and "P" asking Paul what the initials stood for. "Salt and Pepper", he responded. "Sergeant Pepper". By

the time the plane touched down at Heathrow the entire concept was in place.

Of course, what it incredible about this story is that Mal Evans, *The Beatles'* roadie, who had been on every single tour with them from day one never saw a salt and pepper sachet before on any of his previous flights.

But, at least we have one thing cleared up. McCartney didn't come up with the idea for *Sgt. Peppers* in February 1967 or April 1967, it was, in fact, November 1966. Well, not according to what he told biographer Mark Lewisohn.

It wasn't going to be Sgt. Pepper's Lonely Hearts Club Band until Sgt. Pepper's Lonely Hearts Club Band came along. That is, the album was not "The Sgt. Pepper project" until the recording of this McCartney song and Paul's realization soon afterwards that the Beatles could pretend they were Sgt. Pepper's band, the remaining songs on the LP forming a part of a show given by the fictitious combo.

As this song was recorded on the 1 February 1967 it was afterwards that the concept was conceived by McCartney.

That brings us back now to April 1967, or does it?

Ringo Starr who always seems to have a better memory than Sir Paul is on record (no pun intended) as stating that after the original *Sgt. Pepper* song was recorded on the 1 February 1967 they dropped the whole military idea, that is, the band behind another band and that "they just went on doing tracks."

But hang on, didn't I read somewhere that it was James Paul McCartney who came up with the *Sgt. Pepper* idea during their final American tour in August 1966? Ah, yes, here it is on page 184 in *Revolution in the Head* by Ian MacDonald:

> **During the Beatles' final tour, McCartney had been struck by the fanciful names adopted by the new American groups and the Pop Art graphical blend of psychedelic and vaudeville used in West Coast pop posters.**
>
> **Such anarchic free association made "the Beatles" seem as passé as the performing career the group were about to abandon. Musing on this, he conceived the idea of a reborn Beatles in the form of a corporate alter ego: Sgt. Pepper's Lonely Hearts Club Band.**

In fact, it is this final version that seems the most plausible. Perhaps, in honour of his death and in memory of his life, Lennon, Harrison and Starr decided to carry on Paul's dream and create the *Sgt. Pepper's Lonely Hearts Club Band* and inform their millions of fans through numerous hidden messages that James Paul McCartney was no longer with us. Whatever about Harrison and Starr, John Lennon did not want to record anymore with the new and revitalized Paul McCartney after the 24 November 1966. The remainder of their days together would be marred by spite, jealously, contempt, anger and hatred. The brilliant musical partnership was over.

DAVID ELIO MALOCCO

When you have eliminated the impossible, whatever remains, however improbable, must be the truth.

Sherlock Holmes

Paul McCartney has never had plastic surgery, ever. This is what Geoff Baker told me. He worked for him as his press officer for twelve years. So, he should know. In fact, my good friend, Geoff Baker added:

> **He's not that type of person. He hasn't even had that chipped tooth fixed. Remember the one he broke on that moped accident. He still hasn't had**

that fixed. And this is one of the richest men in the world.

You can't buy loyalty like that. Well you can, but Geoff doesn't work for McCartney anymore and hasn't done so for several years. While he is bound by a confidentiality agreement it wouldn't cover the subject of McCartney's broken tooth – but it might cover the fact that he had plastic surgery. In any event, I believe Geoff. I believe Geoff in that he believes Sir Paul McCartney has never had plastic surgery. But then they don't call him Plastic Macca for nothing, or again, maybe they do. Although I also hold great sway in a comment by one of his childhood acquaintances: "Paul is very tight with his money, always has been. He wouldn't buy a coat for £100 if he thought he could get it for £75 somewhere else." But someone, sometime has had quite a lot of plastic surgery and only a Fool on the Hill could deny it.

Still not convinced that there was a conspiracy?

If you are not yet convinced of a *Beatles'* Conspiracy then perhaps some forensic evidence might sway you. In 2009 *Wired Italia*, which had just begun its publishing life, produced a sensational cover story.

Two Italian scientists presented forensic evidence that the Paul McCartney of 1968 was not the same person as the Paul McCartney of 1966. On the very day the article was published Sir Paul McCartney made his very first appearance on the American David Letterman talk show. Although the actual magazine article wasn't mentioned Letterman asked him about the PID theory.

That was the idea that was the other part of it that there was a guy who looked like you taking your place.

To which McCartney replied pointing to himself:

Well no. This is him.

Guests don't just pop in for a chat with hosts like Letterman. Interviews are scheduled well in advance and in the case of someone like McCartney parameters are set as to what they will and will not be asked. McCartney arranged for the interview to take place on the very day the *Wired* article was published. There was a reason for this. But let's discuss the Italian scientists.

Dr. Gabriella Carlesi is a scientist who claims to be an expert in the identification of people using via digital image processing. The article describes her as a forensic pathologist who specializes in identification of people through craniometry, the scientific measurement of the dimensions of the bones of the skull and face. She is also an expert in forensic odontology which deals with the analysis of the teeth. She has been a consultant in a number of high profile cases in Italy including: The murder of Italian journalist Ilaria Alpi and her camera operator Miran Hrovatin (for an Italian Parliament Commission). Alpi and Hrovatin were killed in Mogadishu, Somalia. In 2009 Francesco Fonti, a former 'Ndrangheta member, claimed that they were murdered because they had seen toxic waste shipped by the 'Ndrangheta arrive in Bosaso, Somalia;

The identification of Sergei Antonov in the attempted assassination of Pope John Paul II, in relation to the "Mitrokhin Archive" (again for an Italian Parliament Commission). Sergei Antonov was a Bulgarian airline representative who was accused of involvement in an assassination attempt against Pope John Paul II by Mehmet Ali Ağca in 1981. The case against him collapsed when Italian prosecutors failed to prove that the Bulgarian secret service had hired Mehmet Ali Ağca to assassinate the Pope at the behest of the Soviet Union. Antonov returned to Bulgaria following his acquittal. He refused to speak publicly about his time in prison. He was found dead in his Sofia, Bulgaria apartment in the summer of 2007;

The assassination of Benito Mussolini and his mistress Claretta Petacci (for a historical reconstruction); and the identification of Francesco Narducci, connected to the investigation of the so called *Monster of Florence*. Her partner in this examination was Francesco Gavazzeni who is described as a specialist in computer analyses. Working together with sophisticated computer technology they obtained high precision measurements of Paul McCartney's skull from various photos of his face. We know that certain features of our skull provide effective means for identification purposes and some features cannot currently be altered by surgery.

Obviously because they didn't have two different skulls to examine they had to rely on photographs. They searched for high resolution photographs which had not been digitally altered from before 1966 and after 1966 so that they could compare the differences, if any, between the images.

Gavazzeni indicated that from his investigation he noticed that some photographs taken before 1966 were not properly dated and in some cases different photo agencies had different dates for the same photo.

He also discovered that some of the best photos were copyrighted by photographers who were very reluctant to release them. However, according to Gavazzeni they eventually found two good quality photos dated before 1966 and two after 1967.

You cannot properly compare photographs of a human face until they have been sized correctly so that they match the same scale. The feature most preferred as a factor in scaling is the distance between the pupils. They re-scaled the photographs so that the distance between the pupils was a perfect match.

COMPATIBILITA ANATOMO-ANTROPOMETRICA

MESSA IN SCALA E MAPPATURA DI DUE IMMAGINI DI PAUL PRE 1966

[Italian caption text describing the anatomical-anthropometric comparison methodology used by Caresi and Gavazzeni, comparing pre-1966 and post-1966 images of Paul McCartney, using craniometric reference points per Paul Pierre Broca: 1. Glabella (G), 2. Nasion (N), 3. Centro delle pupille, 4. Punto naso-spinale (SN), 5. Pogonion e gnathion (PG).]

They were then able to lay the photographs on top of each other. Their purpose was to prove that the shape of the skull on each photographs was identical – all other features can be altered by surgery or damage but the size of the skull in an adult of a certain age remains constant. I should add that they had originally intended to prove that pre-1966 Paul and the post-1966 Paul were one and the same person.

The pre-1966 photographs matched one another perfectly.

The post-1966 photographs also matched one another perfectly. That would be expected. However, they were shocked to discover that the pre-1966 photographs did not match the post-1966 photographs in several material respects.

This is what they discovered. The quotations have been translated from Italian to English and thus might lose some of their significance in translation:

In relation to the jaw line of both men:

> **The mandibular curve between the two sets of photos showed a discrepancy of over six per cent, well beyond the acceptable threshold for error. But there was more. There were changes in the development of the mandibular profile: before 1966 each side of the jaw is composed of two curves but since 1967 there appears to be a single curve. There is therefore a morphological difference in the curve.**

For example, the frontal curvature of the jaw was different, that is, the curve going from one ear to the other and passing through the chin, which you see when looking directly into a face, was different.

Furthermore, the jaw arc was also different, that is, the curve of the jaw that you would see if looking downward at the head from above was not the same

Gavazzeni also noticed a common feature of early post-1966 photographs. There was a dark area shadowing the external corner of the left eye. That area displayed something half-way between a scar and something that resembles skin that was stretched as a consequence of cosmetic surgery, or, as Gavazzeni suggests, of an imperfect cosmetic surgery.

Significantly the photographs also showed that in the post-1966 ones Paul's head was more oblong than in in the pre-1966 photographs. Essentially the photographs were of two different heads.

Gavazzeni pointed out that some post-1967 photographs of Paul must have been compressed to hide the fact that the skull was longer.

We can do this ourselves on our computer with any photograph we have. We can make someone's face fatter or thinner, smaller or bigger etc. We don't even need any special tools to do this. A fat person can make themselves look slimmer by elongating their photograph.

In relation to the lips of both men:

> **Compared to the previous picture, that of Sgt. Pepper's shows clearly that the commessura lip (that is the line formed by both lips) was suddenly stretched. This obviously is not possible as whispers cannot be camouflaged. In other words, the phenomenon is all too frequent these days, the lips can be inflated and increased in volume, but the width of the lip commessura cannot vary that much. It may be slight but this is not the case in the photographs examined: here the difference between the before and after is too strong to have been caused by any surgery.**

Carlesi pointed out that the line separating the post-1966 Paul's lips was much wider. In fact that it was so much more wider that it was obvious even after Paul grew his moustache.

She suggests that the post-1967 Paul grew the moustache in an attempt to hide that detail. It should be pointed out that while lips can be inflated and increased in volume, the wideness of their separating line can be altered only to a small extent.

The position, relative to the skull, of the point where the nose detaches from the face, is more significant because it cannot be altered by surgery. According to Carlesi, these points for pre- and post-1966 Paul are considerably different

In relation to the ears of both men:

> **This is technically called tragus: everyone has two ears and the characteristics are different for each human being. In Germany there is a**

recognition procedure called craniometrics in which the identification of the right ear is tantamount to identification by fingerprints. But what is tragus? Tragus is the small cartilage covered with skin that overhangs the entrance to the ear and the ear canal and like the whole ear it cannot be changed surgically. How then can you explain the differences between the right ear of Paul McCartney in a previous 1966 photograph? Things that ordinary mortals might seem irrelevant or unclear, the tragus to the expert allows them to locate and identify persons.

Some features of the ear are also useful for identification purposes because these as well are not modifiable through surgery. Carlesi and Gavazzeni determined that the ears of both men, particularly the tragus, differed significantly.

They had a lot to say about the differences in teeth and palate as displayed in the earlier and later photographs of McCartney:

> The changes that are evident are not impossible but to make these changes would require long and painful operations and the results would not necessarily be perfect. This is especially so if these operations were carried out in the 1960s. Careful examination of the 1966 and 1967 photographs produce amazing results. First of all there is the upper canine. In the 1966 photographs the upper canine is protruding relative to the line of the other teeth. It's the classic case of a tooth that lacks space which ends up as misaligned. It is pushed out by the pressure of other teeth. It is curious that in the

1967 photographs the upper canine is still protruding but for no apparent reason. The images show that the space would have to be aligned with the neighbouring teeth. It's like there was an attempt to recreate an anomaly that was never there in the first place.

But it is in the area of the palate that Dr. Carlesi found the most serious differences.

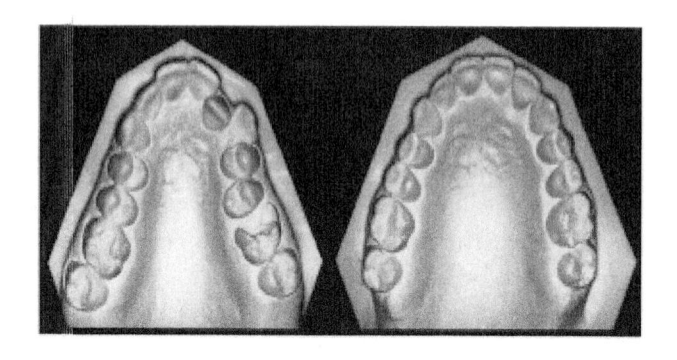

After the publication of the Sgt. Pepper's album McCartney's palate seems to widen considerably to the point that the front teeth do not rotate on the axis as before. A change in the shape of the palate in the sixties was not impossible but would be very traumatic. In practice, McCartney would have had to have been subjected to an operation that would involve the opening of the suture palate, have bones broken and then undergo a long and painful orthodontic treatment...including the use of a fixed orthodontic multiband which he would have to wear for over a year. This would not have been possible to hide and would have obvious repercussions for the performance of a professional singer.

We are aware that the position and slope of teeth can be altered, for example by braces, surgical removal and the imposition of implants and by capping. But Carlesi was of the opinion that not only did the teeth configurations for the two men not match but there was additionally something strange going on.

Just to clarify what Carlesi was saying: In pre-1966 Paul, his upper right canine tooth was pushed out of its normal position because there is not enough room in his jaw for all of his teeth to fit properly.

In the older Paul, that same canine tooth was also crooked, but it was curious that there was plenty of room in his jaw for all of his teeth. As no other teeth were pushing against the crooked tooth, what happened to make that tooth crooked?

In Carlesi's opinion the crooked tooth in the post-1967 photographs was the result of a dental operation to simulate the crooked tooth in the genuine Paul's mouth.

The obvious difference in the shape of the palate shocked her even more. It was so narrow in the younger Paul that some teeth, like the upper canine, were misaligned but the palate of the post-1967 Paul was so wide that the front teeth did not rotate with respect to their axis, or tilt, as was happening for the genuine Paul, with the only exception of that upper right canine (mentioned above) which leaned outward.

Carlesi then tells us that while it was possible to alter the shape of a person's palate in the 1960s it would have required a traumatic surgical operation and necessitated the wearing of fixed dental braces for more than a year.

Following their investigation they concluded. on many different grounds, that it was not the same man and that the post-1967 Paul went to the trouble of having one tooth altered to make it crooked so that he would look like the real James Paul McCartney. But they qualified their conclusions by saying they were not 100% certain but certain enough to make their observations.

In relation to his teeth who would undertake such an operation? Perhaps, their own dentist, the one that introduced Lennon and Harrison to LSD, Mr. John Riley.

Riley was a south Londoner destined for life as an NHS dentist in north London, until heading to the Northwestern University dental school in the US and returning as one of Harley Street's few cosmetic dentists, whose clients also included Dudley Moore.

However, when I went searching for Dr. Riley I discovered that by 1968 he had given up his lucrative Harley Street practice in London and had inexplicably emigrated to Ireland. Further enquiries revealed that he died in 1986 in a mysterious car crash in Ireland only ten miles from where I live!

In relation to the Forensic evidence it should be

pointed out that even at the best of times facial identification and reconstruction is a very complicated process which requires measurements using actual human skeletal remains. Here there is no body.

Identification is estimated on the basis of photographs. And not hundreds of photographs but just a few. We have no way of knowing if the photographs used were authentic original photographs.

We have to take their word for it.

We don't know where these photographs came from. Accordingly we cannot say with any certainty that they have not already been tampered with. They say that the photographs have not been tampered with and I have no reason to disbelieve them.

But what the Italian scientists have tried to do is to examine photographs and apply scientific principles in forensics that are not meant to be applied in that manner.

I don't profess to be an expert in the field of Forensic Science although I have two diplomas in the area and have written a best-selling book on the subject called *Forensic Science: Crime Scene Analysis* which includes a chapter on Forensic Anthropology.

But I can tell you that forensic facial reconstruction and identification is the process of recreating the face of an individual for the purposes of identification from their skeletal remains not from photographs of their skeletal remains.

Because this is not a precise science and involves an amalgamation of artistry, forensic science, anthropology, osteology, and anatomy it does not fall within the ambit of the *Daubert Standard* regarding the admissibility of expert witness testimony during legal proceedings.

Accordingly, their evidence in relation to the comparison of skulls would not be admissible in a court of law.

They also wrote extensively about the differences in ears between the pre-1966 and post-1966 photographs of Paul McCartney. But although ear identification is beginning to be accepted in certain jurisdictions it is far from being universally accepted.

Again, in this instance the scientists are not comparing ears. They are comparing photographs of ears. And again we have no way of knowing if the photographs they are using are authentic genuine photographs which have not already been tampered with.

On three separate occasions I endeavoured to contact Dr. Carlesi to discuss these shortcomings but she failed to reply to any of my emails.

Accordingly, while the study is impressive and a lot of scientific analysis has been undertaken and to a degree positively proved it can in no way be considered proof positive, on the basis of the standard of proof required in a British or American Court of Law, that these are photographs of two different men.

But it certainly makes you appreciate that an impostor may very well be in place.

The trouble with having an open mind, of course, is that people will insist on coming along and trying to put things in it.

Terry Pratchett

And so, there you have it.

The *Paul Is Dead* conspiracy theorists claim that there is unassailable evidence which prove, not just on the balance of probabilities, but also beyond a reasonable doubt, that James Paul McCartney either died or became incapacitated or retired in 1966 and was replaced by the gentleman now known as Sir Paul McCartney.

In fact, Michael Wright, in his comprehensive book *An Investigation into the Beatles, Paul McCartney: His Alleged Death and Cover-Up in Late 1966* (2014), cogently argues that Sir Paul McCartney is a clone and that the technology to clone humans was available much earlier than 1996 when by Ian Wilmut, Keith Campbell and colleagues at the Roslin Institute, University of Edinburgh, Scotland, financed by the biotechnology company PPL Therapeutics, cloned a domestic sheep from an adult somatic cell, using the process of nuclear transfer.

Part of the evidence relates to his mysterious and undocumented disappearance between the 31 August 1966 and the 24 November 1966. James Paul McCartney was supposed to be in France, Spain and later Kenya, first on his own and then with *Beatles'* roadie and minder Mal Evans and McCartney's girlfriend Jane Asher.

His journals and the home movies he shot disappeared; the journals were lost and the movies were stolen, supposedly by fans. They have never surfaced.

Jane Asher was supposed to have been holidaying with McCartney in Kenya that November but she was never there because she was shooting the film *A Winter's Tale* with Laurence Harvey in England at that time.

Furthermore, Mal Evans, in his monthly column in the official *Beatles'* magazine in January 1967 makes absolutely no mention of her in the story about his safari trip with Paul McCartney in Kenya. The small bits of film which exist today have glimpses of a man supposed to be James Paul McCartney but look nothing like him.

McCartney's blue Aston Martin was in a road accident in 1966. But this fact is not documented anywhere.
Why? And what happens when the new and revitalized McCartney returns to England after his sojourn in Africa where conspiracy theorists claim he underwent plastic surgery at a private clinic?

He immediately sacks his live-in butler and his wife. Was this because they would instantly realize that the Paul McCartney who returned was not the Paul McCartney who left?

All through this time Mal Evans was keeping a diary for a forthcoming book he intended to write after *The Beatles* split up. So, what happened the book? The manuscript which was due to be published went missing two weeks before its publication date. It went missing immediately after Mal Evans was shot dead in highly mysterious circumstances which deserve closer examination. Mal Evans knew everything about *The Beatles* in general and McCartney in particular. If ever there was someone who could spill the beans, it was him. But just like his manager, agent, lawyer, best friend, psychiatrist, dentist and business associate, Mal Evans never lived to tell the true story. Because Mal Evans was murdered.

Iamaphoney

Every now and again, pages allegedly from Mal Evan's manuscript, appear on the internet, placed there by someone who calls himself *Iamaphoney*. One is worth particular attention. A photocopy of it is at the end of the chapter. This document appears in the *Iamaphoney* movie and purports to be an extract from Mal Evans book *Living the Beatles Legend*.

In this particular piece Mal writes about the time that McCartney's Irish butler George Kelly and his wife, the housekeeper of his London home, were sacked the day before McCartney arrived back. The clear implication is that their dismissal occurred immediately following the Kenya trip where the new McCartney received plastic surgery and possibly some kind of revolutionary treatment in November 1966.

Ostensibly there were sacked because they sold an article to an Australian magazine but we all know that was not the real reason. This is what the page says:

> **George was not very happy about it. He didn't understand it, but I had no choice. Brian could have sent somebody else to tell him the bad news, but the easy way was letting me tell him, even though I was closer to George and his wife than the others. I felt so bad and was actually crying in front of Brian, begging him to not let me do this. Brian thought that it was a splendid idea to tell George that because of the article we**

could no longer trust him and he was fired. Poor George, he didn't understand a thing. Why, he cried bitterly, why? He kept asking this question again and again. I was standing there as a butcher with his knife. My body was shaking and I was fighting to hold the tears back, but big boys don't cry...It was a pretty (indecipherable) moment not having a chance to tell him the truth. George and his wife left Cavendish the same evening. The next day Paul arrived. We were all there, Neil, Robert, John, Brian, Ringo/Anita, George and Tony. Everybody was excited and stunned. It was amazing. They did a good job in Nairobi.

It was really happening, it was like we had known him forever. Brian was afraid. Neil assured him that he could trust Pete but Brian needed a commitment from him. John was paralyzed. Just don't go there, he said, we don't need friggin Pete involved. I don't need to see him again, just don't let him near us, Mal. I felt bad again, starting thing(s) about Gary, Lily and Babybird (?). I tried to tell that I had to see my family sometime, but Brian and John insisted that I should stay with Paul for awhile. In these days we were so out of it and I see now that I left my beloved ones alone and unsafe. When I was thinking too much about it I felt real low and I had to get high. We all had to get high. It was so unreal and that is why John invented Strawberry Fields. Nothing is real, he said again and again. We didn't really understand it until he showed us what really wasn't real in the lyrics. John is a genius, a real one. It blew my mind when he played it backwards. What a way to tell a story. Paul really gave him a new direction, a new way of art. Good and Bad. Black and White. In

> **November, they started to record the album or what we thought would be the new album. It sounded right, the song, and we were all very pleased with the idea of making a new sound on the album. Paul came up with an idea we already had talked a lot about when we were at the clinic in Kenya. The Sergeant Peppers Lonely Hearts Club Band. We were playing around with the moustache...**

Obviously, the most significant part of this document is the part that contains the following lines:

> **The next day Paul arrived. We were all there, Neil, Robert, John, Brian, Ringo/Anita, George and Tony. Everybody was excited and stunned. It was amazing. They did a good job in Nairobi. It was really happening, it was like we had known him forever.**

This document would be evidence that James Paul McCartney was indeed replaced and the those who welcomed him back were involved in the cover up.

So, who are they?

The alleged author is certainly Mal Evans.

Neil is Neil Aspinall, the Beatles' personal assistant.

Robert is Robert Fraser, the art dealer.

John is John Lennon.

Brian is most likely to be Brian Epstein but it could

also be Brian Jones from the *Rolling Stones* because of the inclusion of "Anita" – see below.

Ringo is Ringo Starr.

Anita can only be Anita Pallenberg who was dating Brian Jones from the *Rolling Stones* at the time and who was in the B*eatles'* inner circle.

George is George Harrison.

Tony is Tony Bramwell the *Beatles'* publicist and press office.
Another interesting line is:

> **Neil assured him that he could trust Pete but Brian needed a commitment from him.**

Who was Pete? Pete Best? Pete Shotton? Pete Blake? No, my opinion is that the Peter referred to therein is Pete Asher, the brother of Jane Asher and till today close friend and confidant of Sir Paul McCartney.

Another point that conspiracy theorists claim is evidence that McCartney died and was replaced is the sheer number of suspicious deaths of those close to him. Remember what the insider told us: *Dead men can't talk.*

MAL EVANS (R.I.P.)

If ever there was a fifth *Beatle* it was Mal Evans who was affectionately called The Gentle Giant. Mal was working as a Post Office communications technician in 1962 when he first heard *The Beatles* perform at the *Cavern Club*. He was soon hired as bouncer, roadie and gofer.

He loved working with *The Beatles*, and making movies and music with them. He contributed to many *Beatles* recordings, received little credit and was denied royalties promised to him. In fact, despite his undeniable loyalty and his genuine love and fondness for each of them, at the end of the day, they treated him very poorly.

When *The Beatles* stopped touring in 1966, Mal continued to work for them and remained their friend. Despite the fact that although he worked seven days a week they only ever paid him a basic wage (the equivalent today of £30,000 per annum.)

You could say they brought him on holidays and paid all his expenses but Mal never earned enough money to be able to buy a home for his family and was always worried about his finances.

An entry in his diary dated the 13 January 13, 1969 is painfully revealing:

> **Paul is really cutting down on the Apple staff members. I was elevated to office boy [Mal had briefly been made MD of Apple] and I feel very hurt and sad inside, only big boys don't cry. Why I should feel hurt and reason for writing this is ego... I thought I was different from other people in my relationship with the Beatles and being loved by them and treated so nice, I felt like one**

of the family. Seems I fetch and carry. I find it difficult to live on the £38 I take home each week and would love to be like their other friends who buy fantastic homes and have all the alterations done by them, and are still going to ask for a rise. I always tell myself — look, everybody wants to take from, be satisfied, try to give and you will receive. After all this time I have about £70 to my name, but was content and happy. Loving them as I do, nothing is too much trouble, because I want to serve them. "Feel a bit better now — EGO?

In 1968 Evans he discovered a group called *The Iveys*, later known as *Badfinger* and suggested that they be signed to Apple. He later produced several of their songs. One in particular, *No Matter What* charted on Billboard's Top 10 in December 1970. He also discovered the group *Splinter* and brought them to the Apple label.

Mal separated from his beloved wife Lily in 1973 and moved to Los Angeles where he continued to manage new bands and produce music. He was working on a book of memoirs called *Living The Beatles' Legend* which he was due to deliver to his publishers, Grosset and Dunlap, on the 12 January 1976. At the time he was living with his twenty six year old girlfriend Fran Hughes in a rented motel apartment at 8122 West 4th Street in Los Angeles

On the 5 January 1976, Mal called his friend and the cowriter for his biography, John Hoernie. He said he was depressed and asked him to come over. He did and later made a statement that Mal appeared "really doped-up and groggy". Before he left Mal told Hoernie to make sure he finished the book. Hoernie helped Evans up to an upstairs bedroom. There was a drunken altercation an Mal is alleged to have picked up an air rifle.

His girlfriend, fearful that he might self-harm, called the police and told them that Evans was confused, had a rifle, and was on valium. Four policemen arrived and three of them, David D. Krempa (30), Robert E. Brannon (27) and Lieutenant Charles Higbie, went up to the bedroom. They later reported that as soon as Evans saw the three policemen he pointed a rifle at them. They told him to drop it and when he didn't Higbie shot him six times, "in self-defence," killing him instantly.

He was cremated on the 7 January 1976, in Los Angeles. None of the former *Beatles* attended his funeral. He had been one of only two witnesses at the marriage of Paul McCartney to Linda Eastman in 1969. His family were so broke that eventually George Harrison gave them £5,000. In 1997 Sir Paul McCartney sued his widow Lily over a copyright matter.

She had wanted to auction off a scrap of paper on which McCartney wrote the lyrics to *With a Little Help From My Friends* thirty years earlier. She found the manuscript among papers left by Mal.
But McCartney served her with an injunction preventing the sale claiming that she was trying to sell something she didn't own.

He claimed that Mal Evans, was holding the lyrics for *The Beatles* as their employee. His lawyers got a legal injunction blocking the sale. Lily Evans, who has worked as a secretary since her husband's death twenty one year's previously, said that auctioneers at Sotheby's had estimated the paper could have fetched up to $100,000.

On further examination of this shooting two serious issued caused me concern. A suitcase that Mal was carrying at the time, containing unreleased recordings, photos, and other memorabilia, was taken away by police as "evidence" during the investigation, and subsequently lost. The suitcase became known as the lost "Mal Evans Archive." Beatles historians have regarded these archives as the holy grail.

Only recently have portions been planted on the internet. But why?

The second issue relates to the identity of the officer in charge when Mal was killed. His name is Lieutenant Charles Higbie of the LAPD robbery and homicide division. In his report he wrote:

> **Officers directed him to put down the rifle. He refused to put down the rifle. The officers then fired six shots, four of which struck Evans, killing him instantly.**

There was something about the name Charles Higbie that struck a cord with me so I searched for his name on my computer. Had I written about him before? I sure had, and so I did a little more digging on this gentleman. In 1987 Higbie retired from the LAPD after thirty years of service. Would you like to know what his role was? For thirteen years he investigated shootings by LAPD officers. On the 1 February 1987 the *Los Angeles Times* wrote:

> **Because his accounts almost always exonerated officers, critics have alleged that his evaluation of evidence was selective.**

By 1968 Higbie was a homicide detective in the LAPD and strangely enough involved in the investigation into the Sirhan Sirhan murder of Robert F. Kennedy. Lisa Pease is a respected journalist who is convinced that Sirhan did not shoot Kennedy.

Pease claims that the fact no official body has ever made a genuine effort to honestly examine all the evidence in this case is nearly as chilling as the original crime itself. This in itself points to a high level of what can only be termed "government involvement".

In the course of her article Sirhan and the RFK Assassination Part II: Rubik's Cube by Lisa Pease *Probe Magazine* March-April 1998 she writes:

> **It has often been said that a successful conspiracy requires not artful planning, but rather control of the investigation that follows. The investigation was controlled primarily by a few key LAPD officers and the DA. Despite Congressman Allard Lowenstein's efforts, no federal investigation of this case has ever taken place. In other words, a small handful of people were capable of keeping information that would**

> point to conspirators out of the public eye. The Warren Commission's conclusions were subjected to intense scrutiny when their documentation was published. Evidently the LAPD wanted no such scrutiny, and simply refused to release their files until ordered to do so in the late '80s.

One of those LAPD officers was none other than Charlie Higbie! And here's the bombshell:

> Charles Higbie, who controlled a good portion of the investigation, had been in the Marine Corps for five years and in Intelligence in the Marine Corps Reserve for eight more.

So, this begs the question, how is it that such a senior detective who had enough power and influence to have played an important role in the investigation into the assassination of Robert F. Kennedy eight years previously, found himself answering a domestic violence dispatch to a motel apartment in 1976? This senior detective insinuated himself into a "routine domestic quarrel" call, attended at the scene, and killed Mal Evans by discharging six shots four of which killed him. And this happened just a week before his book on *The Beatles* was due to be published. Now, I don't know about you, but I find this quite odd.

Others who died.

So, of those referred to in the page which is allegedly

part of Mal Evans' explosive book those that remained loyal to McCartney survived and thrived, i.e. Neil Aspinall, Pete Asher, Ringo Starr, Anita Pallengerg, and Tony Bramwell. The four others, John Lennon, George Harrison, Mal Evans, Robert Fraser and the two Brians, Epstein and Jones were cut down in their prime.

Epstein accidentally overdosed on drugs in 1967 aged 33. Jones was found floating face upwards in his own swimming pool in 1969 aged 27. Lennon was shot dead allegedly by a crazed fan in 1980 aged 40. Fraser died of a mystery illness in 1986 aged 49. Harrison survived an assassination attempt by a crazed fan in 1999 and died shortly afterwards aged 58. None of them died of natural causes.

On top of those, six other people, who became involved in the cover up also died in mysterious circumstances after the replacement of James Paul McCartney was effected.

In chronological order, those six comprise of Kevin MacDonald, MCartney's Agent who fell to his death on the 15 December 1966.

Tara Browne, McCartney's best friend who was killed in a car crash avoiding a head-on collision died on the 18 December 1966.

David Jacobs, McCartney's Lawyer who allegedly hung himself on the 15 December 1968.

Dr. Richard Asher, McCartney's Psychiatrist who also

hung himself in his cellar on the 25 April 1969.

Mr. John Riley, Cosmetic Dentist who died in a mysterious car accident in 1986. Once again, none of these people died of natural causes.

There is a *prima facie* case to answer in relation to these deaths, simply because there are so many of them and they are all connected with *The Beatles*. That does not, for one moment, suggest that *The Beatles* or anyone who worked for them were, in any way, involved, directly or indirectly with these deaths.

But let's look a little closer at these deaths.

KEVIN MACDONALD (R.I.P.)

On the 15 October 1966 the body of Kevin MacDonald, one of three founders of *Sibylla's* Nightclub in London, was found on the concrete canopy over the north entrance to King Charles House, Wandon Road, Fulham, London.

He had fallen eighty feet from the tenth floor of the building. No one witnessed the incident. There were two lifts and one stairways to the tenth floor and anyone could have entered the building and reached the floor without being noticed. The floor overlooks the Chelsea Football Club's ground Stamford Bridge and there was a reserve game being played that day when Mr. MacDonald fell. Mr. MacDonald was not a football supporter and was not in the building to watch a football match.

When he was found he had the sum of £8.14.10 change in his pockets.

The curious thing was he lived in Rectory Chambers, Old Church Street, Chelsea and no one had any idea why he would have been in this particular building.

Fingerprints taken from the windowsill of a window on the tenth floor matched those of the deceased and police gave evidence that the position of the fingerprints suggested that a person had been hanging outside the window by holding on to the top of it.

Evidence was given that he was an advertising executive with certain business interests.
Sibylla's nightclub was not mentioned at the inquest but we know that together with professional photographer Terry Howard and property developer Bruce Higham he had set it up.

Newspaper reports headlined the death as a "mystery" and stated:

> **The mystery of how a young man's body came to be on the entrance canopy to a block of council flats near his home on Saturday remained unsolved this week….The body was discovered by Mr. and Mrs. Ernest Payne at 2.15 p.m. when they were going out for a walk.**
>
> **Mr. Payne (42) thought it was a drunk and called the caretaker, Mr. Robert Hughes (31) of the block next door, Harriet House. Mr. Hughes said**

> 'I took a ladder and found the boy. I could see at once he was dead. There was not very much blood and the only physical thing you could see from the back was that his arm bone had come through his jacket.'...It is believed that he died about noon. There is no suspicion of foul play.

Family relative Teresa Stokes told me that "the Coroner had no absolutely doubt that it was suicide, for example there was no sign of a struggle, and Kevin had been suffering from depression and had previously tried to kill himself with an overdose of sleeping tablets. He had recently been hospitalised for depression and schizophrenia but checked himself out."

In his book, *Once More With Feeling: A Story of Music, Love and Adoption*, Gerry Morris who played with the sixties band *The Cymbaline* wrote an interesting piece about this nightclub:

> **Laurie was really pleased for us and he literally cracked a smile as we left to drive back to Redbridge. He gave us an official contract from the organisation he represented, The Charles Kray Entertainment Agency. (Charlie was the older brother of East London's infamous Kray twins, Ronnie and Reggie.) We couldn't wait to perform at Sybillas.**

The Laurie referred to was Laurie O'Leary, the club's manager. O'Leary formed the agency in partnership with Charlie Kray. It would not be unreasonable to assume that if the club was being run by a Kray employee then the club security would have been supplied by the Kray twins themselves. If not the twins would have wanted, and would have taken, a large cut of the proceeds anyway.

Glasgow crime lord Arthur Thompson once claimed that the Krays had been interested in taking over *The Beatles* from Brian Epstein. Were they the ones who were blackmailing him over information stolen from his briefcase by his onetime American lover Dizz Gillespie?

Conspiracy theorists claim that MacDonald was silenced because he knew that James Paul McCartney had died and *The Beatles* wanted to replace him and was too unstable to keep his mouth shut.

THE HON. TARA BROWNE (R.I.P.)

Next to die in mysterious circumstances was twenty one year old socialite and close friend of James Paul McCartney, the Honourable Tara Browne, heir to the Guinness fortune.

Browne was the son of Dominick Browne, 4th Baron Oranmore and Browne, a member of the House of Lords since 1927 and Oonagh Guinness, heiress to the Guinness fortune and the youngest of the three "Golden Guinness Girls".

On the 18 December 1966, Browne was driving with his girlfriend, model Suki Potier, in his Lotus Elan through South Kensington at excessive speed.

Depending on who you believe he either swerved to avoid an oncoming car which failed to stop or neglected to see a traffic light and proceeded through the junction of Redcliffe Square and Redcliffe Gardens, colliding with a parked lorry. He died of his injuries the following day.

Potier claimed Browne swerved the car to absorb the impact of the crash to save her life. According to her, Browne tried to avoid a car coming straight at him. Why would a car be driving straight at him if only to put his off the road?

He swerved to avoid it and crashed into another one trying to save her. She also claimed Browne was not going particularly fast when he drove down Earls Court Road into Redcliffe Gardens.
He was survived by his wife (Nicky) nee MacSherry, the daughter of a County Down farmer, and their two sons, Dorian and Julian Browne. The couple were already estranged in what was then a very public battle for custody in the High Courts.

Conspiracy theorists claim that Browne was deliberately killed (in the same way as Princess Diana was killed) because he was about to announce that his good friend, the real James Paul McCartney, had been permanently replaced by an imposter. The day of the crash Sir Paul McCartney attended the premiere of *The Family Way* with Jane Asher in a theatre just a few miles from the tragedy.

BRIAN EPSTEIN (R.I.P)

The next person to die was Brian Epstein on the 27 August 1967 supposedly from an accidental overdose of drugs because he was depressed and couldn't cope any longer.

But Epstein was coping very well and his other acts like Georgie Fame, Cilla Black, *Gerry and the Pacemakers* and others were making serious money for him. He had everything to look forward to.

Only those in the inner circle knew the real story about Brian Epstein and his demons. Essentially, Brian Epstein was a kind and caring man who never wished any harm on anyone. Unfortunately for him he was also a homosexual in a time when homosexual acts between consenting adults were illegal.

He was also addicted to prescribed drugs and a compulsive gambler. He suffered from depression and was involved, albeit peripherally, with some of London's most notorious gangsters, including the Kray brothers.

Very few people knew he was a homosexual and it was only revealed to the general public years after he died. But it was an open secret among his friends and business colleagues.

He was known to cruise the gay bars of London dressed as a British army officer and was once arrested for impersonating one.

Epstein himself admitted that his first homosexual experience occurred when he returned to Liverpool after being discharged from the army for being medically unfit (i.e. homosexual.)

He spent a year studying acting at RADA, but dropped out shortly after his arrest for "persistent importuning" outside a men's public toilet in Swiss Cottage, London. McCartney said that when Epstein started to manage *The Beatles* they knew that he was homosexual but did not care. He was an excellent manager who encouraged them professionally and offered them access to previously off-limits social circles.

John Lennon was known to make frequent sarcastic comments about Epstein's homosexuality but only made them to friends and to Epstein personally, and never to anyone outside the group's inner circle.

In fact, *The Beatles* were very protective of him and never allowed people speak about Brian's sexual proclivities; not because it might bring them negative publicity bit out of respect for the man himself.

On one occasion, Ian Sharp, an art school friend of Lennon, made a childish sarcastic remark about Epstein, saying, "Which one of you [Beatles] does he fancy?"

Although he later apologized Sharp later received a letter from McCartney directing him to have no contact with any of them in the future. It was a measure of their loyalty to their manager.

Epstein frequently took weekend holidays to Amsterdam and Barcelona where he engaged in homosexual activity. In his biography, Pete Best, mentions an incident in Blackpool when Epstein made a pass at him. Best politely declined an the incident was never mentioned again.

Rumours were rife that he had a "special relationship" with Lennon but Lennon always claimed that the relationship although special was never anything more. In 1980 he told *Playboy* magazine:

> **Well, it was almost a love affair, but not quite. It was never consummated but we did have a pretty intense relationship.**

Lennon once joked that Epstein's book, A *Cellarful of Noise*, should really have been called *A Cellarful of Boys*.

Almost as soon as he began managing the group he became addicted to stimulants, usually *Preludin*. He claimed he took them only because they kept him alert at night during numerous concert tours. He later developed a dependency on *Carbitral* which is a sleeping pill.

He later graduated to more serious drugs. During the four months when the *Sgt. Pepper* album was being recorded, Epstein spent his time on holiday, or at the Priory Clinic in Putney, where he tried unsuccessfully to curb his drug use.

He left the Priory to attend the *Sgt. Pepper* launch party at his house on 24 Chapel Street, but returned to the Priory immediately afterwards. A frequent cannabis user and supporter he often called for its decriminalization. In June 1967, after McCartney had admitted to LSD use, Epstein defended him to the media, stating that he had taken the drug himself.

Brian Epstein was also a compulsive gambler and a frequent visitor to many of London's gambling clubs including Curzon House where he often lost thousands of pounds by playing *baccarat* or *chemin de fer*. His losses were known to be substantial. It was because of these demons that Epstein was a perfect candidate for blackmail.

The last time Brian saw his beloved *Beatles* was when he visited them at a recording session on the 23 August 1967, at the Chappell Recording Studios on Maddox Street, London.

The following day he asked some friends down to his home Kingsley Hill, Warbleton, Sussex for the bank holiday weekend. Soon after they arrived he decided to drive back to London alone. This was because he had engaged a group of rent boys for the weekend and they failed to turn up, although they did after he left. Pat Conroy was one of those rent boys.

At about 5.00 pm on the following day a "very groggy" Epstein phoned his friend Peter Brown who tried to persuade him to return to his country home and to take a train back down to the nearest railway station, in Uckfield, instead of driving under the influence of Tuinals.

According to Brown, Epstein told him he would have something to eat, read his mail and watch *Juke Box Jury* before phoning Brown to tell him which train to meet. He never called again. On the 27 August 1967 Brian Epstein died of an overdose of *Carbitral*, in the bedroom of his London house.

He was discovered after his butler had knocked on the door, and then hearing no response, asked the housekeeper to call the police. Detectives found him lying on a single bed, dressed in pyjamas, with various correspondence scattered around him. When news filtered through to the group in Bangor they were stunned, shocked and deeply saddened.

At the subsequent inquest his death was officially ruled an accident; caused by a gradual build-up of *Carbitral* in his system, combined with an excess of alcohol.

The death was rule as accidental by Coroner Gavin Thurston. Pathologist, Dr. Donald Teare, stated that Epstein had been taking bromide in the form of *Carbitral* for some time, and that the barbiturate level in his blood was a "low fatal level".

In his memoir, *The Love you Make: An Insider's story of the Beatles* (1983) Brown stated that he had once found a suicide note written by Epstein and had spoken with him about it. Part of the note read:

This is all too much and I can't take it any more.

When Brown confronted him about the note Epstein

asked him not to tell anyone explaining he had, at the time, taken one pill too many but had no intention of overdosing. He also promised him to be more careful in the future.

Although suicide was denied by all around Brian there are strong suggestions that he was unable to cope with the deceit involved in replacing the real Paul with the fake one and decided that he couldn't live with the guilt.

DAVID JACOBS (R.I.P.)

Then there was McCartney's London lawyer, the flamboyant David Jacobs. Like Brian, Jacobs was Jewish, homosexual and another prodigious user of amphetamines. Jacobs had worked for a long time for Epstein and *The Beatles* as well as other famous clients including Marlene Dietrich, Sir Laurence Olivier, Judy Garland, Liberace and Diana Dors.

He was found hanging from a length of satin from one of the beams of his garage in Hove, Sussex in December 1968 after reportedly having turned down the opportunity to represent Ronnie and Reggie Kray as the defence lawyer in their forthcoming trial for double murder. But why would David Jacobs kill himself?

David Jacobs was every bit as theatrical as the clients he represented. At over six foot three, with his hair dyed jet black he cut a suave and commanding figure.

Openly gay at a time when homosexual acts between consenting adults were illegal, he often appeared in court complete with make-up, much to the consternation of the legal profession.

He employed a chauffeur to drive his two-tone pink-and-maroon Rolls-Royce and allegedly kept a table on permanent reserve at Le Caprice restaurant in Piccadilly.

His assistant Peter Maddock described him in the following terms:

> **David was one of those big people who moved like a ship under sail. Quick on his feet. He was a personality.**

Gregarious and highly sociable Jacobs was famous for throwing extravagant parties at his home in Chelsea, and at his home in Hove which he shared with his mum.

As Brian Epstein's assistant Peter Brown once said:

> **There was always an implication that if you need anything, come to David. David knew everyone and could always fix something for you.**

Epstein and Jacobs were close friends and had much in common. They were both were Jewish, addicted to uppers and downers, homosexual and their families were involved in the furniture business. Epstein trusted Jacobs implicitly and told him everything. Was this why he was silenced? By 1968, something was deeply troubling him. According to Peter Maddock who was one of the few who knew he had been admitted to the Priory Clinic:

> **It was all hushed up. He was very much a shadow of himself. He'd lost an enormous amount of weight. There was clearly some major issue preying on his mind, a number of things, perhaps. It was obvious he was in trouble.**

Peter Brown once told the story about how he and society tailor Tommy Nutter were invited to spend the weekend in Hove in November 1968:

> **It was very strange. David was very hospitable, trying his best to be charming and nice to us, but he was very edgy. He was definitely on something. Jacobs's lover, John Barr, was in a different part of the house. We never saw him. It was all very creepy. When we left to go back to London, Tommy said: 'I never want to go back there again.'**

Three weeks later Jacobs was found dead. At the inquest, his brother Basil said that Jacobs had been concerned over tax problems. But Jacobs had left over £105,000 in his will. It was reported that following his death, police had found "almost indecipherable notes" in Jacobs's hand in his red smoking jacket, leading them to question a number of young men and "several well-known and titled people" including *The Beatles*.

A private investigator, John Merry, who often worked for Jacobs told newspapers at the time that there were "certain things" going on in Jacobs's life and that he had telephoned him two days before his death, saying:

"I'm in terrible trouble. They're all after me," and reeled off the names of six prominent figures in show business. When the investigator tried to reassure him, Jacobs rang off.

There were suggestions that shortly before his death, Jacobs was approached by an emissary of the gangster Ronnie Kray, who wanted him to defend the twins in a forthcoming trial involving the murder of George Cornell and Jack "The Hat" McVitie. Jacobs, it is said, refused to help, and had asked for police protection.

However, Peter Maddock doubts the story, or that Jacobs and Kray were acquainted and stated that "David was not involved with gangsters. It wasn't his style."

But Maddock has another story to tell. Shortly after Jacobs's death, Maddock visited the playwright Robin Maugham, a close friend of Jacobs, at his home in Hove. Maugham had something to show him. It was a Christmas card from Jacobs. "All love and best wishes for the New Year. David." It had been posted two days before his death, Maddock says. Hardly the actions of a man who was planning on killing himself.

Another friend was the beautiful young English actress Suzanna Leigh whom he had known since she was a child. Jacobs had advised Suzanna in her film career which had seen her signed to Paramount Pictures by the legendary Hollywood producer Hal Wallis. Following her return from Los Angeles to her home in Belgravia, Suzanna was heartbroken to read in the newspapers of Jacobs' death on the 15

December 1968. A few minutes after she had read the about his death she picked up a postcard which had just dropped through the letterbox. It was from David Jacobs, inviting her to lunch at La Caprice the following week:

> **I was holding the newspaper telling me he was dead in one hand and the postcard inviting me to lunch in the other. It didn't seem right.**

It didn't seem right because it wasn't right. Jacobs was murdered but by whom and for what reason?

JANE ASHER

Jane Asher was Paul McCartney's girlfriend between 1963 and 1968. During this five year period McCartney was also sleeping with at least one dozen other people.

The relationship is particularly significant in the minds of conspiracy theorists as it straddles the all-important time frame during which James Paul McCartney died, became incapacitated or retired and was replaced by the gentleman now known as Sir Paul McCartney.

If such a replacement ever occurred it would not be unreasonable to assume that Jane Asher was aware of it. But she has never spoken of it. In fact, she has for nearly fifty years refused to discuss or talk about or answer a single question in relation to McCartney.

Why?

If everything was alright - girl meets boy, girls falls in love with boy, boy is constantly unfaithful, boy and girl split up – then what's not to tell? Sure, we had a relationship, we were engaged, it didn't work out, we split up. But it is her very refusal to answer a single question about the entire affair which makes the conspiracy theory more believable. Some say her father was murdered and she was told that if she spoke about it she too would be murdered. That would be enough to stop me from talking. But now, fifty years on?

There are suggestions that her father Dr. Richard Asher was involved in Government sponsored mind control experiments involving LSD with two other top London psychiatrists Emmanuel Millar and William Sargent. They were unofficially supplied with drugs from the Metropolitan Police Force and undertook secret experiments on volunteers to determine the effect these mind-altering drugs had.

There are further suggestions, never fully substantiated, that Asher used McCartney as one such guinea pig. It is known that he and his wife Margaret were both psychic and telepathic and never trusted McCartney. Dr. Asher was found hanging in his cellar after having gone missing for a day.

LSD was discovered by Albert Hoffman in 1938. Sandoz AG, a Swiss pharmaceutical company introduced the drug onto the market in 1947. This led to a CIA program called MK-Ultra.

It began in the 1950s and its purpose was to conduct experiments on CIA agents using LSD. Some committed suicide resulting in massive lawsuits against the US government. It is believed that similar experiments were conducted in the UK.

LSD was seen as a wonder drug that would be useful in mind control. One such volunteer was a gentleman called Ken Kesey who went on to write *One Flew Over the Cuckoo's Nest*. Strangely enough, an American called Ken Kesey was employed by Apple Records in London in 1969. This fact is often used by those who argue that *The Beatles* were involved wittingly or unwittingly in Government sponsored projects concerning mind control.

Which brings us back to Jane Asher. Is she really still hiding a terrible secret, a secret that Heather Mills said if revealed would shock people:

Remember what Heather Mills had said:

> **I found out he had betrayed me immensely and I don't mean infidelity or anything like that. Like beyond belief. ...I've got to protect myself. I have to protect myself. People don't want to know what the truth is because they could never ever handle it, they'd be too devastated.**

Is this also how Jane Asher feels? Today Jane Asher is happily married to the same man, Gerard Scarfe, for nearly 35 years and bakes cakes for a living.

Jane Asher was born in London on the 5 April 1946,

to Richard Asher, a psychiatrist, and his wife Margaret. Dr. Asher was a consultant in blood and mental disease at Central Middlesex Hospital in Acton, London. He was also a broadcaster and author of a number of notable medical papers. Margaret Asher was a professor of the oboe at the Guildhall School of Music and Drama. One of her pupils was George Martin, who produced much of the *Beatles'* music. George studied piano and oboe at the school between 1947 and 1950.

Jane was educated at Queen's College in London's Harley Street. She began her acting career at the age of five, playing the role of Nina in the 1952 film *Mandy*. She the appeared in a number of films, including *The Quatermass Xperiment* (1955), *The Greengage Summer* (1961), *The Prince And The Pauper* (1962) and *Alfie* (1966). She also appeared in numerous television programs, including a spot as a panellist on the BBC music show *Juke Box Jury*.

She met James Paul McCartney for the first time on the 18 April 1963, prior to a performance by *The Beatles* at the Royal Albert Hall in London. She was just seventeen. According to McCartney in *Anthology*:

> **I met Jane Asher when she was sent by the Radio Times to cover a concert we were in at the Royal Albert Hall - we had a photo taken with her for the magazine and we all fancied her. We'd thought she was blonde, because we had only ever seen her on black-and-white telly doing Juke Box Jury, but she turned out to be a redhead. So it was: 'Wow, you're a redhead!' I tried pulling her, succeeded, and we were boyfriend and girlfriend for quite a long time.**

They went on a number of dates in London, and their romance became public when they were photographed leaving the *Prince of Wales* theatre after watching Neil Simon's play *Never Too Late*. Thereafter they became a serious item. In her book *A Twist of Lennon,* Cynthia Lennon wrote:

> **Paul was obviously as proud as a peacock with his new lady. For Paul, Jane Asher was a great prize.**

By summer 1963 *The Beatles* had become household names, and found it difficult staying in hotels and walking around London unhampered.

Although they went to plays and clubs, McCartney and Asher often stayed in at her parent' home at 57 Wimpole Street, in Chelsea. It was a six storey townhouse and Jane's mother agreed to let him move into the attic room, on his own. McCartney described his time with the Asher family to Barry Miles:

> **It was really like culture shock in the way they ran their lives, because the doctor obviously had a quite tight diary, but all of them ran it that way. They would do things that I'd never seen before, like at dinner there would be word games. Now I'm bright enough, but mine is an intuitive brightness. I could just about keep up with that and I could always say, 'I don't know that word.' I was always honest. In fact, I was able to enjoy and take part fully in their thing.**

McCartney actually lived at the house for three years. The change of environment greatly broadened his cultural horizons. Here was a working class lad from

Liverpool literally adopted by an upper class culturally aware establishment family. Margaret Asher taught him to play the recorder and provided him with music tuition in a music room in the basement.

It was here that Lennon and McCartney wrote many songs including *I Want To Hold Your Hand* and *Yesterday*.

Paul and Jane often went on holiday together, when their busy schedules allowed. In September 1963 they spent two weeks in Greece with Ringo Starr and his future wife Maureen. There was another holiday with Ringo and Maureen in the Bahamas.
Later on the pair tended to have weekend breaks in the countryside. Ringo thought they would marry:

> **I think we expected Paul and Jane Asher to get married. They were lovers, they were together, and it seemed a natural thing to do. I don't know in the end what actually broke them up. We'll have to ask him about that, or ask her – that's probably more interesting!**

But Jane Asher was an independent, head-strong lady with a mind of her own. She was more interested in pursuing her acting career rather than being someone's girlfriend. This undoubtedly caused friction.

During the course of the entire relationship McCartney remained unfaithful to her. He slept with actress Jill Haworth during *The Beatles'* February 1964 visit to America and also had an affair the same year with actress Peggy Lipton, as well as scores of groupies across the world.

> I didn't treat women as most people do. I've always had a lot around, even when I've had a steady girl. My life generally has always been very lax, and not normal. I knew I was selfish. it caused a few rows. Jane left me once and went off to Bristol to act. I said OK then, leave, I'll find someone else. It was shattering to be without her.

In 1966 Jane helped him pick out a house in Cavendish Avenue, London, and they moved into it in 1966.

In the same year she also encouraged him to buy High Farm in Machrihanish, Campbeltown, Scotland, as a country retreat. The same year he began a three year affair with model Maggie McGivern.

In 1967 Jane began a five-month tour of America with the Bristol Old Vic, appearing in *Romeo And Juliet* in Boston, Washington and Philadelphia. McCartney flew over to America to celebrate her 21st birthday. But, at this stage, the writing was on the wall:

> When I came back after five months, Paul had changed so much. He was on LSD, which I hadn't shared. I was jealous of all the spiritual experiences he'd had with John. There were fifteen people dropping in all day long. The house had changed and was full of stuff I didn't know about.

Paul certainly had changed so much. Was he even the same person? The man who was so violently against LSD was now advocating its use. In an infamous television interview the following exchange occurred:

Reporter:

> So, now you seem to be encouraging your fans to take drugs!

McCartney:

> No, I don't think my fans are going to take drugs just because I did. That's not the point anyway. I was asked whether I had [taken LSD] or not, and from then on the whole bit about how far it's going to go, and how many people it's going to encourage, is up to the newspapers, and up to you.

Reporter:

> But as a public figure surely you've got a responsibility to ...

McCartney:

> I'm not trying to spread the word about this. The man from the newspaper is the man from the mass media. I'll keep it a personal thing if he does, too, you know... It's his responsibility for spreading it, not mine. You are spreading it now at this moment. This is going into all the homes in Britain, and I'd rather it didn't. You're asking me the question, you want me to be honest, I'll be honest. But it's you lot who've got the responsibility not to spread this.

A few days later the *Daily Mirror* published a scathing editorial entitled "Beatle Paul, MBE, LSD and BF (Bloody Fool)," the *Daily Mirror* charged that he had behaved "like an irresponsible idiot," and suggested that he should see a psychiatrist.

Epstein was forced to grant several interviews to journalists the following month, defending the *Beatle's* statements about the drug. But the damage was done. The public had seen a different side to Paul McCartney.

Those who worked with him were astounded by the change in him. Dr. and Margaret Asher were far from impressed and genuinely concerned for their daughter's well-being.

Meanwhile the media carried frequent predictions and rumours of McCartney and Asher getting married. Perhaps because of this pressure they announced their engagement on Christmas Day 1967. Shortly afterwards, in February and March 1968, she accompanied *The Beatles* to India.

But their five-year relationship eventually fizzled out as McCartney's string of infidelities, including Francie Schwatrz and Linda Eastman, became public knowledge around London.

Jane's mother Margaret called around to Cavendish Road to collect her belongings. Jane publicly announced the end of their engagement on the 20 July edition of the BBC television show Dee Time:

> **I haven't broken it off, but it is broken off, finished. I know it sounds corny, but we still see each other and love each other, but it hasn't worked out. Perhaps we'll be childhood**

> **sweethearts and meet again and get married when we're about seventy.**

Asher met the political cartoonist Gerald Scarfe in 1971 at the 10th anniversary party of *Private Eye* magazine, of which she is a shareholder. Their first child Katie was born in April 1974; they married in 1981, and had two sons: Alexander in 1981 and Rory in 1984.

As well as acting, Asher has also written three novels and more than a dozen books on lifestyle, cake decoration and costuming. She has also developed the best-selling Jane Asher range of cake mixes.
About the relationship McCartney once said:

> **I liked her a lot and we got on very well. She was a very intelligent and very interesting person, but I just never clicked. One of those indefinable things about love is some people you click with and some people who you should maybe click with you don't. Whatever.**

While maintaining an affair with Maggie McGivern McCartney then began sleeping with Linda Eastman, an American photographer and groupie who had slept her way around over twenty rock and roll stars and actors on the cover of photographing them. McGivern later described the situation:

> **One day, a little after we returned from Sardinia, I rang Paul and Linda answered the phone. I had seen a newspaper story about him having lunch with her before that, but I wasn't the type to ask questions or get jealous. I remember Paul telling Linda to get off the phone and I asked him who**

she was and what was happening. He said: 'I don't know the scene, man. I don't know what's going on'.

Sometime later McGivern received a very late night and peculiar visit from McCartney.

> He was really down and I couldn't seem to get a word out of him. He was crying and I knew he had been stressed. I stood and held him and asked him to tell me what was wrong. Then suddenly he jumped up and said he had to go. Somehow I knew when I closed the door that night I wouldn't see him again.

Two days later McGivern discovered that McCartney had married Linda Eastman when she saw the headline on a newspaper billboard on King's Road.

Jane's brother Peter was one half of the hit sixties singing duo *Peter and Gordon*. He later went on to become a record producer. He believed that McCartney and his sister would marry, despite McCartney's constant, "just good friends" posturing to the news media.

In an interview in the *Daily Express* in 1967 which would have been after McCartney had been replaced, if you believe the conspiracy theory, Asher was quoted as saying:

> I love Paul. I love him very deeply, and he feels the same. I don't think either of us has looked at anyone else since we first met. ... I want to get married probably this year and have lots and lots of babies. I certainly would be surprised indeed if I

married anyone but Paul.

Was she the only person in London who didn't know he was constantly sleeping with other women? McCartney never spoke much about Asher after the split except for a 1986 *Playboy* interview when he said:

We nearly did get married. But it always used to fall short of the mark and something happened. And one of us would think it wasn't right, for which I'm obviously glad now. Jane and I had a long, good relationship. I still like her. I don't know whether she likes me, but I don't see any reason why not. We don't see each other at all.

Was Jane Asher really threatened into remaining silent about the switch? There is no doubt she, of all people, would have known. It's just that she doesn't seem to be the type of person who would involve themselves in such a massive deceit.

In 2004 she told journalist David Thomas from the *Daily Telegraph*:

Life is bloody dark and awful. It doesn't mean I go round being permanently depressed. But I would if I really started to think about things. I don't think there's any meaning to anything. I have slightly more of an acceptance that you're hurtling towards the abyss. At least you won't know anything once you're in it.

A strange comment to make from a happily married mother of two who makes her money baking cakes.

Have the conspiracy theorists got it wrong?

If James Paul McCartney did not die in 1966 in a car crash, either in the incident involving his *Rolling Stones* friends and his Mini Cooper allegedly driven by Mohammed Hadjij, or in the subsequent accident in his Aston Martin in France, then why did *The Beatles* leave so many hidden messages and clues about Paul dying in a car accident?

There is a reason for everything and there is a reason for this. Earlier in the book we confirmed that it was *The Beatles* themselves that started a rumour in 1967 that McCartney had died, simply by denying it.

Then on the cover of the *St. Pepper's* album there is, for no apparent or explainable reason, a toy car sitting in a doll's lap. The doll wears a sweater reading "Welcome, The Rolling Stones." Also, for no apparent reason, there's a picture of two cars meeting on a darkened road on page 14 of the *Magical Mystery Tour* booklet. If these aren't references to Mohammed Hadjij's accident, or to "Paul's death" (as denied by *The Beatles*), then what do they mean and why are they there?

So, did *The Beatles* use the Mini Cooper incident as the inspiration for the hoax and, if so, why? There has never been an admission that *The Beatles* had a direct hand in the Paul Is Dead rumour.

In fact, they have always denied culpability, but they have never been the most honest in their memoirs and the sheer overwhelming abundance of "coincidences" and "clues" deliberately planted in their five subsequent albums certainly casts doubt on their statements. Clearly something is amiss.

As to why they would even entertain undertaking such a bizarre exercise it's helpful to revisit the time period when all of this happened. Less than a year earlier the band had become fed-up with screaming *Beatlemania* and decided to stop touring in order to concentrate on their music. This involved a huge risk.

Before then no pop band had ever attempted to cross the cultural divide from teen idol to serious artist. And no successful band had ever suddenly decided to stop touring. They were intending to ignore an existing substantial fan base in search of a new one. Would their existing fans take to their new mature style?

Before the release of *Sgt. Pepper's* most critics believed that they would fall at the first hurdle. In fact, the British media had already labelled them as "washed-up" and "out of ideas." A lot was riding on their next move and it was a tense time, make or break time.

Therefore one has to ask if it is really such a stretch to think that four intelligent young men like *The Beatles* might want to take out a little insurance against the possible failure of *Sgt. Pepper's* by cooking up a fantastical scheme as bizarre as the Paul Is Dead Rumour?

They weren't adverse to mischief. They had previously placed backwards singing on "Rain," singing "tit, tit, tit" on the choruses of "Girl" and managed to slip the phrase "Paul's a queer" into the ultimate kiddies' song, "Yellow Submarine?" Is it possible that their theory was that if the *Sgt. Pepper* album failed then the band could slowly reveal the "clues as to Paul's demise" some months, or even years, later in order to spur sagging album sales?

Were they embarrassed at the premature discovery of the scheme? Did this account for their later adamant denials? Come to think of it, it really is a brilliant marketing idea.

Remember what producer Joel Gilbert said:

> **It is clear, unmistakable and undeniable that there were in fact numerous intentional "clues" placed by the Beatles in their music that Paul McCartney had died. However, whether it was just dry British humour of bored Beatles messing with their fans, or for some other purpose, is up to Beatles fans to ponder.**

This raises the question: Has Sir Paul McCartney deliberately and systematically deceived millions of *Beatles'* fans for nearly fifty years by perpetuating a hoax involving his own death in an effort to increase sales? Is this the betrayal Heather Mills spoke about?

Even today the Paul Is Dead controversy rages on the internet, seducing a new generation of *Beatles'* fans and increasing the bank balances of *The Beatles'* vast organization in general and McCartney's in particular. So who is fuelling the hoax on the internet today? Let me introduce you to Mr. Neil Aspinall.

Iamaphoney is central to the PID conspiracy. It is the user name of an individual or a group of individuals that have been disseminating "insider" information for years on the alleged death of James Paul McCartney.

They are so adept in this exercise that they have convinced many die-hard conspiracy theorists that they have secret knowledge that McCartney died and was replaced and that all will be revealed in the fullness of time. It's all very fanciful I hear you say but where's the logic to all of this. In other words who benefits? That's a good question.

If the whole Paul is Dead conspiracy theory is untrue it was not conjured up for fun. Too much work went into it and too much work continues to go into sustaining and renewing interest in it. This leads us back to the question: who does it benefit?

Who owns *The Beatles'* music? The music is owned by the record company for whom they were recorded. EMI is the ultimate owner. The company Parlaphone was a wholly owned subsidiary.

When *The Beatles* began recording on their own Apple label it was purely with the express consent of EMI. *The Beatles* were still under contract to EMI when Apple was set up so Apple could only record unsigned artists. Apple did not own *The Beatles'* music.

Royalties are a separate matter. The songwriter usually receives 50% of the royalty when their song is played.

That means that Lennon and McCartney received the vast majority of the royalties that accrued to *Beatles'* songs. Another lucrative market is the publishing rights.

In February 1963 Dick James persuaded Brian Epstein that forming a company with Lennon, McCartney and Epstein would result in a lot more money in the future.

Lennon and McCartney were either led to believe or wrongly assumed that they would, in fact, own the entire company but that is not what happened. Lennon received 20 shares, McCartney 20, Epstein 10 while James and his partner controlled the remaining 50 shares. The company was called Northern Songs.

The agreement further provided that the company would own the copyright to 56 songs and that Lennon and McCartney would write a minimum of six new songs every year. Another company Maclen Music, which published Lennon and McCartney's songs in the States was also controlled by Northern Songs.

The profits accrued by Northern songs were channelled into another company called Lenmac Enterprises. Lennon owned 20% of this company, McCartney 20% and Epsteins' NEMs Company a further 20% but the company only collected profits from UK sales. In 1965 Northern Songs was floated on the stock exchange.

At the end of the flotation ownership of the company

was divided as follows:

James and Silver	37.5%
Financial Institutions and Miscellaneous	23.4%
John Lennon	15%
Paul McCartney	15%
NEMs	7.5%
Starkey and Harrison	1.4%

Lennon and McCartney then signed a contract binding themselves to Northern Songs until 1973. Realizing that Lennon and McCartney were the company's most important assets Dick James took out life assurance on each of them for £500,000.

If James Paul McCartney died in 1966 one would have expected Dick James to cash in the policy.

He didn't.

Later in 1969 James and Silver quietly sold their shares to Lew Grade's ATV without giving Lennon or McCartney and opportunity to bid for them.

The purchase price was £1,525,000. Several months later ATV offered to buy out Lennon and McCartney for £9,000,000. They declined.

Then unable to buy out ATV Lennon and McCartney

decided to sell out their interest to them but retained royalties from their published songs.

In 1990 McCartney was offered the opportunity to buy back the songs for £20 million but thought the price was too high. Eventually in 1985 a smarter Michael Jackson bought the publishing rights for £24,400,000.

McCartney was furious and felt that Jackson had wiped his eye. But, of course, he hadn't.

What is relevant here, in the context of the conspiracy theory, is that when Michael Jackson bought Northern Songs he also acquired the still valid and unclaimed life policy on Paul McCartney. Jackson later sold out at a vast profit to Sony.

Today control of *The Beatles'* empire is split between Sony and Apple Corps. Apple Corps was conceived by Brian Epstein but after his mysterious death the project proper did not begin until after 1968. The company's first project was the film *Magical Mystery Tour*. It was produced by Apple Films.

In 1969 power in this division was transferred from Alan Klein to Neil Aspinall, a childhood friend of Lennon, McCartney and Harrison.

Within a relatively short period of time Aspinall went from *Beatles* roadie to the managing director of Apple Corps. That was some promotion.

His role in the entire conspiracy theory is pivotal. He

is believed to be the author of the famous "False Rumour" article in the *Beatles'* monthly magazine which started the rumour in the first place. In fact, he was a regular contributor to the magazine. He didn't always write under his own name. Actually, he wrote under the name Billy Shepherd!

More recently Neil Aspinall began contributing to various conspiracy websites using different aliases. One such alias was Apollo C. Vermouth.

This is the name McCartney used for producing a song for the *Bonzo Dog Doo Dah Band*.

As Redwell Trabant writes in *The Beatles Book of Revelations* (2014) :

> **Comments left by this user tended to be cryptic, though supportive, clues designed to further the ever expanding internet fuelled Paul is Dead conspiracy.**

Trabant also tells us that *Iamaphoney* has been heavily involved in the renaissance of the conspiracy theory and has, since 2006, been instrumental in releasing video films which seek to expand the original theory "well beyond its original confines."

Those involved in producing the videos have clearly been financed along the way as the production values have greatly increased since their original debut. Not only that but they appear to have unlimited access to original *Beatles'* archives.

Was Neil Aspinall the man behind *Iamaphoney?*

He is the revisionist who created the *Beatles' Anthology* which rewrote the real history of *The Beatles*. He also had access to the archives. Many believe that Aspinall's company Standby Films was the main financier for *Iamaphoney*.

Both Standby Films Limited and Apple Corps, although they had different directors, shared the same company secretary.

Standby Films ceased to trade in 2009 but a search of the ownership of its website in 2011 showed that it shared the same email address with Apple Corps!

The significance of this is that if *Iamaphoney* was funded by Aspinall's company then it would not be unreasonable to suggest that it was, in fact, funded by *The Beatles* themselves.

Aspinall died a multimillionaire in 2006. So, who runs the *Iamaphoney* Facebook page now? According to Trabant it is owned by Martin Heurlin, Hans Buchardt and Martin Lind. So, perhaps the whole conspiracy theory is a deliberate hoax on *The Beatles'* fans?

Perhaps.

It's time for Sir Paul McCartney to begin answering the questions people have been asking for nearly fifty years.

Is he an imposter or just screwing with his loyal fans

to make even more money for himself? You decide.

Meanwhile, take a look at his extract from the IAMAPHONEY document.

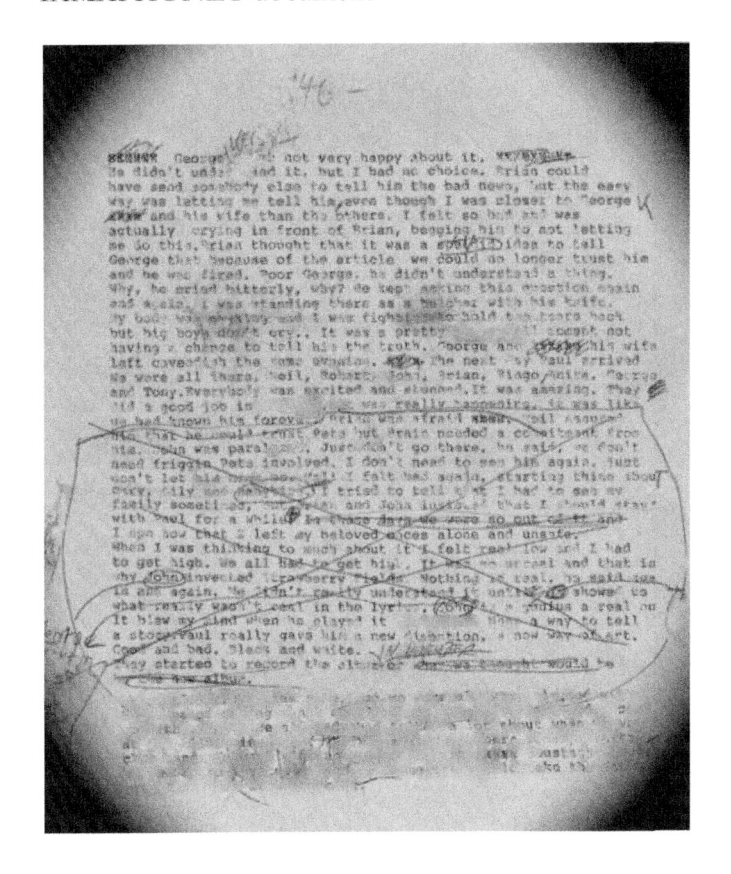

I don't understand you, said Alice. It's dreadfully confusing.

Alice in Wonderland

Yes it is dreadfully confusing, isn't it?

The very possibility that McCartney died and was replaced, if true, would be the story of the century. Is this what Heather Mills was hinting at? Or, was it something more mundane? At this stage, if it were true, the final story will only be revealed after the death of Sir Paul McCartney. There again, maybe it will never be revealed.

Meanwhile the main protagonists just get on with their lives. As of early 2017:

Yoko Ono

In an interview with the *Daily Mail* published on the 29 November 2015 BBC Radio One DJ Andy Peebles gave a very candid account of an interview he carried out with Yoko Ono and John Lennon two days before Lennon was shot dead.

Peebles claimed that by 1980 the marriage between Lennon and Ono was a sham and that Ono was already involved in a long term relationship with her lover Sam Havadtoy. The purpose of the BBC interview was to promote their new album *Double Fantasy* with the objective of restoring Lennon's profile after a five-year absence.

Peebles also claimed that at the time Lennon was immersed in scandal and controversy due to his drug use; was afraid the Nixon administration would boot him out of America and was terrified to travel back to Britain in case the U.S. immigration authorities would prevent him returning to the States.

Peebles found the diminutive artist Yoko Ono to be arrogant and conceited. At 47, Peebles described her as "small and hard, with a slim figure but also very busty". She made it clear to him that the interview would be 50 percent about her and 50 per cent about Lennon The interview was a success. Two days later Lennon was murdered by Mark Chapman.

Thereafter, the grieving widow mounted exhibitions around the world, and expanded her profile as a musician. According to Peebles, she became more creatively active than ever before in her life. He was of the opinion that Lennon's murder was working to her advantage.

He said that " she used John's death to hype her own new record, for example, and rushed to record a sentimental B-side compilation of bits of John talking as a souvenir. She compared John's killing to the assassination of John F Kennedy, and herself to Jackie Onassis, insisting that their influence was greater than that of the Kennedys."

A year after the murder Peebles was chosen by the BBC to conduct a second interview with Ono. At this interview she cried when talking about Lennon but Peebles believed she was insincere. He was aware that she was parading her new lover Havadtoy, who was twenty years her junior, around New York which Peebles found "scandalous".

Havadtoy was a sculptor and antiques expert who had been a close aide of Lennon. It is said that Lennon was aware of the relationship. In fact, one track on *Double Fantasy* is called *I'm Losing You* and many believe that Lennon composed and wrote the song fearful that Ono would leave him for Havadtoy. Peebles claimed that Ono had her lover move into the

Dakota building with her on the same night Lennon was shot. He remained there and took on a new image even dressing up in Lennon's old clothes. The couple remained together for twenty years which was far longer than her marriage to John Lennon.

And Peebles' final verdict on Yoko Ono? "The bottom line, of course, was that she was just an average Japanese artist who got lucky – and wrecked the greatest band that Britain has ever produced."

Meanwhile, Havadtoy relocated to Europe and as of February 2017 was living in Hungary and Liguria, Italy.

In June 2012, Ono received a lifetime achievement award at the Dublin Biennial in Ireland. In February 2013, she accepted the Rainer Hildebrandt Medal at Berlin's Checkpoint Charlie Museum, awarded to her and Lennon for their lifetime of work for peace and human rights. Four months later, she curated the Meltdown festival in London, where she played two concerts, one with the *Plastic Ono Band*, and the second on backing vocals during Siouxsie Sioux's rendition of *Walking on Thin Ice* at the *Double Fantasy* show.

In February 2016, she was hospitalized after suffering what was rumoured to be a possible stroke. Her PR people claimed it was influenza. Every two years, she vehemently objects to the release of Mark Chapman at his parole hearing.

Jane Asher

In 2012 she appeared in *Charley's Aunt* at the Menier Chocolate Factory. In the summer of 2013 she played Lady Catherine de Bourgh in *Pride and Prejudice* at the Open Air Theatre, Regent's Park. In 2014 she starred in the stage adaptation of Penelope Lively's *Moon Tiger* at the Theatre Royal Bath and on tour. In 2016 Asher took on the role of Miss Havisham in Michael Eaton's adaptation of Great Expectations. She still refuses all requests to talk about her relationship with Paul McCartney or even *The Beatles*. She remains happily married to Gerald Anthony Scarfeis an English cartoonist and illustrator since 1981.

Ringo Starr

Still married to former Bond girl Barbara Bach the couple split their time between homes in Cranleigh, Surrey; Los Angeles; and Monte Carlo.[In the *Sunday Times Rich List 2011*, Starr was listed at number 56 in the UK with an estimated personal wealth of £150 million.

In 2012, Starr was estimated to be the wealthiest drummer in the world.

In December 2015, Starr and Bach auctioned some of their personal and professional items to the public via Julien's Auctions in Los Angeles. Highlights of the collection included Starr's first Ludwig Black Oyster Pearl drum kit; instruments gifted to him by Harrison,

Lennon and Marc Bolan; and a first-pressing copy of the *Beatles*' White Album numbered "0000001". The auction raised over $9 million, a portion of which was set aside for the Lotus Foundation, a charity founded by Starr and Bach.

Mark Chapman

There have been quite a number of conspiracy theories published concerning Chapman's murder. They are based on CIA and FBI surveillance of Lennon due to his left-wing activism; on the actions of Mark Chapman in the murder; and, on the subsequent court case.

Playwright Ian Carroll, has staged a drama suggesting that Chapman was manipulated by a rogue wing of the CIA. Claims include that Chapman was a Manchurian candidate, including speculation on links to the CIA's Project MKULTRA. At least one author has argued that forensic evidence proves Chapman did not commit the murder.

Chapman's seventh parole hearing was held before a three-member board in August, 2012. The following day, the denial of his application was announced, with the board stating, "Despite your positive efforts while incarcerated, your release at this time would greatly undermine respect for the law and tend to trivialize the tragic loss of life which you caused as a result of this heinous, unprovoked, violent, cold and calculated crime."

Chapman's eighth parole application was denied in

August 2014. At the hearing, Chapman said, "I am sorry for being such an idiot and choosing the wrong way for glory. I found my peace in Jesus. I know him. He loves me. He has forgiven me. He has helped in my life like you wouldn't believe."

Chapman's ninth parole application was denied in August, 2016, at which Chapman said he now saw his crime as being "premeditated, selfish and evil"

His next parole hearing is scheduled for August 2018.

Heather Mills

In March 2015 Heather Mills appeared on Ireland's *Late Late Show*. In the course of her interview she became agitated when asked about McCartney. At first she refused to talk about him saying she wasn't interested until the host urged her saying: "I think people are more interested than you allow for."

Heather responded: "No, they're not. That's the thing. When I go down the street, I get kids coming up to me, half of them don't even know who he is, that's why he's got to do songs with Rihanna and Kanye West, so people remember."

McCartney had, a month previously, recorded *Four Five Seconds* with Rihanna and West, and the trio performed the acoustic ballad together at the Grammys. Heather then continued: "When I go down the street, it's 'Oh my god, you're a ski-racer or You help the animals.' You know, I own the biggest vegan company in the world. This is just someone I fell in love with who to me was a normal guy that happened to write a few cool songs in the sixties and a few in the seventies. Like everybody that's a partner. You fall in love, you get married, you sometimes then go 'Oh my God, this is completely wrong,' you wake up, and you move on."

Sir Paul McCartney

In January 2017 the Reuters newsagency reported that Sir Paul McCartney has sued Sony Corp's music publishing arm in a federal court in New York. He sought to reclaim copyrights to 267 *Beatles* songs that pop star Michael Jackson acquired two decades before his death.

Jackson had famously outbid McCartney for the publishing rights to the songs in 1985, paying Australian businessman Robert Holmes à Court $47.5 million to obtain the collection as part of a trove of some 4,000 pop music tunes.

The Beatles songs and rest of the collection were then rolled into a joint venture Jackson formed in 1995 with his Sony-based label, creating Sony-ATV Music Publishing, which grew into the world's biggest song publisher.

In 2016, Jackson's estate sold off its stake in Sony/ATV, including *The Beatles* collection, to Sony Corp for $750,000. In the papers filed in Court, McCartney put Sony/ATV Music Publishing on notice as early as October 2008 that he wished to reclaim rights to the dozens of songs he co-wrote with John Lennon from September 1962 to June 1971. The legal writ claims that Sony-ATV has so far failed to acknowledge the composer's rights to terminate copyright transfers of that music, including such hits as *All You Need is Love* and *I Want to Hold Your Hand*, under the US Copyright Act. The lawsuit also claimed that Sony-ATV attempted to stall talks with McCartney until the conclusion of a separate lawsuit involving similar claims by British pop band *Duran Duran* in an English court. The suit is seeking a declaration from the Court that McCartney can reclaim his copyright interests in the songs, as well as all the legal fees due.

ABOUT THE AUTHOR

David Elio Malocco was born in Dundalk, County Louth, Ireland. His father was born in Casalattico in Frosinone in Italy and his mother was born in Monaghan in Ireland. He was educated at the Christian Brothers School in Dundalk and his parents later sent him to St. Patrick's College in Cavan where they hoped he would be ordained as a Roman Catholic priest. But he chose law and business instead.

He received his Bachelor of Civil Law degree from University College Dublin and spent fifteen years as a criminal lawyer before taking a second degree at the Open University, Milton Keynes in England where he obtained a first class honours degree in Psychology majoring in Cognitive Development.

In 1991 he realized a personal ambition and moved to New York where he studied film direction, production and writing for film at New York University. Since then he has written numerous screenplays in several genre and has written, produced and directed several shorts and three feature films, *Virgin Cowboys, Magdalen* and *Jack Gambel: The Enigma*.

He later studied creative writing at Oxford University and since then has completed a Higher Certificate in Psychotherapy; a Professional Certificate in Stockbroking from the Institute of Banking and is currently completing a Masters in Financial Services from University College Dublin..

He is a graduate member of the British Psychological Society; and a member of the Association of Professional Counsellors and Psychotherapists; the American Criminology Society; and, the Institute of Banking.

He has written several books on true crime and forensic science. The books were motivated by dual diplomas he had taken. The first was in the Psychology of Criminal Profiling and the second in Forensic Science specializing in crime scene analysis. But his repertoire of writing also includes comedy, cooking, conspiracy theories and health books.

His publications include:

A Brief History of Criminal Profiling
A Brief History of Psychology
Approaches in Criminal Profiling
Criminal Profiling
Eat Yourself Thin Fat Bitch
How to Commit the Perfect Murder: Forensic Science Analyzed
I am a Cannibal: A Study of Anthropophagy;
Murder for Profit: They Killed for Money;
Psychotherapy: The Top 50 Theorists and Theories
Psychotherapy: Approaches and Theories
Serial Sex Killers: Real American Psychos;
Sexual Psychopaths: British Serial Killers;
The Beatles Conspiracy: John, Paul, George, Ringo and Bill!;
Whacker Hennessy's Fifty Alcohol Infused Classic Recipes
Which Therapy?
Who's Who Serial Killers: The Top 100;
Wicked Women;
The World's Worst Serial Killers;

David is a lifelong supporter of Liverpool Football Club and enjoys filmmaking, writing, drinking wine, cooking and rescuing abandoned and abused dogs.

Printed in Great Britain
by Amazon